AMERICAN NATURE WRITING 1995

AMERICAN NATURE WRITING 1995

Selected by John A. Murray

SIERRA CLUB BOOKS
San Francisco

The Sierra Club, founded in 1892 by John Muir, has devoted itself to the study and protection of the earth's scenic and ecological resources—mountains, wetlands, woodlands, wild shores and rivers, deserts and plains. The publishing program of the Sierra Club offers books to the public as a nonprofit educational service in the hope that they may enlarge the public's understanding of the Club's basic concerns. The point of view expressed in each book, however, does not necessarily represent that of the Club. The Sierra Club has some sixty chapters coast to coast, in Canada, Hawaii, and Alaska. For information about how you may participate in its programs to preserve wilderness and the quality of life, please address inquiries to Sierra Club, 730 Polk Street, San Francisco, CA 94109.

The three quotations on page vi come from a symposium on nature writing edited by John A. Murray that appeared in *Manoa: A Pacific Journal of International Writing,* Fall 1992.

Pages 337–339 serve as an extension of this copyright page.

ISBN: 0-87156-438-6

ISSN: 1072-4723

Production by Robin Rockey

Cover and book design by Amy Evans

Composition by Wilsted & Taylor

Printed in the United States of America on acid-free paper containing a minimum of 50% recovered waste paper, of which at least 10% of the fiber content is post-consumer waste.

10 9 8 7 6 5 4 3 2 1

For my readers,
whose friendship is as sustaining as the Earth

I hope "natural history writing" really signals a shift in direction for American literature, away from a concern with the pleasures, the pains, and the fates of the self toward a concern for the mysterious web of being in which we are all delicately suspended. And that people will someday say our years saw a renaissance in literature, not the resurgence of a genre; a rediscovery of the resilience, the pertinence, and the scope of natural history as a metaphor to illuminate the joy and the terror of human existence. Barry Lopez

Partly to counter the exploitative vision of nature two hundred years of frontier ethics have fostered, contemporary nature writers are writing about relationship, about sense of place, about how we may still find our way out of isolation and into authentic communion with the organic community. If more people read nature writing than ever before, it is because they are following its central theme: the search for a place to stand, a position from which to act responsibly. Pamela Frierson

We are to some extent handicapped in this discussion because we are prone to think of nature as something outside of us and therefore subject to control and exploitation if only we can find the means. It becomes possible, therefore, to speak of "the death of nature." This phrase is by now almost a popular formation, one that tends to diminish understanding. We are unable to see nature for the inclusive force that it is. It is about us and within us, a necessary part of everything we are and can do, of everything we make, even the books we produce. It is in the dust of our carpets, in the spiders and roaches that seek whatever household crack or crevice exists for them, and in the shifting foundations of our buildings. It is in the squalor of the streets and neighborhoods of our cities, where nature, shunned otherwise, returns in the form of random violence and deliberate criminality. It is in the decay of our political systems, and in the confusion and incoherence of our public discourse. Strictly speaking, there is no life apart from nature. John Haines

Contents

Preface

What would the world be, once bereft
Of wet and of wilderness? Let them be left,
O let them be left, wildness and wet;
Long live the weeds and the wilderness yet.
Gerard Manley Hopkins, "Inversnaid"

This year marks the second edition of Sierra Club Books' nature annual, a collection dedicated to bringing you some of the best nature writing of the preceding twelve months. Our 1994 volume met with success and I thank all of you—readers, reviewers, booksellers, nature aficionados—for making it so. For me, the task of assembling one of these collections is always a labor of love, as I am introduced to many wonderful writers and readers whom I would otherwise not know. As in the first year's edition, I have brought a diversity of subjects and styles to these pages. The standard for inclusion has been singular literary achievement and a strong natural content. Some of the authors are essentially unknown (Clarice Dickess and Jim Miller), others are becoming broadly recognized (Brenda Peterson and John Gierarch), and quite a few are widely respected (Jane Smiley and Peter Matthiessen). With only a handful of exceptions, the 1995 volume is a fresh anthology, featuring many nature writers not represented in the 1994 annual. The same overall structure for the book has also been maintained; that is to say, I have alternated male and female voices (twelve men and twelve women) to provide a unique natural counterpoint. I hope this adds to your reading pleasure. This collection includes both essays and poetry, though the former, the primary vehicle of the genre at present, comprises the bulk of the book. Fiction, in my experience, frequently suffers from excision in collections such as we have here. In these pages you can travel on board a research vessel to Antarctica with Barry Lopez, explore tropical Vietnam with Susan Brownmiller, seek out the elusive brown bears of Romania with Rick Bass, explore the erotic in nature with Terry Tempest Williams, fish for salmon in Scotland with John Gierarch, walk the plains of Iowa with Jane Smiley, and observe beautiful Asian cranes with Peter Matthiessen, to describe just seven.

Next year's collection is already being planned. If you have a selection, or know of a selection, that you believe would contribute to that anthology, by all means send it to me in care of Sierra Club Books, 100 Bush Street, 13th Floor, San Francisco, California 94104. I am particularly interested in nature writing (i.e., writings of any genre with a strong natural content) from the following groups: (1) writers known only locally or regionally but with national potential, (2) writers from the Midwest, Northeast, and Deep South, (3) writers with experiences in nature abroad, (4) writers concerned with nature in an urban or suburban context, and (5) writers from ethnic groups offering alternative perspectives on nature (such as African American, Asian American, Hispanic American, and Native American). I promise to respond to each submission. Working together—readers and editor—we can build anthologies in the future that, like this one, hold both literary excellence and thematic and stylistic diversity as the standard.

I have many thanks to give. First, the writers, their agents, and publishers have been extremely cooperative in securing permissions and I thank them all; no anthology is possible without such quick and enthusiastic assistance. My editor, David Spinner, as ever, has been wonderfully helpful; all authors should be blessed with such warm, energetic, and perspicacious guidance. The dedication acknowledges the affection I have always felt for my readers. Your letters, cards, packages, and home videotapes remind me each time that it is for you that we writers exist. In fact, I must admit the first piece of mail

I open is always that with the unfamiliar name and return address on it—experience has taught me I am about to meet a distant reader, a new friend. Finally I must give thanks to the Murray family for their love and support, and especially my son, for whom everything I do is in some way related.

J.A.M.

Introduction

September on the Kenai

I.

That it will never come again
Is what makes life so sweet.
Emily Dickinson

The river was green. Not just green, but bright green. Even with the eastern clouds turning red as the eggs of the sea-run salmon you could see that. I asked Brian the guide about it and he said the Kenai was glacially fed.

"How fast is this thing running anyway?"

Brian strained on the oars, rowing the twelve-foot drift boat toward the middle of the river.

"Between five and six miles an hour."

The water was moving fast. No doubt about that. I had first noticed the current from the bank as we climbed over the gunwales. Now we were out on the flood of yesterday's rain, being swiftly pulled downstream. The speed was noticeable, even exhilarating. At this rate the boat could reach the north Pacific by evening. We were in the middle of the river before long, thanks to Brian's efforts, and I picked up the spin-cast rod and cast the hook with the imitation salmon egg into the nearest slow water. Three lead sinkers carried it to the bottom. The idea was to drift the morsel along the cobblestone, where everything in the universe was feeding on them. I got a bite right away, a two-pound Dolly Varden that flashed vibrantly like a piece of polished metal, and I quickly released it. I looked back and Brian was smiling. And why not? I was another happy client making a payment on his new $4,000 drift boat.

But the cheerful spirit was more than that.

It was a privilege to be out on one of the world's finest streams in September. To smell the wet fish scent of the river and to watch the cold Alaskan sky coming to life. To have everyone back in the cities and the campgrounds empty and the restaurants and bars uncrowded, to enter a time machine, as it were, and visit the mountains of Colorado around Aspen or those of Montana around Livingston in the 1940s. Fifty years from now, when Anchorage is the size of Denver, and Denver is the size of Los Angeles, the Kenai will no doubt resemble the western Colorado of today. Fifty years after that, God help us. Most of what remains of America's wild west will probably appear about as pristine as the chalet and pasture, condo and chair lift country of Grenoble, France.

Truly, we live in those long-ago times people will talk fondly of.

Brian rowed the boat from one slow stretch to the next, each one better than the last, and the Dolly Vardens were ravenous. I was glad we had started early, even if it meant no breakfast. The mature char were striking, with their emerald green flanks and brilliant pink and orange spots. It was hard to believe they once earned a bounty, per tail, simply because they scavenged a few salmon eggs.

Moose season was in progress, and every now and then we heard a distant thump as the winter meat was either felled or sent off like a freight train through the birches.

A king salmon as heavy as a young wolf jumped beside the boat.

"Why do they jump like that, Brian?"

"Nobody knows."

I liked that. The mystery, I mean. The inexhaustible ability of nature to exhaust our capacity to understand it.

We floated around the shoulder of a mountain and a dozen sandhill cranes flew by, only a few hundred feet above the river, their wings beating loudly and their voices calling back and forth.

We watched until they could not be heard.

Brian said they were local birds that summered in the black spruce muskeg of nearby Kenai National Wildlife Refuge. The cranes had been grounded by the rainy weather and were only today moving again. They would follow the Pacific coastline south to Oregon and California.

Another group flew by, this time so low I could see the ashen gray feathers of the outstretched wings and the red caps on the heads and the short dark bills and the loose webbing between the toes at the end of the long slender legs. Their voices were as insistent as the creak of a rusty handle on an old-fashioned water pump.

On either side of the river the cottonwoods and alders still held their summer green. Only a few willows and alders had begun to change to gold and they stood out like prematurely grayed people at a ten-year high-school reunion. Skinny white spruce, the trademark of the auroral country, were everywhere and I felt right at home among them, living as I do up north near the Arctic Circle. They are not much of a tree, but they are all we have around Fairbanks and so you grow to love them. The mist was lifting from the water now and the ancient weathered peaks on either side of the Kenai River were catching the first light. The autumn colors on the heights were fired from the early frost, the orange swales of dwarf birch and the rust-colored bilberry patches on the tundra ridges, and even without the binoculars I could see the white dots that were Dall sheep moving in a line across the black shale below the first dusting of snow. Above it all was the sky, painted a blue like one of those Winslow Homer watercolors from the Bahamas, a blue which says the sea is near.

The boat drifted around a wide bend, past a cow moose and her calf drinking in a quiet backwater. They seemed to realize we were not hunters, and that they were not legal game, and so they ignored us in the dignified way of wild animals.

Their eyes were the color of the forest, and they possessed the same calm.

On the fourth cast into the pool past the moose I caught my first rainbow trout of the day. Brian said they would go much larger. Coming originally from Colorado, the land of sixteen-inch stocked fish, I had never seen one as large. The rainbow is a native to southern Alaska, and so I carefully returned him, flashing silver and purple like something from a William Butler Yeats poem, to his element.

Brian was smiling. Always smiling. I liked that about him. He reminded me of myself in my early twenties, those idyllic days long ago (everything is idyllic in retrospect), working summers as a wrangler near Yellowstone and falls as a hunting guide in the Colorado Flattops. He had the mountains in him, and the rivers too, and so was doubly blessed.

We drifted on, and I lost count of the Dolly Vardens and rainbows. I told Brian this and he chuckled, "There are worse things."

There was a narrow band of deep water near a bank thick with devil's club and bracken fern. The rainbows lived here, and the Dollies, and so we lingered in an eddy.

Brian rested with the oars under his armpits and, as I fished, told me his life story.

He lived across the river in a cabin he built himself. He had grown up here, in Cooper Landing, had gone to school with fourteen other kids. The sweet elderly lady I had talked to in the log house by the state road, the one with the hand-painted fishing sign out front, had been his schoolteacher. She was also his mother. His father had once owned a local moose and caribou outfitting business but sold it to work on an oil rig in Cook Inlet, a lucrative job the hard-working patriarch loathed. Both of Brian's brothers were state troopers and one was lucky enough to be a Game and Fish officer and flew his own Piper Supercub. I decided not to tell Brian about my friends up north who had been cremated on impact, about good-natured Joe Firmin from Fort Yukon, with whom I'd hunted caribou in the Arctic Refuge, who popped a control cable and crashed upside down into Mount Schwatka, or hard-working Lynn Castle from Denali Lodge, who clipped an alder on take-off and cartwheeled into the Wood River, or my former student Billy Campbell, who lost manifold pressure on final approach to the Fairbanks airport and nose-dived into the mosquito bog at the end of the runway.

I asked Brian about winters and he said that in the snowy months he worked as an independent logger in the Chugach National Forest (a forest larger than New Hampshire) and also dove for sea urchins in Kachemak Bay near Homer. I asked him if he was married yet and he said his girlfriend had just left for the fall semester at UNLV, and his voice tensed as he talked about that subject.

Up ahead were rapids and Brian told me to put the rod down and hold on.

"By the way, John," Brian said, "that life preserver is to find your body. Your arms and legs will freeze in thirty seconds."

"Thanks, man."

So much for the cold-water survival course I barely passed in the Marines about twenty years ago.

Brian was proud of his boat and rowed us directly for the most massive wave, a standing monument of four or five feet, and we went right over the top, then down into the trough below, and up and over a couple of more waves. We were backwards now, and Brian rowed us around in the right direction. Brian yelped and pointed to an immature bald eagle with a dirty white hood, staring at us from the top of a dead cottonwood. The eagle never blinked in the time I watched him.

In the long stretch below the rapids some more cranes passed overhead. They beat their wings a little more vigorously once they noticed the eagle.

We were around the bend before long and Brian rowed the boat toward a broad expanse of still water. As we came in, there were countless salmon of three different species in the clear shallows below. Some were as red as a really bad sunburn, and others were the silver of well-used half dollars. A few were dead, heavy with fungus, their fins rotted away. Most were alive, hovering in the twilight between life and death, struggling to keep themselves afloat. One was enormous, about four and a half feet long, and in his flat eyes was the knowledge of the grim joke. For this he had grown big, evaded the salmon sharks and Taiwanese drift nets, battled thirty-five miles up from the sea, attacked the other males so that he alone would orgasm with the female, all for the immortality of fertilized eggs the trout were eating for breakfast.

There were red fox tracks on the bank, and brown bear tracks, and the stray markings of sea gulls. Salmon heads and well-scavenged fish vertebrae littered the sand.

Brian beached the boat and threw out the anchor. He asked if he could fish a special place upstream by himself, and I said sure. He gave me a pair of pliers to remove the hook and told me to be certain to release all king salmon, which are protected during their spawning season.

"Watch their teeth, John. They are like barracudas. They are evil, nasty-tempered things. Especially the males. They are mad at the world. They can take your finger off like that."

He snapped his fingers.

Brian disappeared down a bear trail into the yellow alders, a magnum revolver on his cartridge belt, and I was alone with the beautiful green river. With the sun fully on it now, the brilliant green reminded me of the turtle grass lagoons fringing the Yucatán coast north of Belize, those warm tropical waters and peaceful coconut groves where I spent a wild honeymoon with my first wife, Linda, in another lifetime.

I waded out into the river among the dead and dying salmon, the cold water pressing against the hip waders. I quickly caught and released two rainbows, and then I saw something jump out of the corner of my right eye and cast in that direction. The line immediately snagged on a sunken log. I was about to cut the line and retrieve some more leader and a new hook from the tackle box when the line started to move toward deep water, and I realized I had hooked some sort of fish. This was a size of fish unlike anything in my experience, and I felt the same stab of adrenalin I did as a six-year-old boy back in Ohio, when my father let me catch my first bluegill at Mr. Archibald's backyard pond. This was a Kenai River salmon that lived on everything smaller than it, from herring and crabs to Dollies and rainbows. Although his stomach had atrophied in fresh water, he still would snap at anything that irritated him. I tried to reel the salmon in but the reel turned in the other direction. The salmon was pulling me into the river and I was staggering behind him. I was up to my thighs and the water would soon pour over the hip waders, so I planted my feet among the bottom rock and began the fight. It would not be good to tell my old college fishing friend Greg over the phone that the rod had been pulled from my hands. The salmon sounded in a pool and then the line went slack as he came clear of the water, thrashing his tail in the sun, the size of a freshwater marlin if there were such a thing, snapping his ugly jaws, and then he hit the water on his side with a resonant splash. It was a king salmon alright, a giant chinook born of these ancient green waters, who had returned to spawn and die, and whose temper reflected his fate. He headed upstream for a fallen spruce and I kept pulling and reeling, pulling and reeling, sweating now under the three layers. After a while I had him close to the shore and my arms were tired from fighting him. He was ten feet from me now and I could see he would measure more than four feet. His weight was anybody's guess. Brian said that a spawned-out king can weigh in the neighborhood of ninety pounds. I was wondering what I was going to do with him, how I could possibly get that hook out of his mouth without losing part of my hand, when he spit the hook out and disappeared over the flats toward the middle of the river and left me there, the muscles knotted in my arms and shoulders, my heart pounding.

Half an hour later Brian returned to tell me of the nice rainbow he had caught and released, and we pushed back into the river. It was good to be in the boat again, moving through new water.

There was another boat in the next stretch and the other guide rowed near to us.

"Having any luck?" the other guide called out, a paunchy man with the mottled face and swollen nose of a morning drinker.

"Just like in the brochure," said Brian with a smile.

"Ahh, everybody knows the brochures are full of shit."

The last word, in the surroundings, sounded about like the f-word would in a presidential State of the Union address.

The two anglers in the other boat stared at me dejectedly. They wore blue and gold Lufthansa baseball hats and looked to be cargo pilots on layover from the international airport in Anchorage.

I waved hello and good-bye to the poor captives.

The river went under a bridge and I cast toward the bank and immediately caught a four- or five-pound Dolly with the enameled emerald body and Salvador Dalí pink spots of a mature fish. I held him from the water for a moment.

"What do you think?"

"Naa. You'll catch a lunker yet."

I released the fish.

I'd seen a picture of Harry Gaines, the recently deceased Kenai River guide, on the cover of the 1993 Alaska fishing regulations and asked Brian if he'd ever met him.

Brian said Harry visited his grade-school class once and told them funny stories about the various celebrities he had guided.

"Is that what you'd like to do, Brian, run your own guide service on the Kenai like Harry?"

"Not here. It takes twelve years to get a license. No, I'll start my business up north on the Gulkana. Salmon are smaller, of course, thirty to fifty pounds, but nobody has discovered it yet. It's like the Kenai was twenty years ago when Harry started."

It occurred to me that one day there would be no more new rivers in Alaska, even in the Russian Far East, that they would all be as well known as the Kenai, and I counted my blessings that I lived before that dismal century. I suppose that John Smith in Massachusetts and Meriwether Lewis in Montana and Aldo Leopold in New Mexico had all made that revelation, that they were seeing a world that would never be again.

A mile farther on we approached a large forested island that split the river into separate channels and Brian chose the left channel and beached the boat. He went downstream and I walked upstream to the head of the channel, where he said the salmon would be stacked like cordwood. On the fifth or sixth cast I caught a much larger Dolly than the one at the bridge, but lost him in seconds. It was my fault. I began to reel before I set the hook. I decided to cast in another area and then return to the place where I'd hooked the Dolly. While I let the egg drift I ate part of a chocolate bar, the first food all day. After a while I cast to the same spot and the fish immediately hit the egg and I snapped the rod back and began to work on him. The Dolly was a heavy fish with a strong tail and put up a courageous fight, exploding from the depths and thrashing over the surface before making a run upstream and then a run downstream and then back again, trying to get behind or to the side of the hook and work it out. The rod was nearly doubled over, and each time I glimpsed the fish I grew more excited. I wanted to look downstream to see where Brian was, to see if he could get the net from the boat, but instead I concentrated on the fish, holding the rod at an angle, making certain he didn't free himself. I did not want to lose this fish a second time. When he was in the shallows I wished for a net. I had no choice and so I risked breaking the line and heaved him over my shoulder onto the shore and grabbed him there in the grass, a thirty-inch monster surging in my hands.

"Brian," I yelled, "I think I caught a big one!"

I felt like I was ten years old again.

That's the whole point, isn't it?

We pushed off and Brian rowed us toward the center of the river. Once we were in the main stream he anchored the oars under his feet and rubbed the back of his neck with his hand. His neck muscles were cramped from rowing the better part of seven miles and he tilted his head back to relax them.

"Hey, look at that."

He pointed upward.

Far above, a flock of cranes was forming up. They had circled on the rising heat of the Earth. There were perhaps five or six hundred of them. As we watched, the leaders guided the others into an arrowhead-like formation. Every once in a while the air stilled and we could hear them calling. Hundreds of voices, as from a distant county fair. After a while the flock angled south, toward the bright blue of the sea.

II.

I believe very much in what I call hidden art—art in which the reader doesn't quite see what you have done—he only feels it's a good story.

Norman Maclean

Later that night, sitting alone at my fire in the Kenai River campground (the sole occupant among fifty-seven spaces), I reflected on the similarities between fishing and nature writing. Fishing stories are among the oldest narratives in the world. We find them throughout antiquity, and their telling no doubt predates historical times, from the crocodile-infested banks of the Nile to the dolphin-haunted delta of the Yangtze. Beyond that we can say that all narratives are grounded in nature, because nature consists of endless stories. We have the epic migration of salmon and cranes, the passing of the days, the building of great storms, the procession of the seasons, the waxing and waning of the moon, the transit of the constellations, the life and death of stars and galaxies, the life and death of the universe itself. These stories exist, have existed, and will always exist, separate from human experience. They are part of the elemental narrative structure of the universe, which is based in turn on linear time and causality. Writers, in this sense, produce artifacts that are akin to the fisherman's lure, creating an illusion that pulls readers into a dream, into an artificial world being formed with words. To sustain that effect requires all the skill and patience of the fisherman; to create narratives that flow naturally requires a knowledge of how rivers proceed from rapid to pool, from steep canyon to wide meadow, always moving surely from origins through climaxes to endings.

Two fishing selections were included in last year's nature writing annual. The first, by the late Harry Middleton, dealt, at least on the surface, with big-game fishing in Baja. The second, by Russell Chatham, related a lifetime of fishing experiences, a sort of extended pilgrimage by water, in locations as diverse as Iceland and California. This year we are fortunate enough to have an essay by John Gierarch, who, with Jim Harrison, Tom McGuane, and several others, is among the senior anglers in American literature. In his essay "Scotland," Gierarch takes readers to a highland stream far to the north of England where no one catches any fish, and yet everyone deals with the absurdity of the situation philosophically. The humor and intelligence displayed by these dislocated Americans are reminiscent of the élan found in Mark Twain's hilarious European travelogue *Innocents Abroad.* In writing about this subject area Gierarch, Middleton, Chatham, and the others are following a long tradition in the national literature. Thoreau, for example, wrote fondly about salmon fishing, and he often augmented his monkish diet of garden vegetables by fishing for perch in Walden Pond. His contemporary, the darkly brooding Melville, wrote the longest fishing story in history, *Moby Dick.* A century later America's first millionaire author, Zane Grey, discovered deep-sea fishing as a sport, and his popular books of the early 1920s inspired a younger member of the guild, Ernest Hemingway, who in 1954 was awarded the Nobel Prize for his Gulf Stream marlin saga *The Old Man and the Sea.* More recently, Norman Maclean's novella *A River Runs Through It* was made into a beautiful film about angling and family life in the northern Rockies. In nearly every case, including Gierarch's "Scotland," there is a deceptive simplicity to the piscatorial narrative, as the author, like some latter-day Confucius, seeks to convey a whole philosophy of life through what appears to be a passing anecdote about a matter of little consequence. Harry Middleton put it this way: "Fishing is not an escape from life, but often a deeper immersion into it, all of it, the good and the awful, the joyous and the miserable, the comic, the embarrassing, the tragic, and the sorrowful."

Water, or the absence of it, runs thematically through many other selections included in this year's annual. Three essays, for example, concern cranes, a wading bird dependent on large freshwater marshes scattered across migratory routes spanning entire continents. The eminent naturalist and novelist Peter Matthiessen, who is preparing a book on cranes, writes in his essay "At the End of Tibet" about the plight of the species on the Asian continent, where explosive human population growth and widespread habitat destruction are imperiling many plants and animals, not to mention people, dependent on extensive low-water areas. Susan Brownmiller, well known as one of the leading feminist writers of our time, takes us to Vietnam, where the destructive 1963–1975 war left the delta of the Mekong River, and other critical crane habitat areas, in a seriously degraded state. Back here in the States, biology doctoral student Jim Miller explores the flood plain of the Platte River in western Nebraska, where every spring half a million sandhill cranes stop to rest. Eventually, as Miller points out, these birds move to nesting areas in northern Canada, Alaska, and Siberia. In recent years, minimal water levels on the Platte, one of the most abused rivers in the country, were imperiled by the controversial Two Forks dam project in Colorado. Fortunately, the ill-conceived project was killed several years ago by EPA Director William Riley during the Bush administration (Bush is an avid fisherman). Cranes, like so many plants and animals in the natural world, are an "indicator species," whose presence tells us the habitats they occupy—habitats that human communities also depend on—are still healthy. In this sense, their preservation is consonant with our own, and that of our children.

Pulitzer Prize–winning novelist Jane Smiley writes, like Miller, of environmental issues on the Great Plains, a vast ecosystem whose character has been defined by the paucity of precipitation. Smiley, who teaches at Iowa State University in Ames, focuses on what she calls the "paradox" of the prairies—that grassy regions appear to be fertile but in reality exist at the margins. At one time in the late nineteenth century, Smiley recalls, an act of the Iowa legislature actually "asserted that the drainage of surface waters [was] presumed to be of public benefit." She argues vigorously for the preservation of prairie wetlands, which act as vital reservoirs to replenish the surrounding biotic and human communities:

> It is not "politically correct," or "morally right," or even "necessary" to heed the warnings abounding in the soil and water of the prairie. It is intelligent. Whether we do so or not is the measure of whether we have progressed beyond the Mesopotamians of four and a half thousand years ago, or whether we are, in fact, still caught in a comforting illusion of familiarity.

Jim Miller's half-million sandhill cranes are but one avian species that would benefit from Jane Smiley's heartfelt plea to save the many endangered wetland areas, and dependent species, in the water-scarce interior of North America.

Five selections were inspired by the oceans. Barry Lopez takes us aboard the *Nathaniel B. Palmer,* an icebreaking scientific research vessel en route to remote waters off the coast of Antarctica. Despite the austerity of the polar climate, Lopez finds the Weddell Sea teeming with life. He notes "large numbers of crabeater and Weddell seals, fur seals, and predacious leopard seals; chinstrap, Adélie, and emperor penguins; sei whales, minke whales, and orcas." Compared to the "heavily-utilized seas to the north," the "Weddell [seems to him like] a refugium," and Lopez's essay reminds us that once the temperate latitude seas were as rich with life. In a similar vein to Lopez, Woods Hole marine biologist Cindy Van Dover describes her adventures as chief pilot for the *Alvin,* the deep-sea submersible used by world scientists to explore geothermal vents and other phenomena of the seafloor. California naturalist David Rains Wallace rides a craft to the Farallones near San Francisco, in waters where blue whales were once regularly seen. Upon arriving at the islands, Wallace observes northern elephant seals, a species nearly extinct when Wallace first arrived in California in the 1960s, but now making a comeback. He humorously remarks of the giant twenty-foot-long bulls: "Thoreau wrote that we need some life pasturing freely where we never wander. I'd add that we need some life rampaging, shrieking, and stinking freely out there, too." Retired submariner Gerard Gormley, author of an acclaimed earlier work on killer whales, takes readers to the secret world of the humpback whale and provides us with a breathtaking view of the birthing process. In the last selection in the book, Alaskan marine biologist Eva Saulitis describes a necropsy she performs on the carcass of an adult killer whale washed ashore in Prince William Sound. It was in these once-pristine waters, first seen by a European only two centuries ago, that one of the world's worst oil spills occurred in March 1989.

Harvard University professor Edward O. Wilson brings together many of the diverse themes of the collection in his essay *Biodiversity Threatened.* Wilson, an entomologist who is increasingly mentioned as a Nobel candidate, has devoted his scientific career to chronicling the most significant natural disaster of our time, namely, the widespread loss of life forms resulting from unprecedented human population growth. Most often, he writes, this mass extinction is caused by clear-cutting forests, especially in tropical regions. In his essay, the two-time Pulitzer prize winner informs us that "one fifth of the species of birds worldwide have been eliminated in the past two millennia," that since World War II "population densities of migratory songbirds in the mid-Atlantic United States dropped 50 percent," and that "about 20 percent of the world's freshwater fish species are either extinct or in a state of dangerous decline." He calls the current situation in which seventy-four species vanish every day "one of the great extinction spasms of geological history" and recommends aggressive action to prevent the further impoverishment of Earth's biota. Contrary to popular belief, these species are not all obscure fungi and insects, but also include animals of higher biomass, such as the blue whale (largest animal ever to live on the planet), of which there are, at this writing, only 450 remaining in the world. By the time my son enters college in the year 2006, the blue whale may, like the passenger pigeon and other recently widespread animals, be found only in natural history museums. Wilson's essay is a depressing but necessary call to action, and reminds us that our children may well ask of us what we now ask of those generations who lived during the period of institutionalized slavery, or during the genocide of the American Indian wars, or during the Holocaust of 1930s and 1940s Germany—Why didn't the good people organize themselves early on and stop it?

III.

The great tragedy of life is not that men perish, but that they cease to love.
W. Somerset Maugham

After the fire dwindled to a bed of coals, I walked through the spruce forest to the edge of the Kenai River. The clouds had blown off and the stars were out. The moon was rising from the east. It would be full in a day or two. The cold light fell as from a lantern. Everything was clear. The floating aspen leaves on the surface of the river. The smooth rounded stones along the bank. The dying spikes of fireweed at my feet. On the heavy ridge across the river I could see the individual rocks in the talus slides, and the columnar outcroppings of Jurassic cliffs, and the gray bulking mass of the tundra. The wind roared against the peaks in a cold uncaring way that made me glad to be on the valley floor.

I had my binoculars with me that night and lay on the grass and traveled among the stars. Orion the hunter was not up yet. The constellations were still those of summer. Pegasus the horse. Cygnus the swan. Pisces the fish. The red beacon of Aldebaran and the faint blue cloud of the Pleiades. No planets that night. No northern lights. Just the pale white moon reflecting the light of the sun. As I moved from one lovely nest of suns to another I wondered if there were rivers and seas on those worlds as beautiful as those on this one, and if writers of a kind lived there, as well, trying to put the beauty of nature into something resembling words.

Whatever we are doing as writers, it is bound up in something larger, part of a mode of thought just being born, a way of being that will one day, after many ages, prevail. Each of the writers in this book is a part of that movement, a slow transformation which began thirty thousand autumns ago in the caves of Lascaux, and will end somewhere up there, among the stars whose distant campfire light calls us home. Every person needs something larger than life to devote his or her years to, something to love, as Maugham phrased it. What the writers in this book are trying to tell us is that we only have to look outside to find something worthy of our devotion and love.

Peter Matthiessen

At the End of Tibet

from *Audubon*

Among all of the earth's far-flung cranes, the species most difficult to see is probably *Grus nigricollis,* the black-necked or Tibetan crane. Largely confined in breeding season to remote regions of the Tibetan Plateau, as high as 16,000 feet, it migrates in winter to high mountain valleys of remote southwestern China and Bhutan. These migrations are more altitudinal than geographical—the hardy birds descend an average of 5,000 feet. A very few breed across the Tibetan border in Indian Ladakh, where a mummified bird collected about 1805 by an early explorer still hangs in front of a religious painting in Lhyang Monastery. A few formerly wintered as far east as India's remote northeastern state of Arunachal Pradesh, from which the crane disappeared in the mid-1970s, when the last known pair, alighting near Hang village, were killed for the pot within an hour of their arrival.

Since all of these regions, until recent years, were closed to foreign travel, very little was known about this species—so little, in fact, that in 1984 it was estimated by one Indian authority that only about 100 birds survived in Tibet and Ladakh and that, barring immediate intervention, the black-necked crane would be extinct by 1985. Other authorities agreed that these Tibetan cranes—once common in a Buddhist country where wildlife was generally protected—had been mostly exterminated in the drastically increased human, industrial, and military activity that accompanied China's seizure of Tibet in the 1950s. Even the more optimistic feared that there might be only 700 left, making it the second-rarest crane species on earth, after the whooping crane of North America.

Following the general assault on wildlife that characterized the so-called Cultural Revolution, China reversed its policies in the 1980s in an effort to save what little wildlife it had left and created refuges throughout the country and in what the Chinese government calls the "autonomous region" of Tibet. Among the immediate beneficiaries were the several endangered Asian cranes, among them the black-necked crane, which had eight locations set aside for its protection on both wintering and breeding grounds in Tibet and China. Between 1990 and 1993, new surveys by an American researcher, ornithologist Mary Anne Bishop, indicated that the population estimates had been unduly pessimistic. Today the crane has an estimated population of 5,500 birds, though they remain as difficult to go see as ever.

Meanwhile, the Royal Government of Bhutan decreed protection for the birds in the three known places where wintering black-necked cranes had been reported, including a remote glacial valley in the Black Mountains near a monastery known as Gantey. It was this flock that in January of last year [1993] we went to see.

Though less remote than China's mountainous western provinces of Sichuan and Yunnan, Bhutan remains some distance from the beaten track and somewhat difficult to enter. Its few towns are small—a country the size of Switzerland, it has a population of about 1 million. Not until 1962 did the first road connect this small country to the outside world—or more specifically, connect Thimphu, the capital city (or small town, or large village, according to the eye of the beholder), to Phuntsholing, on the Indian border. For another 12 years the country remained virtually closed to foreigners; even today it has sensible restrictions against foreign writers and other troublemakers and limits its tourist visas to 3,000 per year.

On this rare late-January day, on the flight from Delhi, the bright wall of the eastern Himalaya passed in review, from Mount Dhaulagiri and the Annapurna Cirque (the five-mile-high portals of the Kali Gandaki gorge, through which demoiselle cranes migrate on their way south from central Asia) to great Lachi Kang (Mount Everest) and Jhomolhari, the conical 24,000-foot peak that separates Bhutan from southeastern Tibet.

Bhutan, or *Bhot Ant,* is generally translated "Eastern Bhot" or "End of Bhot"—that is, End of Tibet, with which it shares much of its history and religion. In fact, the people of western Bhutan are known as Ngalong, or "First to Rise"—first, that is, to turn to Tibetan Tantric Buddhism.

The Paro Valley, about 40 miles southwest of Thimphu, is the only one in western Bhutan that is wide enough and long enough to accommodate an airstrip. Even here the strip is disconcerting, being rather too sudden and too short even when not closed down entirely by the rivers of thick cloud that can fill the small dark valley. Thus the flight that arrives on auspicious days from Bangkok or Delhi is not one the visitor is likely to forget, since the aircraft operated by Druk (dragon) Air must curve around a mountainside on the way in as well as the way out.

The town of Paro lies at about 7,000 feet, in what is known as the Inner Himalaya, and Thimphu is approximately 600 feet higher. This region, where most of the population is located, though somewhat higher than the Nepal midlands, is also wetter, and Paro therefore has orchards of apples, plums, and peaches, as well as asparagus and rice, which in Bhutan can be grown at elevations as high as 8,000 feet. There is also more snow than in most lands of the Buddhist Himalaya, and in consequence, the flat roofs—used for storage of fuel, fodder, and dried food—are fitted with steep, open-sided, peaked roofs of slates, shingles, or corrugated iron, held in place by heavy stones.

Paro is a one-street town with willow trees that bend along the gray torrent of the Paro Chhu River. Along the river the next morning, the sharp eye of my traveling partner, Victor Emanuel, finds the rare and beautiful shorebird known as the ibisbill. After the black-necked crane, which the Bhutanese know as *cha trung trung* ("bird with long legs"), it is the species that our wildlife group wants most to see. The ibisbill superficially resembles a pearl-gray curlew, with a black-and-white breast band and a bright-red, decurved bill. It is strong enough to breast swift glacial currents on its way across a shallow channel between islands.

Paro's eighth-century temple, Kyichu Lhakhang, is the oldest in Bhutan, and the national museum in the round guard tower of Paro Dzong contains superb Buddha figures and also *thangkas,* or religious paintings, cloth on silk. But since 1988, foreigners have been excluded from most of Bhutan's holy sites, not only to protect the ancient art from the thievish proclivities of strangers but also "to prevent any commercialization of the religion and to preserve the sanctity of its ceremonies"—both excellent reasons, as looted and trampled traditional societies throughout the Buddhist Himalaya can attest.

High on the sheer cliff face of a mountain up the valley is Taktshang, or "Tiger's Nest," the famous monastery perched on a ledge where by all accounts the great Padma Sambhava, or Guru Rinpoche, arrived from Tibet in 747 A.D. and rode on the back of a tiger, the better to banish the old B'on religion and affirm the Buddhist faith. The Drukpa, or "Thunder Dragon," sect (thunder was once thought to be the dragon's roar) of the Kagyu school of Tibetan Buddhism was confirmed in the 12th century as the official religion of Bhutan, which is known to its own people as Druk Yul, "Land of the Thunder Dragon."

A fine walk up through mountain oak and rhododendron and andromeda, to the rush of waterfalls and the ring of bells struck by prayer wheels turned by steep streams, and the squall of nutcrackers and the song of laughing thrushes (mercifully, not in the least like laughter), with lavender primula in sheltered sun patches and red cotoneaster berries higher up, and everywhere the smell of cow dung, fire smoke, and spruce, brings one out at last on a ledge bedecked with prayer flags. Here three black mastiffs rush to meet me, and I stoop to pick up rocks. But Bhutanese mastiffs are smaller than their Tibetan kin and less eager to attack—another virtue of this country—and we make friends as I continue to the teahouse, from which a superb view of the white *gonpa* of Taktshang may be obtained. Below the monastery a flight of snow pigeons circles the black cliff face and settles like a sudden crop of strange white fruits in a dead tree.

Our guide will be Ugyen Dorjee, and his assistant is called Karma. Like all Bhutanese men, both wear the traditional central Asian *kho,* or long formal robe, which can be hitched up with a belt for riding horses. Next day we head southeast to the Wang Chhu River and the main east-west road across the country.

With its small population and ample rainfall, Bhutan is still 65 to 70 percent forested, yet the country is dedicated to sustained reforestation, a farsighted precaution that other Himalayan lands such as Pakistan and Nepal have failed to take. In a world spinning out of ecological balance, this country is as refreshing as an oasis in a desert, especially to travelers en route, as we are, from India to China, the two most populous and battered landscapes in the world.

Simtokha Dzong, at the entrance to the Thimphu Valley, is the oldest monastery in the country and is now used as a Buddhist school. The huge fortress-monasteries, or *dzongs,* at towns and other likely places on these mountain rivers are one reason why throughout the centuries, despite small wars with Tibet and India and even Great Britain, Bhutan has stubbornly maintained its independence. In 1907, when Great Britain was meddling extensively in Tibet, Bhutan's traditional leader was replaced with a royal family. Since then, a hereditary king of the Wangchuk family (the incumbent is Jigme Singye Wangchuk) is the nation's Druk Gyalpo, or "Precious Ruler of the Dragon People." Monarchy or no, the country is roughly democratic, with no caste system as in India and Tibet and full women's rights. (It is, however, under increasing international criticism for human rights violations against the indigenous Nepalese population in the south.)

From Simtokha Dzong the road climbs a pretty valley with brown winter-rice fields and the pale greens of winter wheat, arriving at last in the colorful main street of Thimphu, where the government buildings are located and the Druk Gyalpo has his residence.

That night it snowed, and it was still snowing when we departed the next morning, passing a village of Tibetan refugees and climbing slowly through hemlock, spruce, and fir to the Dochu La Pass, at 10,200 feet. On this cold, heavy winter day, the fine view of the northern peaks promised by our guide, Ugyen, cannot be seen. (On our return, however, the entire snow-peak border with Tibet lay in full view, from Jejekangphu Gang to Gangkar Punsum, otherwise known as White Glacier of the Three Spiritual Brothers. At 24,596 feet, it is the highest mountain in Bhutan, and climbing to its peak is not permitted.)

Beyond Dochu La Pass the road descended from the conifers into the oak-rhododendron forest. Birds were numerous—finches, redstarts, and laughing thrushes of several species, the large, dark-blue whistling thrush, and the lovely gold-billed magpie. Here and there along the narrow winding road were primitive huts of Bangladeshi peasants brought in to maintain these mountain roads, which have a tendency to fall away into the gorges. Gradually, with the descent, the forest softened, a plantation of walnut trees appeared, and soon we were back in temperate forest at about 5,000 feet.

In the village of Mesina, in the Punakha Valley, all manner of communal house building and wheat threshing and garden preparing were in progress. No nails are used in the skilled construction (which is why the roof slates are weighed down with heavy stones), and the walls are erected in wooden forms or molds into which clay is pounded by teams of singing, stamping girls using big pestles.

According to Karma, one song they sang was called "The Flying of the Cranes," composed (if I understood him correctly) by the fifth Dalai Lama, who is said to have been something of a poet. A prisoner sentenced to death is enclosed in a box and thrown into the river, from where, through the slats, he espies two flying cranes and implores them to lend him the help of their wings. Asked if they did so, Karma shook his head in regret. "I suppose that prisoner was a romantic sort of fellow," he said.

Our route turned off to the northeast, up the beautiful Dang Chhu tributary into the Black Mountains, climbing gradually along high cliffs above the river. In a ravine at about 6,500 feet, in the dense forest, we were witness to a wonderful outbreak of wildlife behavior. The small bus had stopped on the next incline for a striking bird not seen before—a spotted forktail, working a rivulet that came down through fern and moss off the steep mountain. Here dense forest climbed steeply to lost canopies above and fell away just as steeply from the downhill side of the road, so that the crown of a large red-fruited tree was just at eye level. This tree and lesser trees and vines and tangles all around had attracted an extraordinary array of brilliant birds. Both adjectives are used advisedly, and I'll list the general names just to give the feel of it: barbets, bulbuls, woodpeckers, laughing thrushes, sibias, yuhinas, sunbirds, fantails, and the shy, infrequently observed barred cuckoo dove.

The excited travelers were not the only ones drawn to the melee, for while we watched enraptured from the roadside, looking down into the trees instead of up in the usual neck-breaking birder way, I heard from behind a rush of air and leaned back in time to see the beak and folded wings and talons of a goshawk pass right over my head, aimed (I decided) at the bright green of a great barbet or the bright gold of a small yellow-naped woodpecker, both of which stood out prominently at the treetop. At the last second the accipiter flared off, no doubt taken aback by the brightly hued big mammals on the road, and kept on going down the mountainside; but where it had come from, up the ravine, a second goshawk passed between the trees, and there was some red where a flared pheasant, presumably a tragopan, careened into the hillside brush.

At some point in this interlude there came a sharp cry from a woman in our party who had chosen this moment to slip behind a bush. A terrific fracas, filled with eerie squalling, had broken out in a tree over her head, and running down the road, I saw an otter-size animal out on the very tip of a bouncing branch, where it had been driven by two more that were snarling and spitting from nearby branches—tawny white-chinned animals, yellowish along the throat, set off at one end by a long black bushy tail and at the other by a glossy mask of purest black that looked as triangular as an adder's head when the beady eyes turned toward us. This creature was the yellow-throated marten, a very large arboreal weasel that is common enough—I had found its scat on the path down from Taktshang two days before—but infrequently seen, at least by me. In hundreds of miles of walking in the Himalaya I had never seen it, which caused me to add an enormous bellow of excitement to the general din.

The martens far exceeded my expectations, not only in size but in speed and fierce demeanor. The attacking animals were aware of us and displeased by the distraction, racing up and down the tree and whisking back and forth among the rocks as if seeking reinforcements, only to swiftly reappear and race up to the attack again. So intent were they on their own business that we watched their acrobatics at close hand for several minutes, until finally a rough vehicle appeared and its driver, poking out his head, kindly offered to shoot them. "Make a nice hat," he said. The offer, translated, was spurned with loud cries that confused the martens, and the beleaguered one took advantage of the moment to shoot past the others and off the tree in a great leap toward the mountainside, up which his ill-wishers pursued him with those wild, ugly, tearing cries that seem peculiar to this evil-tempered family.

As for the vehicle, it departed too, leaving a miasma of black fumes in the ravine. We followed slowly. Just up the hill a rhesus monkey, and shortly thereafter a small barking deer, peered out from the roadside. This bountiful region, Ugyen says, is the king's hunting preserve for both tiger and leopard, including the melanistic form called the black panther.

At Pele La Pass, at 11,000 feet, it is already snowing, and the clouds have formed a beautiful frosty mist on the usnea lichens. From somewhere in the snow comes the *chirr* of nutcrackers and the rumble of a rockfall, caused by one of the skittish yak-cattle crossbreeds known as *dzos,* which wander everywhere through these steep forests. Our road—no more than a muddy track in this wet weather—must climb still higher, to Lawala Pass, in order to cross over into the Phobjika Valley, where the *cha trung trung* are said to be. The cheerful Ugyen has arranged for a four-wheel-drive pickup truck to haul us up in relays through the silent snow forest to the final pass, from which we can trek down into the valley.

From the pass, Phobjika Valley looks strange and empty, with dark forest and rough pasture of coarse growth shrouded by snow. At these altitudes, the valley's inhabitants are seminomadic yak herders who spend most of their year in the black yak-hair tents that squat here and there like boulders. But gradually, as the road descends, scattered farmhouses appear in the valley mists below.

In late-afternoon light, in a snow mist, I make out three large, pale shapes in the dark plowed corner of a field two miles away. Then Victor comes up with the second group, and we stand quietly on the mountain road, enjoying these black-necked cranes together, for the *cha trung trung* is the only one of the eight Asian cranes that neither of us has ever seen. We continue down the mountainside, locating a few more distant cranes along the way.

It is nearly dark when we walk the almost empty street of the 15th-century village of Gantey (*gang* is "mountain," and *tey* is "summit"), passing the ancient monastery. Gantey Gonpa, founded in 1613, is the only monastery of the Nyingma-pa (the "Old Sect") west of the Black Mountains, and it shelters 10 monks and 140 lay disciples of the high lama, Gantey Tulku Rinpoche, who according to Ugyen is on a spiritual retreat of three years, three months, and three days.

In the dusk, the ancient roofed *chorten,* or Buddhist reliquary, in the village square seems full of mystery. Gantey is located on a ridge that sticks out like a narrow butte into the valley, and using flashlights, for the dark has come, we make our way downward on a rough and narrow footpath through the forest, meeting the road near a bridge that crosses the small Phobjika River. Beyond the bridge, on a low rise, is a guest house where we spend the night. On the colorful walls of the main room, where an excellent supper is prepared, is a collection of ancient weapons from 17th-century wars with Tibet.

The local people say that just 10 years ago, when perhaps 20 black-necked cranes were first reported from this valley, the birds were still being hunted, mostly by boys out practicing archery, Bhutan's national sport. Far from being revered, as they are in many countries, the native cranes were dismissed as "the thing with a bird's head and a sheep's body." Not until they were finally adopted by the Royal Society for the Protection of Nature did all hunting cease, mostly because the penalty for killing one is now life imprisonment. In recent years the winter population has increased to about 200 birds—the actual count for 1993 is 210—with another 100 birds or so in the Laool Valley, across the main ridge to the east, and another 100 in east Bhutan. In addition there are or were four birds that wintered near Bumthang—in short, perhaps 400-odd birds in the whole country.

Apparently the cranes roost each night at a place within sight of this guest house. Anxious to see and count them before the flock scattered for the day, I got up at six and walked out on the road, where I was soon joined by Victor. The dawn was cold, perhaps 20 degrees Fahrenheit, but clear and windless, and sure enough, the crane flock was in view, though far away across the wet frozen meadows of the Chhu Nap, a stream that winds down through the marshy valley.

Heads beneath their wings, the birds stood hunched on a swale at the foot of snow-misted pasture hills that rose to a forest of blue pine. Though we tried to move closer, it turned out the marsh was not hard-frozen after all, and both of us broke through and took ice water in over our boot tops before clambering free of the half-frozen mud and making our way back up to the road, with mud, pants, laces, and boots already frozen into one hard bond.

By now a cold dawn light had appeared behind the hairline of black conifers on the eastern ridge. Even as we stamped and watched, the dark heads of the cranes started to come up, and one bird called, perhaps to the unsociable few that were hunched here and there farther down the valley. In the great silence, an occasional far-off dog or rooster could be heard. No smoke rose from the scattered farmhouses, which were as empty as Gantey itself, since most of the people at this time of year move away to make a rice crop in a lower valley.

A number of cranes were calling now, and from a distance the double call—*aw-owk,* followed by a two-note response—seemed less like the unison call of other cranes, more like duetting. But we were too far away to tell. After breakfast we crossed the bridge over the Chhu Nap and walked along the pinewood edge to a place where the marsh, with a few leaps, might be crossed dry-shod. On the far side the land rose again to a sort of grassy small plateau, at the end of which two cranes, heads raised, stood with their backs to each other, silhouetted against the mist in the warming valley, the early-morning silver light reflected from their backs. Three others took wing, only to alight by a grove of pines, but the rest were still on or near the roost, a piece of flat ground by the marsh edge, scarcely 200 yards from where we crouched to watch them. Over the shining marshland flew an upland buzzard and a pallid harrier.

In our strange company the cranes were restless, as they had not been when two local men walked past the flock scarcely 50 yards away, and Ugyen had warned us that they might fly off, alarmed by our bright colors. The Bhutanese are smaller than Westerners, and here in the mountain backlands their worn *khos* are of dull earth tones, by design or by attrition, and their walk, after many seasons here, and centuries too, is not so separated from the earth as the walk of strangers. Whatever the reason, there seemed to be no doubt that our presence on the bluff unsettled the birds, though we were careful to move slowly and sit quietly.

Through telescopes, the black-neckeds were so close that we could study the golden orb with the white spot behind, which makes the eye of this species look enormous, and the frontal red patch of bare skin, smaller than in most *Grus*—perhaps a cold-climate adaptation, like its legs and neck, which are noticeably shorter for its size than in other species. For the same reason, this crane is heavy, big, with less heat-losing surface for each pound of weight; its bustle, too, is large, perhaps to help warm its rear end. (The immature birds are dingier, and speckled on the back, with a brown bustle.)

Eventually the cranes forgot about us and went on about their preening and calling, their brief flurries of February dancing—leaping up, wing posturing, elevating their tertial bustles. But soon the calls and bugling grew louder, and one family group after another ran a little and danced into the air and moved out over the winter farmlands where the cranes forage. According to the local people, they also feed on roots and tubers of the coarse local tussock grass called mountain bamboo.

The bright, clear mountain day was warming rapidly, and the conifers lost their white frosting of snow. With most of the cranes gone, we returned upriver to the bridge over Chhu Nap. The last crane I saw in the Gantey Valley had circled high over the ridges to at least 12,000 feet, calling and calling, as it will do later in February, as it gathers its flocks for the flight north to the Tibetan Plateau.

According to the Gantey villagers, the birds arrive in late December, always in the midday period when the sun is highest, and circle three times over Gantey Gonpa, crying out as if to win the lama's blessing before gliding slowly down into the valley. Only a few arrive each day, so that their arrival is spread out across a period of two or three weeks. The departure, when it comes, is much more urgent. The northbound birds fly off in groups of 40 or 50 at a time, so that they vanish within several days, but even then, despite the urgency of spring, they do not neglect to circle three times over the gonpa.

Jane Smiley

So Shall We Reap

from *Sierra*

One of my favorite stretches of highway is Interstate 35 south of Minneapolis–St. Paul. There is always a moment when I realize that the dark, mysterious embrace of the North Woods is well and truly behind me. I look around at the brilliantly sunlit fields spreading in every direction, rich green burnished with late-summer gold, and I sense the continent shift eastward. I am out on the prairie now, and it feels important—not as if I got up this morning and drove for a few hours from our lake house, but more as if I've left one world and entered another. I like to think of this momentary feeling as a ghostly echo of what the European settlers of the 19th century felt when they first saw a sight unprecedented in their lives—pure terrestrial space, pure unmediated land, a vision of absolute largeness guaranteed to disorient, terrify, and inspire.

Of course, what I see bears almost no relation to what the first settlers saw. I see the wide double ribbon of the highway flowing silver-gray between squared-off fields of tasselled corn. I see a ten-foot windbreak of hackberry that curves along the highway for a quarter mile. I see a blue farmhouse to the right and a giant antique emporium to the left. Just past the antique store, I see a Lutheran church on a bluff, and then the Iowa state line, which runs beneath an overpass, over which three cars are passing.

Mostly I see the crystalline blank blue of the sky, so large and all-encompassing that no single storm, no pile of cumulonimbus can fill it. Only the leading edge of a front, advancing in a sheet of platinum cloud-cover slowly but steadily from the Pacific to the Atlantic, can block so much sky, and that has the effect of bolstering my sense of enlargement—rain may soon begin, and is likely to pour down in torrents that seem impossible for my car, or the land, to withstand. This sky, these clouds, these cataracts, perhaps all this is something the early settlers experienced. Otherwise, the land around me is the result of those settlers' dreams—peaceful, productive, domesticated, ordered—as entirely delivered over to human purposes as any urban landscape in America.

Our relationship to the Great North American Prairie, especially the tallgrass prairie, is a paradigm, perhaps *the* paradigm of our relationship to Earth, for on the prairie we have had our way in almost everything, and every potential our ancestors saw for fertility, productivity, and European-style settlement has been fulfilled. The prairies have, almost resistlessly, given every gift. On the *tabula rasa* of millions of acres of flat land, we have finally worked out the logic of our technology, our religion, our moral beliefs, our social and economic priorities, and our appetites. If, as it sometimes seems, we have destroyed ourselves on the prairie, we have nothing, and no one, to blame but ourselves.

About five miles north of my house in Ames, Iowa, is a state-designated "prairie remnant," a 25-acre piece of land that escaped the plow. In mid-September of a very wet year, the dominant color here is rich green. The five- or six-foot-tall stems of Indian grass are fully headed-out—tan seed heads wave and rustle in the stiff westerly breeze. Other vegetation, mostly partridge pea, with its small yellow flowers and vetch-like leaves, clusters and creeps around the base of the taller grasses, entirely covering the soil beneath. Behind the stand of grass is a grove of trees, a few evergreens and some oaks.

A crow sits on the uppermost branch of a dead tree, steadying itself against the breeze.

Through a space between the trees, I can see the lowlands in the distance. The shadow of a cloud crosses the tasselled-out but yellowish corn, then darkens a gray patch of soggy ground that this year failed even to support the poor crop surrounding it. At the edge of the field, another stand of trees rises in sunlit, leafy humps. Against the trees stands a Happy Chef sign. The wind in the Indian grass and the surging and then ebbing sound of cicadas and crickets is almost as loud as the roar of wheels passing south on I-35. According to the historical marker, the distant trees shelter an old graveyard where the Swearingen family is buried, six members of which were overtaken in their covered wagon by a prairie fire on their way through this area in the 1840s. The prairie remnant is small, the cornfields in the distance are large, but it's hard not to notice, in this flood summer of 1993, that the grasses are thriving and the corn is weak.

These are the southern reaches of the prairie-pothole region, a huge area of small lakes (called potholes) and undulating low rises that aren't quite hills. Originally an estimated 6 million acres of tallgrass prairie and wetland, the pothole region resisted settlement 50 years longer than other parts of Iowa. Areas that have become farm fields used to be sheets of shallow water that ran for miles (the earliest settlers reported boating, or, in the winter, skating, from farm to farm). Although crisscrossed by numerous tributaries of the Mississippi and the Missouri rivers, this land was so new—only as old as the last ice sheet 11,000 years ago—that the rivers had not yet formed it, and most of them wandered, slow and wide, over the flat land.

To the first Europeans, the prairies looked, above all, inexhaustible. In addition to inexhaustible space, and inexhaustible soil fertility (the deepest topsoil in the early days was to be found in an area north of Marshalltown and in northeast Iowa, where it measured 20 to 25 inches), settlers found abundant wildlife. "Prairie-chickens [numbered] in countless thousands and their nests often covered acres of the prairie," writes Bohumil Shimek in *Iowa's Natural Heritage*. "The long-billed curlew, now unknown in Iowa, everywhere hovered over the prairie, an easy mark for every pot-hunter; great clouds of golden plovers, or 'prairie-pigeons,' swooped down seemingly out of nowhere, apparently to alight, but only to sweep away again like a turbulent wave; the white and the sandhill cranes danced merrily (and awkwardly) before their mates, and the borders of swamps and 'sloughs' were often lined with the nests of ducks of several species; pelican eggs could be collected in favored spots by the boat-load; and practically every muskrat house supported the nest of a wild goose."

By and large, the prairie states were settled by European farmers whose native regions were mountainous, forested, stony, and cursed with poor soil or unfavorable weather patterns (not to mention absentee landlords, overcrowding, and social unrest). Story City, Iowa, for example, is still self-consciously Norwegian. Elkhorn, Iowa, is the home of the Danish Immigrant Museum. Until World War II, the public life of Manning, Iowa, was conducted entirely in German—a friend's Irish ancestors who settled nearby had to learn to speak German there just to get along. Czechs, Finns, Swedes, Luxemburgers, English, Irish, Dutch, and numerous other European groups are scattered over the prairie, mostly in enclaves of homogeneous nationalities and religions.

Each group of these settlers brought its own habits, manners, cuisine, and dress. Many of them also brought European-style agriculture, which was based on mono-cropped fields and animal power. In Europe, climate and poor conditions put a natural brake on what it was possible to grow. In his study of daily life in the Middle Ages, Fernand Braudel estimates that one wheat seed planted in a field in France would produce, at best, four grains, whereas today's wheat yields a minimum of 30 grains from a single planted seed. And much of Europe was best suited for pasturing animals or hunting, which meant that Europeans had grown accustomed to more meat and dairy products in their diet than many populations living in milder regions. Braudel estimates further that in the 15th century the average European ate meat five times a week. While this average fell considerably over the subsequent centuries, especially for the general population, the ideal remained, modeled in the feasting of the upper classes—course after course of fish, fowl, and meat, leavened with some pie crust or bread, accompanied by wine and ale, finished off with some fruit.

Along with their tastes and know-how, Europeans brought belief systems that were hostile to difference, diversity, and alien forms of knowledge, and that portrayed nature as separate from and subordinate to men. They brought the habit of supporting large cities, which entailed an emphasis on productivity as well as the continuous export of a locality's best goods, be they milk, meat, lumber, or children.

Bent on reconstructing the lives they had left behind, the first settlers saw around them inexhaustible emptiness, a daunting wasteland to which they could bring the familiar—farms, towns, cities, wheat, apples, cabbages, cattle, hogs, chickens, capital investment, import-export relations with the cities further east, and speculation. (Studies of settlement on the prairies make clear that townsite speculators came first, followed by merchants of building materials, clothing, and other supplies. Moderate mercantile success allied with considerable boosting through local newspapers brought in the railroad, and only then did the settlers begin to come, pioneers, perhaps, but customers first and foremost.)

Early leaders promoted Iowa as an agricultural paradise, where "a delicious fragrance fills the air, which impresses the mind with a sense of realization of its fondest ideal of the 'land of flowers.'" Even the climate, though bracing, was perfect: "Almost imperceptibly, these golden days merge into winter, which holds its stern reign without the disagreeable changes experienced in other climes, until spring ushers in another season of life and beauty. And so the seasons pass, year after year, in our beautiful and healthful Iowa," was how it was touted in a pamphlet printed by the General Assembly of 1872 in English, German, Swedish, Dutch, and Danish and widely distributed in the United States and Europe. The potential of native grasses was recognized—blue-joint grass rated a mention for being both nutritious and productive ("It often yields over three tons per acre"), but the great draw, in the view of those hoping to attract immigrants, was the way introduced plants and livestock throve in Iowa—wheat, oats, flax, buckwheat, barley, rye, onions, parsnips, carrots, beets, cabbage, lettuce, apples, grapes, morello cherries, cattle, hogs, sheep, horses—the catalog of the familiar was obviously meant to reassure settlers that they could bring their old lives with them. Even corn, "Irish potatoes," beans, and pumpkins were imports—native to the Americas, but not to the prairies. The promise was that all the immigrants had to do to realize a life just like the one they were leaving (but far more prosperous) was to clear away the native vegetation and bring in the plow.

Although the prairie-pothold region in Iowa was settled relatively late, by the late 1880s and early 1890s the hunger for land made it profitable to invest in the arduous undertaking of digging tile-ditches, laying tile, and draining off the waters. The act of the Iowa legislature establishing drainage districts in 1872 asserted that the drainage of surface waters would be *presumed* to be of public benefit. As Richard Bishop and Arnold Van der Valk remark in *Iowa's Natural Heritage,* "[T]his eliminated much of Iowa's water storage capacity—our natural sponge. No longer would these temporary sloughs hold water for nesting ducks or retard runoff. Tile carried water as rapidly as possible to drainage ditches or creeks and on to rivers which flowed into the larger Mississippi and Missouri rivers." In some places, the surface watercourses were too shallow and slow to carry the drainage water, so the tilers devised drainage wells that sent the water underground, into the aquifer.

The land revealed by the draining of the marshes was unprecedented in its fertility. As the wildlife and the space that had been hallmarks of the prairies began to vanish by the end of the century, it appeared that they could easily be dispensed with, for the familiar could be planted in their place and prosperity itself would be inexhaustible.

The most important lesson of the flat, fertile lands is that appearances are deceiving.

While the agricultural industry nearly always promotes itself as a rousing success (usually in terms of one farmer feeding some mind-boggling number of other mouths), American farming on the prairies has had only one golden decade out of fifteen, and that was before and during the First World War, when, of course, agriculture in Europe was in collapse. Many historians assert that the effects of the agricultural depression of the 1920s and the Great Depression of the Dust Bowl '30s reach well into our era—serious bad times have been followed by moderately good times, but neither the policymakers nor the farmers have succeeded in putting back together the prosperity of the early years of this century.

Today it is clear that the prairies not only *look* different from what the settlers found, they *are* different. The last hundred and fifty years have seen the erosion of half of the original topsoil, topsoil the settlers rightly viewed as a priceless treasure. This erosion not only continues 60 years after the lessons of the Dust Bowl and the development of soil-conservation districts, techniques, and plans, but is happening faster than ever. The prairie has suffered a precipitous decline in genetic diversity of all types of plants and animals, and the rapid depletion of some of the world's largest aquifers. We have witnessed the failure of efforts to control the continent's great inland rivers, the chemical contamination of surface and underground water supplies, the rise of pests and diseases that depend on large stands of mono-cropped food plants to establish themselves (as well as the emergence of resistant strains of these pests and diseases), and the deterioration of rural life for the people who live here. These are not merely signs of mistakes in the application of farming methods to the prairies—they are evidence that those methods are inherently destructive and self-limiting. Of the successive geological epochs of life on the prairie, no doubt the couple of hundred years that humans have tried farming it with plows and other machines will be the very shortest.

But when I emerge from the North Woods and look around at the sunlit cornfields I feel what everyone who lives here feels—how tempting it is to go on with the familiar. There is water in some of the low spots, but the familiar order of the rows of corn and beans, the familiar pleasure of the highway urge me to overlook what I know is happening out here. The effort of embracing something new and alien seems too great today, too difficult, too hard to understand.

Over in Kansas, where the prairie is neither so rich nor so forgiving as in the pothole region of Iowa, Wes Jackson and his colleagues and students at The Land Institute are busy embracing something new. In fact they are doing a simple thing, though not an easy one—they are looking at the prairie and seeing, not an inexhaustible wasteland, but an ecological system of limits and balance. They are asking how the prairie plant community succeeds not only in maintaining itself, but in building its soil base, which ensures future success.

One way is evident at the prairie remnant north of Ames: the most profound difference between the cornfield beyond and the stand of Indian grass nearby is an obvious, physical one. While there is bare soil between the rows of corn, in the prairie remnant the Indian grass and its leguminous companion plant, the partridge pea, cover the soil completely, matting it over and rooting thickly into it. They protect the soil from the impact of rain and wind, and the soil, in turn, protects the roots and seeds of these plants from fires (commonly caused by lightning) of the sort that killed the Swearingen family in the 1840s.

The paradox of the prairie is that though many prairie grasses are related to domestic grasses such as corn and wheat, they are perennials rather than annuals. They put the energy they receive from the sun into deep roots and herbaceous growth rather than setting large seeds. It is the concentrated energy of seeds that humans have heretofore valued in their food crops, but another deception of appearance is that the energy carried in the seeds is mere surplus and can be exported to, say, Chicago, without degrading the ecosystem that produces it.

Prairie perennials grow in small patches that are interspersed with many other sorts of perennials, protecting each other from infestations of insects and diseases and preventing a boom-and-crash cycle in the populations of individual species. Another surprising effect of mixed growth is "overyielding." When planted alone in large stands, potential perennial food crops produce considerably less than they do when planted with others. Land Institute researchers Judith D. Soule and Jon K. Piper report that when wild senna (a grass) and Illinois bundleflower (a legume) were planted in alternate rows, their yields increased by 51 percent over three years, but when they were planted alternately within the same rows, their yields increased 161 percent, and these yields remained stable.

Here in the prairie-pothole region, it may seem as though we have plenty of time and plenty of soil; if we cannot go on exactly as we have for the last century, it does seem as though we can tinker a little bit and buy time. According to Iowa's Department of Soil Conservation, the worst farming practices (fall plowing, planting up and down hillsides, leaving no crop residue on the surface) would use up eight inches of topsoil (which may have taken 7,000 years to create) in 36 years. Contouring, terracing, giving up fall plowing, and leaving crop residue on the surface all year long would make that eight inches last 2,224 years, which seems like more than enough to let our generation off the hook of reconceiving agriculture. Unless, of course, you consider that on a natural prairie there is not only no loss of topsoil, but a net gain.

Agriculture, according to British historian Clive Ponting, is inherently a boom-and-crash operation. When all goes well, the human population dependent upon the crops booms, but when the growth in the human population begins to overstress the surrounding ecosystem, a crash is inevitable. In *A Green History of the World* (St. Martin's Press, 1991), Ponting quotes archaeologist Leonard Woolley, who excavated the Mesopotamian city of Ur, writing in 1936, "Why, if Ur was an empire's capital, if Sumer was once a vast granary, has the population dwindled to nothing, the very soil lost its virtue?" Ponting goes on: "The answer to Woolley's question is that the Sumerians themselves destroyed the world they had created so painstakingly out of the difficult environment of southern Mesopotamia." In the early years, the wheat-and-barley surplus afforded the independent city-states armies, bureaucracies, and war. After awhile there were no virgin fields to be plowed, and all crop production declined, rendering the Mesopotamian cities vulnerable to external conquest. "What is remarkable," Ponting writes, "is the way that the political history of Sumer and its city-states so closely follows the steady decline of the agricultural base." Subsequent civilizations in the region were never able to solve the agricultural puzzle—intensive interference with the water system of the area, through irrigation, always produced a short period of prosperity followed by agricultural collapse and conquest by outsiders.

The application of technology to agriculture on the North American prairies has not, so far, exempted our culture from the biological forces that have destroyed earlier civilizations. It is clear, rather, that big machines and strong chemicals have speeded them up.

There is some movement in the agricultural world toward a more sustainable way of raising food. The Sierra Club, in particular, has worked hard to shape federal agricultural policy so that it reflects environmental concerns. One area of particular success has been the "swampbuster" and "sodbuster" provisions written into the 1990 Farm Bill, which penalize farmers for conversion of wetlands to fields, as well as for plowing steep, highly erodable ground. Other parts of the bill provide more funds for research into sustainable agriculture, promote soil conservation, and regularize the introduction of organic produce into the marketplace. These steps, of course, are important, especially in contrast to some previous federal policies that supported real agricultural evils, such as planting corn year after year on the same fields. But they are only the beginning of coming to terms with what the prairie is and how we can best live with it as well as upon it.

Personally, I like bread, chicken, a good steak, corn on the cob, and a melting pork stew made with yellow potatoes and flavored with onions and allspice. I've never tasted the seeds of Eastern gamagrass (a perennial that can cross with corn), Illinois bundleflower (a perennial, nitrogen-fixing legume), leymus (a member of the wheat-barley-rye family), or Johnsongrass (a relative of sorghum), all of which are being studied at The Land Institute as potential food crops. Not only that, I rely as much as anyone on the export of prairie energy in the form of large seed-grains like corn, wheat, and soybeans. I live in a town. I am a part of the expensive superstructure that weighs upon the soil and depends entirely on the gifts of nature for its existence. For most of human history, the superstructure was like the top of a pyramid. Every soldier, artisan, administrator, and person of leisure was surrounded by the many peasants whose agricultural work supported him or her. In our time, the pyramid is inverted. The enormous superstructure of American society rests on a tiny point—the point where fewer and fewer farmers with larger and larger machines mine as much food as they can out of fields that are less and less what they once were.

The scope of what has been almost entirely lost in the prairie-pothole region is glaringly obvious at the Kalsow Prairie, on a little dirt road north of Manson in Pocahontas County. This 160-acre prairie preserve is one of the oldest in the state, as close to virginal as it is possible to find. This is prairie the way you imagine it—the land is flat under the dome of the heavens, thickly growing goldenrod, big blue-stem, sunflowers, Indian grass, clover, bentgrass, and milkweed. Myriad other grasses and broadleaves (as they call them in the weed-killing business) rise and bend in the gusts of the west wind. Brilliant autumn yellows bloom everywhere against a background of late-season browny-green, though the summer's rains seem to have given the prairie an extra season of lushness. One or two shrubby trees grow among the grasses from seeds that in a natural course of events might have succumbed to prairie fire. The ground underfoot is entirely firm—a mat of roots and plants that tangle into humps and dips beneath my feet. But a hundred and sixty acres is only a quarter-section, after all, and the named and preserved Kalsow Prairie is entirely surrounded, as far as the eye can see, by fields of corn and beans, cut square by country roads, dotted here and there with houses and barns.

Immediately across the road from the prairie is a cornfield. The crop stands six or seven feet tall, blocky and graceless, awaiting enough dry weather for harvest. Between the road and the corn is a strip of wet, black soil, unprotected, ready to be washed or blown away. The crop looks better than almost all the corn I've seen on my way here—at least it is green rather than yellow, tall rather than sickly. The farmer who owns it may survive another few years.

The words commentators used to describe last year in Iowa, Illinois, Minnesota, and Missouri, the heart of the agricultural region and the region of the long-lost tallgrass prairie, are big words: "disaster" gave way in June to "catastrophe" in July. Right here, in the prairie-pothole region, where some creeks and rivers drain into the Missouri and some drain into tributaries of the Mississippi, right here is where floods at Kansas City, St. Louis and Ste. Genevieve, Des Moines and Iowa City, are born. The floods we have seen are not an act of God, but a result of history, a result of choosing technology for an intensively tilled, monocultural, cash-crop-based agricultural system designed to satisfy the demands of ever-expanding markets, as well as an appetite for a meat diet based on feeding animals grains rather than herding them. More immediately, they are the result of altering the water-holding capacity of the soil. More importantly, they are a warning that we have taken too much from the prairie without giving anything back.

Many forces drive us to ignore the warning. One of them is that most of the media commentators know little or nothing about agriculture or the history of this region. Another is the unexamined conviction, shared by most people in our society, that agriculture as it has been done is agriculture as it must be done. Still another is a belief, promoted by those who are invested in the present agricultural methods, that the prairie (or California's Central Valley, or the farmlands of eastern Washington and Oregon) can all be made by technology to perform the way it looks like they should perform—as if they were man-made machines for the production of food—through the application of a little more force. Still another reason is greed, which is merely the conviction that humans have the right, God-given in the eyes of many, to possess and exploit every corner of the earth, that every square mile and every plant and animal species must "pay for itself," that the human life supported by agriculture is intrinsically valuable while other forms of life are not.

It is not "politically correct," or "morally right," or even "necessary" to heed the warnings abounding in the soil and water of the prairie. It is intelligent. Whether we do so or not is the measure of whether we have progressed beyond the Mesopotamians of four and a half thousand years ago, or whether we are, in fact, still caught in a comforting illusion of familiarity.

Barry Lopez

Offshore: A Journey to the Weddell Sea

from *Orion*

I. *Port Fourchon to Balboa, Panama*

Towering magentas have faded from the clouded sky like an exhalation. An open lattice of cumulus shadow glides the moon's manganese swath over black water beyond the bow. I've just stepped outside, barefoot in shorts and a T-shirt, and see below me the port hull wave rising up from a jade base, turning turquoise across its shoulder and breaking brilliant white. High overhead in the port bridge wing, a row of tall windows, misted with the pale red glow of night-vision lamps, projects sharply into a blue-dark sky by the moon.

Behind, in my room, I've left blueprints of this ship—the icebreaking scientific research vessel *Nathaniel B. Palmer*—to flatten beneath a weight of books and bits of dive gear. Deck by deck, I am trying to grasp the order of its design, as one would trace the interior of a pyramid or climb in a cathedral from crypt to spires. I turn the ship on its axes in my imagination, exploring the cleave of its prow, the logic of its engines, the harrowing complexity of its bottom-mapping equipment and its satellite receivers, equipment understood completely by no one. In *The Log from the* SEA OF CORTEZ, John Steinbeck calls such a working ship "the greatest and most important of all tools." Each day as I walk it or sweep it with my hands, I know he could as easily have called it the largest tool we make that possesses the haunting and attractive elements of personality.

This afternoon a Cuban fighter plane dogged the *Palmer* in the Yucatán Channel, dragging its flaps and making two low passes, inquiring. Had the pilot ever seen an icebreaker in the Caribbean? With such a massive forward wall to its superstructure, this one might have mimicked an Aegis-class missile cruiser on his radar. After a while he or she lifted up and bore away in the drab creature. I watched it depart with a Chilean deck hand named Marcelo Mera, and we continued south at thirteen knots affected by the world's wariness.

The *Palmer,* I could reflect, was too new, too obscure, for very many to know about. This was her initial voyage, a shakedown cruise down the west coast of South America to the Strait of Magellan, and then across the Drake Passage and into the Weddell Sea in Antarctica, where she would rendezvous with Russian and United States scientists on an ice floe, deep within the winter pack.

No one before had ever built an icebreaking ship as advanced, as specialized, as the *Palmer,* and only a few such research vessels could compare—Germany's *Polarstern,* Russia's *Akademik Federov,* Australia's *Aurora Australis.* What sets the *Palmer* apart is an ability to gather automatically a wide range of precisely fixed atmospheric and oceanographic information; and also the intention of her sponsor, the National Science Foundation, to employ her year-round in a single task—scientific research in Antarctic waters. She differs from the other vessels, too, in the greater variety of scientific projects she can accommodate, in maneuverability, and in the sophistication of her computer network. Three-hundred-and-eight feet long, sixty feet wide, the *Palmer* is designed to operate in air temperatures as low as −50°F and in the terrific winds and long-term winter darkness that characterize the Antarctic Ocean. With the aid of bow and stern thrusters, the ship can hold steady above the same spot on the ocean floor in twelve-foot seas with thirty-knot winds and a crosscurrent of two knots.

Operating primarily from Punta Arenas on the Strait of Magellan, the *Palmer,* with a crew of twenty-six, can support thirty-seven scientists on cruises as long as seventy-five days. These people will eventually include biological, physical, and chemical oceanographers; marine geologists and geophysicists; students of the history, structure, and dynamics of sea ice, of marine mammal behavior, or the lives of oceanic birds; and design engineers, analyzing the performance of research platforms like this. (The immediate importance of an Antarctic Ocean study lies principally with accelerating an understanding of global climate patterns and biological activity in Southern Hemisphere seas. Antarctica's waters have a profound effect on both.)

Each evening now before going to bed I stand like this at the port railing, on the second of five decks that rise above the main deck, to gaze at the sea, the ship, and the stars. Recalling our course penciled in on a set of maps, I can picture where we are at this hour: Misteriosa Bank, sixteen nautical miles to the west, fifty-five feet underwater. Grand Cayman Island, 120 nautical miles to the east. In thirty minutes we'll cross over the crest of Cayman Ridge; its south slope will then plunge more than three miles down to the wide floor of the Cayman Trench. Between us and that montane bottomscape tonight move all manner of creatures, the catalogued, the unsuspected, and those suspected but, so far, irretrievable.

No other ships appear on the moonlit sea. I recall the first time I saw the *Palmer,* in bayou country in rural Louisiana where she was built. A violent, heavy rainstorm had tapered off. It was late at night and I'd had a difficult time locating an unmarked road, potholed, paved with oystershell, that led past looming warehouses into a dim and gateless shipyard on the Intracoastal Waterway. Around a corner of one warehouse I suddenly came on it broadside at a dock, sheered from the night by its incandescent lights; its orange hull and ivory-colored superstructure were vivid as an infant's eyes and as alien in the dark swampland as a spaceship. Wind whipped steam from shrouding on portable light gantries on the aft deck. Welding's blue-white light smoldered in its portholes. The air, swollen with rain and pneumatic hissing, was heady with paint fumes, sucked from the ship's interior by roaring fans. Sheets of red-orange sparks flared from disc sanders and dwindled in the mist. Over the sounds of air compressors and electric generators, I heard ball hammers peening steel, the clatter of lumber, and half a conversation shouted in Cajun French by someone standing alone at a bulkhead.

The scale and extent of hand tasks, the boldness of the ship against the night sky, and bursts of damp wind that swept through made the ship seem fresh, self-possessed. From the port side she looked athletic: the massive thighs of a sprinter and the lean whip of a long-distance runner. In my motel room that night, I wrote a friend that even in repose like this the *Palmer* bristled with ability, the way a weasel bristles with speed and litheness when it turns its head and its eyes gleam at yours.

In the days following this first encounter, I climbed and crawled through the ship, studying arrangements I'd never seen before and asking questions. As much as I wished to learn the ship and about its construction, I wanted to hear people working on it share whatever they struck upon. They chose precision welding and Finnish naval architecture; offered a succinct reminder—flip the Flinders bar in the magnetic compass at the Equator; debated the savor of brown versus white shrimp from the Gulf and the intractable (some insisted) turmoil of marriage; and said to expect resiliency in the 1⅝-inch steel bow plates even at −60°F. Altogether a fine gumbo, day after day beneath hot, cool, and fretting Louisiana skies.

I stayed on, to speak with the ship's owners, Edison Chouest Offshore, a family-owned business building and operating specialized offshore vessels; and to attend a blessing of the *Palmer* by a young Vietnamese priest, a man who stood joyously in the rain, unaware of the mud welling over his polished shoes, to lead bareheaded shipyard workers and office assistants in a ceremony so ancient it transcended religion.

Two months later I returned. The *Palmer* had finished her sea trials. Ten thousand meters of five different types of wire had been wound on her winches. The drawers in her steel storage lockers were crammed with bolts, valve seals, pipe fittings, light bulbs, wipe cloths, and other spare parts; her small tanks had been topped off with glycol and helicopter fuel; the shelves and floors of her galley storerooms were stacked tight. Her paint was aboard. And the Coast Guard, the American Bureau of Shipping, and insurance agents had signed off on her seaworthiness.

Following a dedication at Port Fourchon, an international shipping terminal fifty miles southwest of New Orleans, the *Palmer* moved offshore to take on hundreds of thousands of gallons of fuel and fresh water, and to address a problem with her bow thruster—its rotating grate, mounted flush with the bottom of the hull, had jammed. The port engineer, a diver, had gone ashore; the captain, who heard I was qualified when I came aboard, asked if I'd go under the ship to see if I could discover what was wrong.

I wanted to see the ice ship from underneath, hung against the bright Gulf sky; but the water was cloudy with sediment and darker still under the hull. Using a knifeblade and a watertight flashlight I located something wedged between the grate and its housing. I memorized the way the grate was askew in the housing and the angle of the jammed object relative to the keel. As I left, the sweep of my light bounced from three urethane bottom panels, small windows that protect separate clusters of transducers within the ship. (Transducers convert electrical impulses to sound waves and the returning sound waves back to electrical impulses.) Depending on the emitted wavelength, a transducer's sound waves can penetrate muddy bottoms to locate tectonic plates twenty thousand feet below, or contour a delicate midwater lens of plankton, or differentiate among a deep crosshatch of ocean currents. The equipment is part of the ship's permanent array of sensors and probes.

I saw, too, as I departed, the eerie pit of one of the ship's seawater intakes; and shuttered openings from which forward-looking sonars would descend to help the *Palmer* navigate along uncharted coasts. As I rose twenty-two feet to the surface, my hands slid up the hull like satin on glass—a vinyl-like paint, Inerta 160, cuts the ship's resistance to water, ice, and snow by about ten percent.

We left our anchorage at ten o'clock one March night, headed for Panama; but the process of leave-taking felt days old by then. Before the *Palmer*'s dedication ceremonies I'd walked off into the marshes east of the wharf, to watch birds. Great blue and Louisiana herons hunted; northern shovelers and green-winged teal floated; snowy egrets and black-necked stilts stepped delicately. Killdeer cried. In the marsh reeds, red-winged blackbirds teetered and sang, a rush of bell notes that fleshed the air and suited the balmy temperatures. I go out of my way to hear birds. Even as their populations wane I find the notes, the phrases, hopeful not poignant. At dawn, from tiers and crossbracing in a signal tower next to the ship, I heard a great rise and fall of song from common grackles, red-winged blackbirds, and brown-headed cowbirds, like running water braided over a river bar. The reason for the chorus, like the pattern time makes in their lives, is ungraspable. I imagined it that last morning a blessing.

We saw thousands of birds as we put to sea that day—flocks of laughing gulls, fast, high-flying ducks, white and brown pelicans in lugubrious wings. At the mouth of the bayou we passed a great egret rookery, perhaps a hundred birds nesting. I recall the afternoon as a meld of brisk winds, bright sunshine, and wild birds. Also calm salutes from the decks of shrimp boats, local men who'd heard of the icebreaker built in the bayous and, here, assumed she was away.

A few days later, out in the Gulf, two purple martins came fluttering around the bridge, ticking the windows with their claws and beaks. Like most anyone far at sea, I marveled at the curious mix of stoicism and confusion that seems to characterize errant birds on blue-water ships. Innocent of their navigational skills and their intents, one feels tenderly toward them, and regardful. They've come out from the invisible shore to which one hopes to return.

The two birds reminded David Martin, the mate on watch, of two other birds that once landed on a ship of his. The crew began to feed them. Later, an owl traveling aboard a freighter sailing a parallel course flew across to the ship. It killed the birds, ate them, and flew back to the freighter.

Some evenings I stand at this railing for more than an hour. Often in that time something happens: a fish breaks the surface of the sea; a meteor blazes for a few moments; or a sweet odor blooms, the breath, perhaps, of whales. Separately the events might seem trivial. But they form a pattern in space and through time, an assurance that the world is animate beyond any human influence. On a boat so heavily engineered as the *Palmer* the feeling is an occasional relief.

I lay my ear to the rail and hear with great clarity the running detonation of the diesel engines below. I am drawn to them in the way one is curious to see the thrash of hurricane winds or to stand beside a river's cataract. Turning over at nine hundred revolutions per minute, the four of them are driving the ship through the Caribbean against a one-knot current. The engines are matched in pairs, through reduction gears, to each of two propeller shafts. The shafts are turning at 140 revolutions per minute. At the end of each shaft a four-bladed, stainless-steel propeller, thirteen feet across, churns inside a nozzle, a shroud that protects it from sea ice and increases its thrust. (To back the ship up, the pitch of the propellers, not the rotation of the shafts, is reversed. Increasing the variable pitch of the props increases the ship's speed, fore and aft.) The wash from each propeller flows across a rudder; the twin rudders, independently steerable, function like high-performance airplane wings, changing the ship's course quickly.

The *Palmer*'s propulsion and maneuvering system is designed for agile, precise handling and to provide the great thrust at slow speeds necessary for breaking ice. Given the variability of prop settings and the way diesel engines can be adjusted to produce more or less horsepower—more to break ice, less to transit the open ocean—the combinations of engine speed and propeller pitch for efficient fuel consumption become unmanageable without computer assistance. (Computerized adjustments also protect the system against excessive loads during icebreaking or maneuvering in heavy seas.)

In extreme circumstances, the *Palmer*'s engines will produce nearly fourteen thousand horsepower. Learning to use some or all of it economically is one of the most complex tasks facing the ship's engineers on the voyage.

I lift my ear from the rail. Nowhere in the ship do you lose completely the sound of the engines, a distant tattoo that changes pitch and tempo slightly as the ship flexes through the water. (The quietest spot I've found aboard is in a compartment forward on the lower deck, piled high with galley stores. The sound that dominates here is a soft creaking of cardboard boxes, like the sound a wooden sailing ship makes in easy seas. I come to believe it is the same cellulose—in the cardboard.) In some parts of the ship, the engines' concussion is the rataplan of taiko drumming. Their vibration is apparent to the touch in the ship's every steel plate and pipe, even in small brass wiring brackets, like barely audible thunder. The closer one draws to the gleaming, heated blocks below, the more sensual the vibrations become.

I feel the grit embedded in the green deck paint against my feet as I walk forward on the second deck, crossing from port to starboard by the anchor winches. I pause briefly to listen to the bows crash the swell, then come aft on the starboard side. Far away, off the stern quarter, lies the Yucatán Peninsula. In recent years the peninsula has grown larger in my mind, not for late revelations about the Maya or for knowing of the collapse of the northward migration of songbirds from its stepping-stone shores, but for the presence of a bolide impact crater located beneath the town of Chicxulub. This deep geological structure, about 185 miles across, was discovered in the 1950s by PEMEX, the Mexican national oil company, though it was not satisfactorily explained at the time. Many scientists now believe the crater, which dates to exactly sixty-five million years ago, marks the spot where a huge meteor or comet slammed into the Earth and that this event caused or abetted the mass extinction of life we know occurred at the end of the Cretaceous.

Yucatán is too distant to see. I finger a fresh cut on my left palm. Miles back, this afternoon, we crossed the track of Columbus's fourth voyage; tomorrow we should cross it again, entering Limón Bay at the entrance to the Panama Canal. He passed that close to the Pacific, only another forty miles over the hills.

I enter my room. The blueprints look as though they will stay flat now. I remove the weights and push aside the books—*Neruda: Selected Poems* and Bowditch's *New American Practical Navigator*—and swing the sheaf of heavy paper up to the bunk above my own, which is unoccupied.

The last image before my eyes each night is a reflection of foam and scud, the ship's wake, in the smooth red-orange bottom of the lifeboat outside my porthole. The last sound is often a human voice in the passage—speaking Spanish softly, or Tagalog, creole French, or the English of Maine, of Boston, or Louisiana.

The number of ships changes with the seasons, but an average of thirty-five vessels a day passes through the Panama Canal, paying about thirty thousand dollars each to do so. The *Palmer* rode placidly at anchor in a north wind for two days while Canal authorities, using a complicated formula, computed her "Panama Canal tonnage," the figure against which a toll would henceforth be assessed.

While we waited I read Columbus's correspondence from the fourth voyage. In November and December of 1502, he was pinned down by a furious storm about twenty-five miles up the coast from where we now stood by. It held him for twenty-nine days in a small harbor, called today Nombre de Dios. When the storm abated, Columbus sailed into modern-day Portobelo, eighteen miles from us, to refit his ships. The voyage, which he had called *el alto viaje,* the High Voyage of success, was to have been his vindication. Columbus's long letter of explication to his sovereigns is defensive and self-pitying; his spiritual muddle and the derangement bred by his frustrated search for wealth and personal advantage are as disturbing as the rhetoric of modern schemers after wealth and power. And sobering, sitting at anchor at a canal whose European history is dominated more by plots of greed and plans for war than by the one thought a passenger might have—how convenient.

More than twenty ships wait at anchor with us in the several anchorages of Bahía de Limón: oil-bulk-ore freighters, a liquid propane gas tanker, car carriers, a tuna seiner, refrigerator ships—*Reefer Jambu*/Singapore; *Necat-A*/Istanbul; *CGM Renoir*/Le Havre; *Lincoln Universal*/ Colombo [Sri Lanka]; *Iver Swan*/Larvik [Norway]; *Asian Senator*/Hamburg; *Chaquita Queen*/Nassau; and the seiner—*Grenadier*/ Port Vila [Vanuatu]. Unlike commercial aircraft, ships have no standard sizes or shapes. Each is different, wilder than any airplane. Laundry snaps in the breeze with a dozen flags.

In a sort of orphan anchorage just east of us, a small, piebald coastal freighter, the *Alpine,* floats catatonic, an embodiment for me of B. Traven's battered *Yorikke* in *The Death Ship.* Beyond it, smoke seeps from the hold of a Panamanian break-bulk ship, the *Ocean Sky.* Its cargo of waste paper has been burning like a mine fire for three days. Past that, in forested hills above the city of Colón wildfire towers in flame and subsides, towers and subsides. At night the fires will look like orange holes, molten and writhing, on the dark perimeter where the sky is finished.

Capt. Russell has given everyone permission to jump into the eighty-seven degree harbor water to cool off. I decide instead that these languid hours will be the time to talk with Dave Nergaard, a technician, about the ship's scientific equipment. We decide to look at a gravity meter, one of the first instruments to be squared away on the ship.

(Slight differences in the Earth's marine gravitational field can expose tectonic activity or reveal the general shape of the sea floor.)

The ship's computer network—to which the gravimeter is linked—is divided into two sectors on the main deck. Receivers for the ship's permanent sensors, and for a wide range of temporary and expendable ones, are located on the starboard side, a data-gathering station often called the network's "real-time" side. The data are manipulated in a companion lab on the port side in a room outfitted with DOS, Macintosh, and Unix workstations, and with silicon graphics machines, a plotter, and printer. The "user-side" workstations are connected to each other and to a service network, which stores all the information the ship gathers. On this cruise to the Weddell, technicians are settling instruments into the computer network, calibrating them, determining what's "noise" and what's signal in the information they provide, and writing related programs for shipboard scientists to use.

The capability and sophistication of the *Palmer*'s computer system is staggering, some of it barely within the theoretical grasp of the people managing it. And some of it, of course, is quite beyond anyone's imagination. Like other systems of its kind in business as well as science, it's dazzling and confounding at the same time; and its eminence is strange.

Nergaard, a man in his fifties, has an intriguing and practical knowledge of many things and likes to elucidate theory in physics with pedantic ironies and engaging anecdotes. He can recall, almost instantly, the routing of several hundred miles of instrument wiring through the ship. And he's delighted to explain what he calls, precisely, the "ship-borne gravity meter."

The force of gravity varies from point to point on the surface of the Earth. The gravimeter, one of half-a-dozen such free-standing instruments on board, measures these fluctuations and can automatically store the information while the *Palmer* proceeds back and forth over the ocean. The actual measuring device, an extremely delicate, fused quartz spring with a weight on it, is isolated inside a pressurized chamber, a sealed oven, in effect, that eliminates the need to correct for changes in temperature and barometric pressure. The chamber is suspended within a self-levelling platform, which uses gyrostabilizers and servo-amplifiers to compensate for the ship's pitch and roll. The platform, in turn, is suspended within an aluminum frame, the motion of which is damped by small shock-absorbing pistons and bungee cords.

"It's the sort of machine you turn on on Saturday night to use Monday morning," says Nergaard, as we wait forty-five minutes for it to finally level itself. (Later, I'll come down to watch the gravimeter compensating to keep itself stable in heavy seas, deft as a surfer.)

To be useful, each signal from the gravimeter must be tied to a particular time and place. Before it's stored, therefore, this steady stream of data, like streams of information from other instruments aboard the ship, is tagged with a latitude and longitude from the vessel's Global Positioning System and with a Greenwich Mean Time coordinate.

Bill Terry, an affable man and one of the few technicians enthusiastic about the world of water and animals beyond the ship's railings, has walked me several times through the *Palmer*'s data-gathering systems, from instruments atop its midships mast, 108 feet above the water, down to the uncontaminated seawater intake below the engine room. One day, while he was trying to isolate a problem in one of some 250 sensor wires entering his lab, he paused and looked up to say, "There's an amazing amount of stuff to remember about this ship." In a more philosophical mood at another time, he tried to convey a sense of the difficulty people face in measuring things, even with very sophisticated instruments. "We can measure time extremely well," he said. "We can measure distance very well. But we can't measure velocity—change over time—very well. Once you have motion, the motion of the ship, the motion of the Earth itself, tides and currents. . . ."

I thought immediately of Darwin, that Charles Lyell had given him the geological time in which to ponder; and that he'd had on the

Beagle's far-flung voyage the space, the geographic expanse, in which to work; and that he had arrived, then, at his theory of change-over-time, a pervasive insight that continues profoundly to affect Western culture. In certain of its applications, the theory weighs heavily upon us; the coordinates of every human life, like those of culture, change, causing disbelief, sorrow, and mistrust. Darwin, adding the authority of science to the acuity of philosophers, told us there was nothing to be done.

The sun is setting when finally we enter the fairway leading to the locks that will elevate us eighty-five feet in three stages to Gatún Lake. The tropical night arrives complete and suddenly. The machinery that begins to lift and convey us over the hills on this water bridge seems sedately colonial; and as we rise, in warm air that carries the perfume of orchids in its dense folds, I think of the death this ease extracted. Between 1906 and 1914, more than five thousand workers died or were killed here, mostly blacks, mostly from Barbados and Jamaica, mostly from malaria, pneumonia, typhoid fever, and accidents—dynamite explosions, landslides, drownings, train derailments.

The *Palmer*'s captain, Russell Bouziga, a heavy-set man, self-educated, hard-nosed, generous, a savvy manager of people, tells me he never makes this crossing without acknowledging those who died, without feeling admiration for the feat of engineering.

From the top of the Gatún Locks, we sail twenty-three miles across Gatún Lake in a series of seven reaches to the village of Gamboa, running on two engines, making an easy ten knots. The pilot, speaking in a subdued voice and standing close behind the helmsman, orders numerous, brief course changes, some as small as a single degree. (The pilot takes his night bearings from green-colored lights on staffs in the hills surrounding the lake.) Against the placid water, the windless air, the engines are quiet, only a murmur. Across the lake's glassy surface comes the ratchet of cricket-like insects; from the catwalk outside the bridge I hear an occasional cry from a startled bird, the rasp of a radar unit turning on the roof of the wheelhouse.

At Gamboa the eeriness becomes surreal. The lake ends; an ebony channel of unrippled water bears on. We pass as if down the village's main street; but the ship—hushed, enormous—moves through like afternoon clouds, seeming to disturb no thought or leaf. With its sleeping dogs, creaking screen doors, and desultory street conversation, Gamboa seems tipped out of some other dimension of mountainous Central America. I watch small pools of human life animated beneath bare porch bulbs receding in the foliage. An immense white ship, its deck lights extinguished like ours, as massive and quiet as I imagine us to be, enters my lingering gaze, headed the other way, cutting Gamboa off. The ship is only a dozen yards away. On the stack a red hammer and sickle. On the stern, *Kropotkin*/Murmansk.

Inside the wheelhouse the air is dry, cool. Long-wave-length red light bathes the instrument panels. Television monitors report green numbers in neat columns. The stout, shadowy figure of the pilot speaks in a voice meant not to startle, to convey one piece of information once: "Steady one-ten."

From Gamboa we follow a second series of seven reaches, leading through the Galliard Cut (in the continental divide) to Pedro Miguel Lock and a thirty-one-foot drop to Miraflores Lake. Capt. Russell, who often gazes from the bridge in solitude for an hour when we are at sea, points silently to the two-hundred-foot high walls in the cut, at the long, thin ghosts of boreholes hammered into the limestone then packed with dynamite to blow a wall of rock away—revealing yet another wall.

We glide on, nearly wakeless, in a mechanical silence we've been taught by movies reigns in space aboard galactic cruisers, from which in some moments we hardly seem to differ.

Capt. Russell asks if I was in Vietnam, where he served two tours. I must say no.

At the south end of Miraflores Lake we make a fifty-three-foot drop to Balboa Reach, sail under the high Bridge of the Americas and enter the Pacific. It is after two in the morning. A launch comes alongside to take the pilot. The chief engineer brings the other two engines on line, the first mate increases the pitch on both props to one hundred percent, and at a speed of about fourteen knots we make for a way point at 1°00′S and 81°14′W, twenty miles off the coast of Ecuador.

To the north I locate the pointer stars of the Big Dipper, but we are too far south here to easily see the North Star. To the east lies Golfo de San Miguel. It was to those waters that Vasco Núñez de Balboa carried the pieces of a small fleet of ships which he then assembled on the beach and with which he began the European exploration of the Pacific Ocean in 1517.

The bill for our passage across the isthmus is $16,363.99. It's been sent on to Edison Chouest in Galliano, the Louisiana town painted in blue on our stern and sited twenty-five miles inland from the Gulf, on a bayou too shallow for the *Palmer* to sail.

II. *Panama to Punta Arenas, Chile*

In the evening off the coast of Peru it's just cool enough now for a long-sleeved shirt. I've come to the stern, the loudest spot on the ship when we're under way. Added to the exhaust noise back here, from the engines and ventilator fans, are clangs and foghorn blasts—the noise of water cavitating around the props and hydraulic rams making small adjustments constantly to the rudders, instructed by the automatic pilot. I watch the convoluted boil and mounding of the prop wash for a while and then go forward where it's quieter.

The sea—we're riding gently over long swells that have come up from the Antarctic Ocean—stretches away to the horizon, untouched by a light. We are a tiny, lighted object, moving south through a hemisphere cloud of darkness headed west. I recall the daylit colors of the sea: olive green, yew green, cerulean, and indigo at sunset. Some of the blues were glycerine, deeper and more transparent than any printer's ink. But what is here now is the black ocean. Even at night it's apparent that no surface is more complicated by the strain of gravity than the ocean's. Watching fish rise and disappear in it by day, I know the water is very like conscious memory, and it is easy to imagine this is where the language of dreams incubates. By day the ocean's ability to erase and to conceal seems more benign than it does now; at night it seems more intimate.

I can see other waves moving through the southern swell, the history of events in other parts of the ocean far away. These histories pass through each other like radio waves; and to them our wake is now added. All this will break indecipherably on the shores of Peru and Australia.

I cross the helicopter pad—from its spaciousness this evening, I saw the sun set brilliantly in tobacco-ash skies, in shades of lemon and salmon—and pass up the starboard side of the ship to the bow.

Eventually my eyes are drawn up to the high, clean arch of the Milky Way. Enthralled by the constellations, I drift from the *Palmer*. I hear nothing. I feel only the breeze steady against the side of my head, and see only the vault of nuclear furnaces winking blue and gold and pink in the deep of space, and then the stars are the round, white breast of a bird, slowly fanning its wings and watching me like an apparition of the Paraclete. I wait—a gull, a swallow-tailed gull, hovering in the weak rays of the foremast light. Beyond are five or six more, their dark bodies barely visible, flapping against the stars. They're the only gulls that hunt at night.

We're riding now above the Nazca Plate. It stretches away to the west, where it meets the Pacific Plate at the East Pacific Rise. The floor of the Pacific, looking away from the starboard bulwark, broadly resembles the topography of the United States. The moderate rise of the East Pacific Ridge suggests the Alleghenies; then comes the abyssal plain of the Midwest, then the "front ranges" of the Line Islands and the Tuamotu Archipelago. Beyond these are the deep canyons of the West, the Mariana and Tonga trenches, and steep mountain ranges that terminate in the Gilbert and Marshall islands. Immense submarine plateaus, entire unto themselves, and smaller, mesa-like features called guyots, rise from the abyssal plain, along with sharp pinnacles that break the surface of the water at a height of eighteen thousand feet or more, forming islands higher than any peak in the Rocky Mountains.

Two hundred miles to the east of us, the Peru-Chile Trench descends over fifteen thousand feet. Here, the Nazca Plate, moving east with the steady expansion of the East Pacific Rise, is overridden by the continent of South America. Beneath, the descending edge of the plate is liquefying in the hot rock wax of the asthenosphere, under the Andes.

There are fifteen or so swallow-tailed gulls now, flying loosely together alongside the ship at the periphery of its deck lighting. Occasionally a wingtip dips into the penumbra. They are close enough to fill the lenses of my binoculars with their ghostly movement. It leaves an afterimage on the glass, or in my eyes.

I often finish my evening walk three levels up on the bridge deck, which I have come to call the scorpion deck. Aft of the span of the bridge, this deck is less than twenty feet wide. It stretches back past the midships mast to the ship's stack which, generously interpreted, rises like a scorpion's stinger. At night, looking forward from darkness by the mast, the hammerhead of the bridge seems inherently calm and hermetic behind tall, slanted windows that would look opaque but for the red glow within. A picket of white antenna wands marks out the bridge roof's perimeter. With them stand five dormant searchlights, turreted on posts, and two radar antennas, their white cross planks turning robotically on stanchions. The radars spin before the slender column of the ice-conning tower, which rises twenty feet to a small, darkened observation room underneath the white spheres of two dome antennas.

The bridge, its wings cantilevered over the ocean on either side and its vast ability to communicate and to navigate so implicit in its mute antennas, nearly fills one's field of vision. Above it and beyond tonight is the blackest blue sky riven cleanly by the familiar tingling spine of suns, the Galaxy seen edge-on. Watching the bridge move under the stars, feeling the ship's engines thrum in my legs, and standing in a breeze high above the ocean's smooth, dark plain—and then sensing the plunging depth, the shadowed plain of the Peru Basin below, the complex signal codes of bioluminescence winking there above the basin floor like stars—I thought, this must be sailing.

Our first morning off Peru, I came on the bridge at four to watch the sun rise. Just to the north of the spot where it would come up, a crescent moon rode horns up in the dark blue. Just to the south Venus glittered like a crystal, fifteen degrees above the horizon. The narrow space between was soon filled by a fan of alternating bars of pale rose light and intensified sky-blue. Then a flush of greenish yellows and saffron oranges spread the horizon. With the color came horizontal depth: I saw beneath a deck of elongated cumulus cloud a farther horizon, and the space above the ocean swelled and deepened. I felt the planet carrying us broadside into the light. The sun was soon shimmering so violently in the clouds I couldn't look at it.

I wondered what lay beyond the horizon, for I knew it was this and not a boundary. A city. Lima, where, long before its discovery, Darwin first heard rumors of Machu Picchu. Pizarro's Ciudad de los Reyes, sacked early by pirates, levelled by earthquakes; a bastion of Spanish conservatism, of resistance to Bolívar's dreams of independence and unification. A seat of the Inquisition, site of the first university in the New World. A city that lost its libraries, the contents of its museums, and its scientific collections to rampaging Chilean soldiers during the War of the Pacific (1879–1883). Darwin's letters from here to family and friends in the summer of 1835 reveal his disdain for Lima and its people; others have written of its brutal isolation in the desert, its squalid barrios, of dreary winters when the city is entombed in mist.

In every city, however, the patient visitor finds something to offset whatever is depressing, and it is not different here. In the seventeenth century Lima was a home to saints, the most widely known of whom are Isabel de Flores, or Rosa de Lima, the first person from the New World to be canonized; and Martín de Porres, a mulatto abject with miraculous powers of consolation and, like Isabel, a mystic and ecstatic. The Church insists upon the virginity and extreme virtue of these two people, but one does not read far in the history of their lives without encountering a love so strange it goes beyond such tenets. It seems to me that Isabel and Martín might have become lovers in their love of God. Such love would place their glory within the grasp of ordinary people.

I sometimes imagine the *Palmer* as a wind-blown stage, empty but for a few chairs, from which one can observe by an exaggeration of scale the distant continent, and contemplate what is marvelous or beautiful or dark while drifting its shores. I read Darwin's correspondence from 1834 and 1835, a life of Porres, and the poetry of Cecilia Vicuña and feel as if I am reading these books in the libraries of Lima.

Our first day south of the Equator I didn't come to the bridge until after eight. I'd been there until very late the night before, staring intently into the darkness, watching for small fishing boats. The sudden sight of the daylit ocean was momentarily bewildering. To the west, the water was thronged with cloud shadow and pools of light. The horizon had retreated, and in that huge and more vertical space a bluish-green sea rolled north with the Humboldt Current. Over Ecuador banks of lofting cumulus reflected the color of the land.

We'd watched a single squid-fishing boat last night work for hours. Burning with the blast-furnace light that draws its prey, it had been visible to us like a shining satellite long before our radars found it. When we were near enough, we studied the ship through binoculars. It was surrounded by a welter of birds. The sea over which its light booms were suspended churned with life, and streams of fish were being pulled in over its sides. Soon the air was rank with the fetid odor of this vacuuming and sorting operation. Now, four of these ships were clustered on the water. They looked primitive and dark in the sunlight, with their jury-rigged catwalks and winches of hook-bearing line. Low, gray hulks, stained with rust and offal.

The first mate said, "These bastards take everything in the sea. They never heard of the law."

I don't know that this is true; but it is true that fleets like this now strip the ocean in a frantic and lethal way. And out of fear of giving offense—for it cannot be out of ignorance—no one with influence has the will to stop it.

The most striking change in the world's oceans since the nineteenth century is their emptiness. Since leaving Panama we had seen only a few pilot whales, a few dozen porpoise, one or two schools of tuna breeching the surface. It is not the wrong season, or bad luck, or inattentiveness on our part. It is what everyone sees in these heavily-fished waters now—nothing.

Disconsolate, I went aft to the helicopter deck to wash away my commonplace anger in the wind. I was as weary as anyone of the threnodies that arise over this and which were now reverberating, I knew, in the mess, where people finishing breakfast were cursing the suspect nations. But the ordinary beauty of the world, in every corner of it I have seen, is being devoured. And it is for profit most often, not sustenance.

From where I stood the ocean looked kind. The water next to the ship was dark blue-green. Beyond, it turned blue-white, then blue-black, serpentine green, and finally at the horizon silver-gray. From the horizon back to the ship, the same pattern of relative shading was apparent in the banded sky.

I remembered we were headed south to the little known Weddell Sea. I recalled that the first birds we saw circle the ship in the Pacific were, to our amazement, South Polar skuas. And I reminded myself that the world is not anywhere free of harm. In Peru, since 1980, 25,000 people have been killed by the government and its opposition, Sendero Luminoso.

Recast, I went below to paint in the holds with the deck crew—Juan Melendez and Curtis Dantin, and Pedro Ledesma and some of the other Filipinos. Juan confides to me a strangeness in the world: one of the Filipinos has penis labrets.

We came upon the Equator late one afternoon. The captain stopped the ship, to let some of us jump in and swim across the line. From there, on that day, we looked north toward spring and south toward fall. The daylight-saving time most of us had gone off the previous fall we would, in a few days, go off again, without in the meantime having gained an hour. Joe Borkowski, the ship's first officer, flipped the Flinders bar under the magnetic compass. And Trevor Masters, a computer programmer from New Zealand creating some of the ship's software, told a story meant to illustrate the hilarious intractability of his work.

A display Trevor had developed, available on screens throughout the ship, showed a model of the *Palmer* moving in pulses across a grid of latitude and longitude. (Surrounding the grid were panels posting the ship's speed and course and other ship and weather data.) When the model hit the Equator it bounced off and sailed north at ninety degrees to the ship's true course. Trevor had used positive numbers for northern latitude and negative numbers for southern latitude in writing the program. It would have worked fine had the first southern coordinate the computer encountered not been an impossible number, −0.0, which it rejected.

This was one of a half-dozen straightforward instances of fallibility, or programming failure, that we would see aboard the ship. Harmless, funny, but oddly unsettling given the authority of the technology, its doyen status on the *Palmer.*

I kept a record of the *Palmer*'s track on a set of charts I'd brought with me, laying it off each day with dividers and a parallel rule. David Martin, the second mate, taught me how to use the calculator in the ship's Global Positioning receiver to determine the distance we traveled every twenty-four hours and also our course-made-good. These calculations were the first I'd ever done where I'd no idea of the underlying mathematics. I trusted, and even found attractive, answers that for all I knew could have been an illusion.

The ship's unblemished and confident charts, each carefully scribed with practical information, with navigational hazards, harbor approaches and the like, numbered over five hundred. (In spite of the recent date-of-issue of most of them, Martin and Mike Watson, the third mate, had to append 274 additions and changes to our charts of just the Chilean coast to bring them completely up-to-date.) Secure as I felt with the rectitude of these charts, I found myself turning to other sources. In "El Gran Océano," Neruda calls the sea "a still solitude replete with lives." He wonders at its "furthest reaches watched by night and air" and at the "white dialect" and "demolished purity" of its breaking waves. I remember a letter from a friend, the poet Pattiann Rogers, who asked, "Is the ocean ever still? It might seem to talk and talk and never lie still."

No skein of figures or plot of rhumb lines can bring the ocean completely within its domain. James Weddell, toward whose eponymous sea we sailed, writing in *A Voyage Towards the South Pole, Performed in the Years 1822–24,* names and praises the individuals who built his chronometers and azimuth compass. But he also describes there a sudden encounter with a whale's bloated carcass, saying that such an anonymous object "seen imperfectly in the night" can be alarming. By that much did his confidence fall shy of complacency.

In Valparaíso, a 450-year-old city with many ties to Antarctic discovery and exploration, we loaded fuel barrels for the ice station, boarded two pilots, and turned south for Isla Chiloé, six hundred miles down the coast. From there we'd follow Chile's inland waterway eight hundred miles to the Strait of Magellan. An outside passage in these latitudes could be very rough; the inland passage was calm, also spectacular.

A second practical reason to take the inside passage was a need for work on the engines. The engineers had discovered the wrong exhaust valves had been installed. Replacing them while the ship was under way in heavy seas would be prohibitively dangerous. Three mechanics had boarded with the pilots in Valparaíso; as soon as we passed around Isla Chiloé and into the placid waters of Golfo de Ancud they would go to work. We would travel on three engines while the mechanics tended the fourth. They thought it would take two or three days for each engine, but the work went faster.

I was drawn daily to the engine room on the ship's lowest deck. The engines, Caterpillar 3608 marine diesels, sat four abreast, with a wide pass between the middle two engines, narrow passes between the pairs, and wide passes on the outside. The noise here defeats conversation; and when our air conditioning failed in the tropics the heat was almost unbearable. (I recorded 134°F between the engines and 126°F in the room's other workspaces with a temperature probe.) But it was this very heat and noise, in combination with the savage, concentrated power of the engines, that made the room so intriguing. You could *feel* the horsepower driving the reduction gears. Stepping through a watertight bulkhead, you could see the massive propeller shafts turning in their shaft alleys. At the far end of the compartment, the power passed through gland seals in the ship's hull and into the sea.

The mechanics, from Louisiana Power Systems in Broussard, Louisiana, were skeptical when I said I wanted to lend a hand. I stood by and watched at first. As sometimes happens, by offering the right tool at the right moment, or by seeing that some unthought-of thing will be needed and fetching it, or by anticipating and diffusing danger, I was wordlessly brought into their realm, which I appreciated.

It took five days to finish the engines. The exhaust valves, about three-and-a-half inches in diameter and with fifteen-inch stems, were installed in pairs in each of an engine's eight cylinder heads. An engine was disassembled until its 450-pound heads could be pulled free with a chain hoist (the only really dangerous step); the valves were then replaced and the engine reassembled.

All the while they worked, the mechanics listened with uncanny astuteness to the sounds the engines made. On that basis, and using readings from sensors in the engines, they tuned them finely. One mechanic, Mike Truxillo, told me he could hear the cylinders popping on the ignition stroke best from the shower stall in his room. So, each morning he went down three levels to work with some idea of what had to be done.

With the help of Dave Munroe, the chief engineer, I soon learned where most every pipe, wire, and air shaft in the ship went, and what it was for. The *Palmer* was like a creature we lived within and upon. And as we steamed south it seemed that, just as engineers, mechanics, and technicians were refining the ship, the ship was discovering itself. Because it felt increasingly alive to me, I wandered through it every day and touched it everywhere. Its steel surfaces were as different as burlap and silk. I bent down in the morning to taste salt crystallized on its bulwarks. I carried a stethoscope into its deepest recesses, trying to find the sound of water against its skin. I listened to wind rifling its corridors when a door was left open. I watched flying fish explode from its forcing bow, sail, and hit the water again like a squall.

The *Palmer* was elaborate with misleading simplicities. Like many ships, it produced four waves, port and starboard, as it moved through the water. These Velox wave systems originated at the bow, at the ship's forward and aft shoulders, and at the stern. These are the wave trains one observes behind a ship, a vee widening toward the horizon. The subtle way in which the waves reinforce or cancel each other is complicated, related to the ship's speed and changes in its draft and trim. Some days I would concentrate on trying to understand this aspect of the ship. It did not seem necessary to be able to use or apply the information. The attention was related, rather, to the kind of pleasure once takes in a fascination with someone, a complicated person one wishes to know.

We hit our first rough weather northwest of Golfo de Penas, about six hundred nautical miles north of Punta Arenas. We entered the gulf from the open ocean long before dawn, heading for the north end of Canal Messier and protected water. Fifty-knot winds which had shredded our American and Chilean flags during the night now whipped froth and spray from wave crests. The *Palmer* pitched and rolled in confused, sixteen-foot seas, but the ride was surprisingly gentle, or "tender" as one of the mates said. (The *Palmer* was designed to sustain a steady one-hundred-knot wind and could right herself from a ninety-degree roll.)

We were all curious to see how the ship would handle in big water; but these waters were not big enough to make the bridge anxious or the ship seem in the least pressed. Once we were well inside Canal Messier the seas dropped. An hour or so later the fog had dissipated. Low clouds lifted to perhaps a thousand feet and we were sailing on calm, wind-ruffled water. As heavily forested coastal islands—Isla Penguino, Isla Sombrero—began to close in on us, black-browed albatrosses and sooty terns that had been looping the ship and riding the storm with such aplomb turned away, back towards the ocean.

The Southern Chilean canals, or Canales Patagonicos, a series of channels and straits that form a remarkably direct interior route along four hundred miles of the Chilean coast, compose a narrow passage through a landscape so steep and silent it feels remote even when one is deep within it. From north to south, the tree line descends toward the water's edge until, on this western flank of the Andes, evergreen beech forests truncated by the wind and dense as a bear's fur run out against bare stretches of tundra and sheer slabs of speckled granite. Lone streams pitch hundreds of feet, disappear in slopes of heath, then pitch again, thin, wind-blown cascades, white against escarpments dark as basalt. The waterfalls, fed by heavy rain in the north, then by snow, finally turn pale blue and aquamarine beneath hanging glaciers in the south.

We came quickly to the tightest passage on the route, the English Narrow, only 260 feet wide. Mike Watson steered the *Palmer* cleanly through the thousand-foot curve on a slack high tide to polite applause from the bridge. Marcel Nuñez, one of the pilots, raised his eyebrows, smiled, and nodded once in appreciation.

A small statue of the Blessed Virgin, white and about three feet tall, stands on an islet at the north entrance to Angostura Inglesa. It was placed there, perhaps sometime in the forties, by Alacaluf Indians living nine miles south at Puerto Edén, the only settlement on Canales Patagonicos. They salvaged it from a wreck in the Strait of Magellan. *Gracias Madre* they have written in black letters at its base. Marcel explains it is to welcome people back after a trip across Golfo de Penas—after the Gulf of Sufferings, glad to be alive.

Six miles past Angostura Inglesa, on an islet called Isolote Ollard, stands a pale-yellow, wooden building, perhaps six-by-eight feet with a faded mauve door and a low-pitched, slate roof. Buried here, in the late seventies Marcel believes, was the last full-blooded Alacaluf Indian, at his own request.

The shrine and this monument are some preparation for the small settlement of Puerto Edén, a redoubt of remnant Alacaluf and others. We edge in toward shore. Several blasts of the ship's horn, which sound garish and rude, bring three skiffs speeding out from the village. The first to arrive is a man in his twenties in a bright red jacket with a trussed mass of shelled mussels to sell. He looks humiliated when the captain says no, no shellfish. The second to arrive is a man in his forties with a lively dog like a border collie. He has fresh fish and two kinds of crab. We barter with him—fifteen-pound bags of rice, sacks of sugar, dry milk, and flour, and cans of tomatoes handed down for his fish and crabs. The captain instructs once and then more sternly that some of these staples are to go to the young man in the first boat. A third boat arrives with three men and a boy. They hope to trade handmade bark canoes and animal pelts for cigarettes, liquor, gasoline, paint. The captain offers only food.

Half the crew and most of the technicians are crowded at the low stern railing. One or two people eagerly offer inconsequential objects—Mardi Gras buttons, Ice Station Weddell shoulder patches, coat hooks—in exchange for the canoes, embarrassing and insulting the people. Jamie Scott, a marine technician, offers two pairs of leather work gloves for a coypu pelt, then returns it and waves off the return of the gloves or the offer of anything else. At the very end, almost surreptitiously, Marcelo slips two bags of clothing over the side and throws the boy a jacket.

We are there, holding the *Palmer* against the current, for only twenty-five minutes. I sketch the Alacaluf boats—beamy, about eighteen feet long, with a rising sheer in the bow, a narrow transom and closely-spaced ribs—and try to take in the village, about fifty wooden houses set square on uneven ground and painted pastel shades of pink, blue, and green. They are set at the foot of a steep, stepped slope of heath and green tundra that rises more than four thousand feet to snowfields. Marcel says about two hundred people live here.

Few indigenous people, anywhere in the world, have been as pitied as the Alacaluf and their neighbors, the Yaghan (Yámana) and Ona (Selk'nam). The French author Jean Raspail, in an anguished and compassionate historical novel called *Who Will Remember the People. . .* , writes of them as the "farthest flung spray" of human migration, "tossed down into the last place on earth"; a people with a hundred words for distress but no word for happiness; a people fearful of "not being sufficiently numerous to dominate the solitude."

The pity of European explorers grew from their perception of the Alacaluf, or Kaweskar, as a technologically impoverished people with little or no social organization, living in terror in a landscape Europeans found the apotheosis of melancholy and psychic depression. Darwin, Cook, Weddell—almost everyone who encountered them here thought they were the most primitive and wretched of people.

Whatever gifts the Kaweskar—together with the Yámana and Selk'nam they are sometimes called "Fuegians"—had to offer humanity, it is now a culture only lately and little studied, and largely excised. One might justifiably speculate that their metaphysics, their epistemology, eluded those people the Kaweskar branded with the epithet "pektchévés"—strangers; and that, sensitive to the horrible residue of colonialism and unthinkingly respectful of others, we shy away today from the confounding savagery and cruelty woven into this and every human culture; and that the Kaweskar lived tightly within the land, that they found it renowned and animated, as alive as their own flesh and as mysterious as any human emotion.

The country of the Kaweskar, into which we now passed, suggested the fiords of southeast Alaska, but it was a country entirely its own. The skies, which had been overcast, began to lift, and we saw the high granite domes and ramparts of the tundra-hided ranges streaked with waterfalls, and slot valleys crowded with dark trees which fell straight to beachless shores of lead-green water.

It seemed a country of rock, water, and plants, empty of animals save for steamer ducks, penguins, shags, kelp gulls, and once, I was told, a pod of Chilean or black porpoise. It was a untenanted landscape, neither bleak nor austere but hinting at the biological termination of Antarctica, at the autism that characterizes that continent.

We passed under Fairway Rock and its lighthouse late one afternoon, then turned south and east into Paso del Mar, the expansive western entrance to the Strait of Magellan. I looked back up Smyth Canal until it disappeared behind the Straggler Islands at the tip of Peninsula Muñoz Gomero, and Isla Turner. The landscape we had spent these last days in seemed the haunt of original spirits to me, not ghosts, a land to which one could become enthralled.

Paso del Mar became Paso Largo and then, as the mountains squeezed in closer on both sides of the strait, Paso Tortuoso. I went to sleep thinking, What of the Kaweskar? Is a contemptuous dismissal of their way in the world ever to be rectified? Is it plausible now, at nearly the bitter end of degradation for hunting people in the Southern Hemisphere, that there will be a reprieve, a second Enlightenment, one not so obeisant to reason? Is it within the power of human politics to restore dignities as well as to instigate economies?

The colonization of a people, we now know, is in some way indistinguishable from colonization of the land they occupy. Curiously, the unpopulated continent toward which we were headed, a place with no history of either indigenous people or colonialism, has begun to illuminate the issue. A plan for mineral exploration in Antarctica, strongly promoted in recent years by the Reagan and Bush administrations, was soundly defeated by other Antarctic Treaty nations in Madrid in the fall of 1991. This condemnation of economic exploitation in modern international affairs bodes well for humanity, even if it comes late for the Kaweskar. And, if nations can decide not to exploit landscapes to which they have access, perhaps they can also imagine it possible not to wrench and exploit the humanity that has risen up, indigenous, in so many places.

Somewhere in his novel, Raspail calls this part of the strait "a blind alley of the Stone Age." I've read descriptions of the landscape as a "rain-sodden mass" and "a ruthless desolation of tundra." Darwin wrote, "Death, instead of Life, seem[s] the predominant spirit" in southern Patagonia; but he also said it was a "peculiar and very magnificent" country. I couldn't wait to see it.

We rounded Cape Froward in the night, sailed up Famine Reach and anchored in a roadstead off the town of Punta Arenas at about six-thirty. At this latitude—53°S—in April the sun rises on a slant, prolonging dawn. The scene over Tierra del Fuego was beautiful. The dark western sky still held stars. Overhead, that blue-black gave way to cobalt and lapis blues which came down to a lighter blue in the east, a bright violet, a band of greenish-blue, and finally saturated hues of yellow.

The growing light gave Punta Arenas a marvelous aspect. Its pastel houses, ranging up shallow hills and gathered together on the Patagonian prairie, were luminously etched, as if after a rain. The town looked fresh and neat and healthy, brighter and more welcoming than I had expected. It seemed like a good place at the end of the Earth. In the days ahead I would become fond of its tattered sidewalks and brave trees, and come to feel sad over its history.

At 7:35 A.M. the harbor pilot, a Capt. Henrichsen, came aboard and at 7:54 the first line went ashore on the west side of Punta Arenas's concrete pier. From Port Fourchon we had come 5,528 nautical miles, or 6,357 of the statute miles peculiar to land.

III. *Punta Arenas to Ice Station Weddell*

By five the sky was pitch dark. The *Palmer* had driven up into the protection of a large ice floe and docked for the night. We were 360 miles inside the frozen Weddell Sea, about a hundred miles from the ice station. (At night, even with the ship's five searchlights, it was too difficult to be sure of the most effective route of travel, through thin ice or down an occasional lead of open water, so we didn't move after dark.)

A thoughtful Steve Schrader, manager of the user side of the computer lab, had just thrown a thermos of hot chocolate and coffee overboard to a group of us on the ice. It was well after midnight, and we still had a few hours of work to do on a project we'd started at six that evening. The wind had dropped but it was cold, about −10°F.

Four of us—David Crane and Mark Brandon, young scientists from Scott Polar Research Institute in Cambridge, Jamie Scott, and myself—were assembling a long string of oceanographic instruments and lowering it through a large hole in the sea ice. On nine hundred feet of cable below us hung a sediment trap, current meters, and devices to measure the water's chemistry. We were now installing the last cluster of equipment, sensors designed to measure salinity, temperature, and biological mass. A separate cable from a ship's deck crane held the weight of the research string already in the water while we worked on this final, slack section, fastening the instrument package in place and measuring and routing electrical wire so it wouldn't bind when the whole line finally came under tension beneath a bright orange buoy. Sitting like a cork in the ice hole, the buoy would drift with the sea ice and then hold the line in suspension when the ice melted, one or two summers hence. Atop the buoy, along with ice sensors and a small meteorological station, was an antenna to send down-line information back to Cambridge via Argos satellite.

Working in the cold, sometimes barehanded, with materials that stiffened and became balky, was trying; but the four of us appreciated each other's company and kept up a humorous banter about our clumsiness and weariness. We finished about three-thirty in the morning. Mark, whose enthusiasm for science was idealistic and genuine, and who had been in a state of euphoria about Antarctica since he boarded the ship in Punta Arenas, now gazed at the "boy" (as he pronounced it) as though he could believe neither the polar coordinates nor the evidence of his accomplishment.

We were the only ship in the million or so square miles of the Weddell Sea that night. The single other human gathering was at Ice Station Weddell (ISW), an international group of scientists in a scatter of huts and inflatable buildings set up on a two- or three-year-old ice floe. The station had been put in two-and-a-half months earlier by the Russian icebreaking research vessel *Akademik Federov.* The floe, more than a mile long and three quarters of a mile wide, and now an almost indistinguishable part of the consolidated pack, drifts north about two miles a day on a current called the Weddell Gyre. It's the first such ice station established in the southern oceans.

The oceanographers and meteorologists at ISW (the U.S. party includes a German, an Argentine, and a Swiss; the Russian, a Ukrainian) are focusing their research in four areas: physical oceanography, especially the development of water in the Weddell Sea; sea-ice growth and behavior; how the atmosphere—wind, say—affects ice formation and sea-water chemistry; and the annual cycle of biological activity. Some of the Americans think the Russians' research methods are too slam-bang and that their instruments are too unsophisticated. The Russians look with mild contempt at the Americans' expressed need for hot showers and with wonder, and some envy, at their financial resources.

The research is being conducted in the Weddell for two reasons: these waters play a central role in the formation of bottom water in the oceans of the Southern Hemisphere (and, so, too, in the biological activity of those oceans and in the atmospheric chemistry associated with them); and because, due to its remoteness and the severity of its climate, it is the least understood sea on the planet.

The Weddell was discovered by a thirty-six-year-old British sealer, James Weddell, in the austral summer of 1822–23. On February 20, 1823, he reached a latitude of 74°15′S, a southing no one would approach again for nearly a hundred years. (He also initiated scientific research in the sea when, three days later, he dropped a watertight bottle overboard in hopes of learning the trend of the current.) In 1912, a German research ship, the *Deutschland,* reached the head of the eastern Weddell. In 1915–16, members of the British Imperial Trans-Antarctic Expedition became the first to enter the western Weddell. Their ship, however, the *Endurance,* was beset and eventually crushed. Camped in tents on the sea ice, the crew of twenty-eight drifted anxiously north (on the same current that now carried the ice station, one of the reasons for locating it where it was). One-hundred-and-seventy-one days after they abandoned ship they reached the Bransfield Strait and launched their lifeboats. Led by Ernest Shackleton, they all survived.

In recent years, partly in response to growing concern about the extent to which the planet's atmosphere has been disturbed by human activity, organizations like the National Science Foundation have tried to secure funds and find the means to conduct basic research in the Weddell—thus ISW and the *Nathaniel B. Palmer* (a young Connecticut sealer, one of the first to see the Antarctic mainland). In 1968, an international team aboard the U.S. Coast Guard icebreaker *Glacier* made the first scientific study of the sea, at the fringe of the pack ice in summer. In 1981 a Soviet ship, the *Mikhail*

Somov, took another international team in search of an area of perennial open water thought to exist in the eastern Weddell, a polynya they were unable to find. The German research vessel *Polarstern* made the first winter cruise, in 1986, but still in relatively light ice to the east. The *Polarstern* joined the *Federov* to make an initial study of the eastern and northern reaches of the Weddell Gyre in 1989. The *Palmer,* on its first Weddell cruise in 1992, would sail farther west and south than any vessel had ever been in winter. (One measure of how little known this area is—the Weddell is about the size of the Mediterranean—is that scientists at ISW discovered the edge of the Antarctic Peninsula's continental shelf about thirty-five miles west of the position marked for it on modern maps.)

The Weddell teems with large animals in the austral summer; even in early winter, when the *Palmer* entered pack ice on its northern perimeter, we found large numbers of crabeater and Weddell seals, fur seals, and predacious leopard seals; chinstrap, Adélie, and emperor penguins; sei whales, minke whales, and orcas. After the barren vistas of heavily-utilized seas to the north, the Weddell seemed like a refugium. Knowing that whales one had only the vaguest notion of—the Southern bottlenose whale, Arnoux's beaked whale—roamed here along with the largest animal that ever lived, the blue whale, made some of us keenly observant. We studied every patch of open water.

Soon, however, our world became little more than sky, nearly continuous ice, and only a few animals. Orcas, minkes, and sei whales, emperor penguins, and small flocks of snow petrels still appeared, hundreds of miles from the ice edge; but it was the ice, the Weddell's hard ceiling, that began to dominate. Antarctic sea ice differs from ice in the Arctic—the pressure ridges are fewer and less formidable; the snow cover is deeper; and the ice is not as thick, not as hard. It's less obdurate, less wrinkled; but it is as anchoritic—it imposes stillness and a terrestrial vastness over the water. The plain of its sameness, to be sure, is an illusion. The variety in its texture and shading, the histories traced and beaten in its surface by the wind, the lines of rubble left by its stirrings, hold the eye like detail in a slab of quartz or a raw pearl.

In Punta Arenas we had taken on 175,000 gallons of fuel, exchanged a few technicians and crew, and boarded seven scientists, five of them bound for the ice station. We made brief trips out of town along the coast, ate and danced in the town's restaurants and night clubs, and shopped for fresh food.

On a clear, windy, April afternoon we backed away from the pier, pivoted 180 degrees using the bow and stern thrusters—"My God," said the new ice pilot, a German named Ewald Brune, "you could waltz with her"—and bore north and east up the strait. At Angostura Primera a racing automobile caught up with us and sent two boxes of helicopter parts for the ice station out with the pilot launch. The launch away with our last Chilean pilot, we sailed into Possession Bay, the eastern entrance to the strait. High winds which had been blowing spray over the bridge (sixty-two feet above the water) began to lie down. On my evening walk I watched gas flare-offs from oil wells all along the coast, wild surges of flame, light up the belly of the overcast sky.

We had worried about the Drake Passage. It's the stormiest stretch of ocean in the world, with big seas of thirty feet or more common. We crossed its six hundred miles on water flat as a tucked sheet, passed between the South Shetland Islands and the South Orkneys and, at eight-thirty on a Sunday morning, sailed into the open pack of the Weddell Sea. It was a very sharp line of demarcation: open water here; there, relatively small floes of lighter first-year ice, a five-tenths cover. People on the bridge and in the bow cheered, applauded, and shook hands. The *Palmer* was making thirteen knots. The ship neither changed course nor slowed and seemed implacable, bumping ice out of the way, running over it, splitting the larger floes. After a few minutes people new to the experience began joking—"Radio the ice station, tell them we'll be early"—a cavalier boast that, like whistling on the bridge, brought an irritated frown of disapproval from Brune.

The idyllic feelings that prevailed on the first day were understandable. The ice floes abounded with seals and penguins, startled and bewildered at our presence. Half the horizon was ringed with glowing icebergs; fulmars, albatrosses, and southern giant petrels wheeled overhead; prions and delicate storm petrels swooped stretches of matte-black, open water. Sei whales blew and sounded in the distance. All this animation, the clear, bracing weather, the ship's straight, swift course, the fall and reflection of majestic light in the dustless air, created an intoxicating atmosphere. It was the energy of aspiration, a volatile pairing of power with images of innocence.

We made eighty-two miles in the ice the first day; forty-two the next; then sixty-six. Our route, however, was indirect, so we gained less in distance to the ice station, still nearly three hundred miles away. Brune thought it best to work farther to the east before trying to come back to the southwest; it clearly was going to take longer to get there than most, including Brune, had guessed. Calm, somewhat aloof, constantly vigilant on the bridge, Brune was given to philosophical shrugs and laconic observations about our arrival time. "A bad ice year," he observed once, "the same for Shackleton." He invoked an ice pilot named Anders Jacobsen: "The ice is telling you what to do and not you are telling the ice what to do."

When one hung out over the bow, the sounds of the ship making its way in the ice were like the sounds of woodcutting: the thud of a splitting maul in the end of a log; the screak of wood fibers twisting; the clean pop of straight-grained wood flying apart; the *twik* of a limbing ax. Inside the ship the noise was louder, more ominous: the long pull of a glasscutter's knife down a windowpane; the surging racket of an engine about to throw a connecting rod. In the galley, where this brawling sometimes undid conversation, we heard elephants trumpeting in panic before they were run over, the *KABAM-*

bam-bam shading to a fine ticking against the hull. Silence, another sudden, horrendous bang. A metal rasp across a barrel. We listened rapt and fearful.

Breaking ice hardly affected the ride of the ship, except for an occasional unexpected tip or a sudden sideways surge. The design of the *Palmer* encourages a helmsman to weave and finesse not bull his way through. (Capt. Russell likened the ride in a Russian icebreaker, where the prevailing theory is tremendous power and straight ahead, to "driving down a washboard road dragging a refrigerator.")

When the *Palmer* got stuck, as happened, or when pressure in the pack closed off her keel water (the open seaway behind), or when she was nipped between floes, she had several remedies. She could rock and tip her way out, shunting thousands of gallons of water very quickly from side to side and shifting ballast water to elevate or depress her bow; or she could use a combination of her thrusters and her prop wash to clear herself.

During our first day in lighter ice in the eastern Weddell, the ship sometimes sailed as it had that humid night on Gatún Lake, a swift, unperturbed glide. We'd leave one enormous patch of smooth gray ice, cross an open lead like a rain-washed, blacktop road, and enter another vast plain of thin ice. It was like gliding the townships of Iowa.

Peter Wilkniss, then head of the Division of Polar Programs at the National Science Foundation, a nuclear and radiochemist by training, had come aboard at Punta Arenas. Wilkniss is very enthusiastic about antarctic science, and is generally regarded as someone who has worked assiduously and astutely to improve the United States Antarctic Program. He is thought by some, however, to be difficult to approach and hard to please. As our progress toward the ice station slowed—down to nineteen miles one day, thirteen the next—shipboard tensions, which had been smoldering for weeks on the *Palmer* and were catalyzed by Wilkniss's presence, came to a head.

Technically, the National Science Foundation sponsors scientific research on the *Palmer* through Antarctic Support Associates (ASA), a private company that had contracted with Edison Chouest Offshore to build and operate the ship. The normal run of disagreements among people about how things should be done was exacerbated by ASA's somewhat overweening concern as the cruise began with issues of authority—they often seemed more interested in asserting their contractual prerogatives than assisting in the routine, but exasperating, business of making a huge, complex machine run properly.

When Wilkniss came aboard, he listened to both sides of the disagreements and then tried, especially, to get some people in ASA to understand a larger picture—the importance of antarctic science in a world in dire need of a better understanding of global climate; the United States's effort to establish international cooperation in the wake of the Cold War; and a need for deference and ease in a remote endeavor like the *Palmer*'s.

An immediate problem for Wilkniss was the poor quality of ice maps Ewald Brune had available to plot a course. The ship received ice information from nine different satellites, but it was relatively crude, large-scale data and no one on board was skilled at refining it. At a staff meeting one afternoon, Wilkniss challenged ASA and people from EG&G (an ASA subcontractor handling most of the computer network design and programming) to use every communication system on the ship to reach any government or university ice-mapping center that might help; and to contact any programmers with relevant expertise. He urged them to explore even a link up with the Russians, widely thought to have the best polar ice information.

Capt. Russell and Dr. Wilkniss, in spite of their different backgrounds and temperaments, gravitated easily toward each other. The captain had had to sort out a crew en route to Punta Arenas, one that could work smoothly together. Like the computer technicians, he, too, had to deal with dozens of false alarms and with breakdowns triggered by programming glitches, many of them in the *Palmer*'s steering and propulsion systems. He appreciated Wilkniss's enthusiasm and his emphasis on a large frame of reference.

On May 1, Wilkniss, after conferring with a dispirited Capt. Russell and a philosophical Ewald Brune, regretfully announced a change of plans. The ice had gotten thicker and harder. Pressure ridges were up to sixteen feet thick now, and we were regularly breaking six feet of ice, sometimes eight or ten feet. We had burned more fuel than expected. In the past three days we'd come only 7.1, then 4.0, then 3.3 miles. We were thirty-seven miles from Ice Station Weddell. Looking carefully at the ice ahead, Brune judged it would take another three or four days to get through. Wilkniss decided to stop where we were, at 67°38′S and 51°57′W. We'd use the ice station's helicopters to ferry people and supplies back and forth. We'd unload fifty drums of helicopter fuel, pay a quick visit to the station, and head north.

Bad weather and helicopter breakdowns added to the strain of almost everyone's disappointment. But the ship itself had performed valiantly. While people fretted over who was responsible for providing ice maps or who should have authorized a larger fuel order at Punta Arenas, the *Palmer* had hammered at the ice, making another two hundred feet, or perhaps only a hundred feet, at each run. Her momentum sapped by the thick ice and by layers of snow that dragged at her sides like wet laundry bags, she'd back into her keel water. Ice fragments would fill the channel in front of her like a movie run in reverse. The power of her prop wash would drive chunks the size of an automobile up onto the ice behind her. Then she'd come again, gaining half her length before being dragged to a stop. I asked Brune later what he thought. "Better than expected," he says. "Better than the 'steady three knots in three feet of level ice' as advertised. I anticipated that, looking at the test-tank results. What surprised me was her acceleration, zero to seven knots in her own length. And how well she maneuvers. Very graceful."

I make the twenty-five minute jump to the ice camp with six others. It's only about two in the afternoon, but darkness will set in soon. We have just thirty-five minutes to look around warns Wilkniss. Ice Station Weddell looks like a camp of snowdrifted huts on an expanse of tundra, not on six feet of ice floating two hundred miles off the Wilkins Coast.

I put my head in at several science huts where experiments I'm interested in are under way, then wander about, looking at the unpeeled pine logs from Siberia that carry 110-volt (United States) and 220-volt (Russian) power lines sagging over the snow. At the mess hall I peruse a message board. I try unsuccessfully to locate two Russian divers, then follow a young Russian—perhaps his name is Alexander Makshtas, I do not catch it in the gusts and cold—to the Russian meteorological hut. On a pole in front of the hut are two flags, a small Soviet flag at the top and a much larger flag of the state of Vermont below it. Alexander explains that the Soviet flag is not "political." It is a souvenir from a cruise with other Russian scientists aboard the research vessel *Professor Multanovskiy* during the weeks of the Soviet Union's collapse. He says they fly it here in memory of that time together, and out of feelings of patriotism too difficult to explain to a stranger who does not speak his language. "It is not political, this flag," he says again softly in English. He gestures around the camp. I take him to mean the flag represents human beings, not a philosophy of state.

The motto of Vermont is emblazoned on the lower flag: *Freedom and Unity.* In that moment, the hunkered, ramshackle ice camp seems worth whatever has been spent to allow these people to do their work, and for a small group of us to come south a thousand miles from Tierra del Fuego to pay our respects. We shake hands. "Do svidaniia," I say. "Do svidaniia."

My nightly walks are now across decks packed with wind-hardened snow, and it is getting colder, down to thirty below zero. But I enjoy going outside. We pull up inside a large floe each night so the shifting ice will not pinch us or close off our keel water, leaving us without steerage. We shut down one engine on each shaft and set just enough pitch on the props to keep the *Palmer* nosed up in her dock during the night. In the morning, if the weather is clear, no fog, no blizzards, we start the other two engines, bring the props to full pitch and press on.

This evening I watch five emperor penguins surfing, whimsically it seems, in the ship's prop wash. Emperors, the largest penguins, stand about three feet tall and weigh as much as ninety-five pounds. They are the only penguins to winter in Antarctica. I don't think I've seen another animal as self-possessed in a landscape so austere and inhospitable to human eyes. Perhaps only oryx, a kind of antelope, in the Namib Desert.

On several nights I've walked away from the ship with a few companions, always sensing a flicker of rebellion in the organs of my body, the tensioning of an invisible tether the farther out on the sea we go. The snow chirps beneath the scuff of our boots. We probe for weak ice and struggle over wind-crusted drifts. From a distance, the *Palmer* seems like a locomotive idling in a desert. Its sharp lines softened by a coating of hoarfrost, its hull sheeted with snow, the high, white shafts of its spotlights nailed to the ice, its yellow deck lights shining through scarfs of steam rising from its vents, it is the machinery of angels.

Wilkniss is sometimes about outside at night and this evening I find him alone on the scorpion deck. He's refreshed by having been able to trace out the true and false Southern Crosses, which he reiterates for me. I volunteer that, despite its lack of amenities, Ice Station Weddell seems something to be proud of.

"We paid for the Cold War," he says, shrugging. "We're both broke. But we're coming through here."

I ask what he thinks the *Palmer* will be doing in the next few years. Among the projects he singles out as important are research into the effect of UV-B light on phytoplankton reproduction in the Antarctic

Ocean—getting a handle on what the ozone hole really means for biological life on the planet. Taking a look at *any* antarctic coastal area in winter. Studying the productivity, chemistry, and currents of the seas fringing the continent. Tying atmospheric research to oceanographic research at the same locations.

Then Wilkniss becomes more animated, talking about the *Palmer* working in concert with new ice stations, with the *Federov,* the *Aurora Australis,* the *Polarstern,* and a new British ship, the *James Clark Ross.* Much better ice imagery for navigation, he says, will soon be available, from synthetic aperture radar aboard the ERS-1 satellite, and from a new series of NASA Earth Observation System satellites. Night vision equipment might mean icebreakers will no longer have to shut down in darkness.

What Wilkniss is groping for, however, is something past all the technology. He believes science, with tools like the *Palmer* to use, is poised to put information together in a striking new fashion. People are going to understand their physical environment he tells me, and how much a part of it they are, in ways that until now science has never spoken of.

Standing there in the frigid night air it is hard not to like Wilkniss. He is passionate, practical, disciplined, and, of course, someone with a vision.

Little by little—thirty-three miles, sixty-eight miles, twenty miles, twenty-five miles—we make our way farther north each day, through a sea with no swells, a sea in whose rigid shield we have quietly ridden out storms that, encountered on open water, would have heaved and rolled us. We sail over an unknown, uncharted bottom ten thousand feet below, through a sea that formed when Africa bore off from Antarctica into the Tethys 135 million years ago. The scientists from the ice station now returning with us offer lectures in the evening, and conduct the first shipboard experiments, confirming at points farther and farther from the ice station the salinity, dissolved-oxygen, and temperature profiles they'd been seeing in their part of the western Weddell.

I take to going out on the bow in the afternoon to watch the sun set. The sunsets linger and are sometimes beautiful. During the short day we often see solar iridescences and pillars, sun dogs, halos, and other solar phenomena. And then in the "evening," maize yellows and diaphanous violets, sometimes a streak of green, appear in the limpid orange sunsets, all of it, save one blooded sun setting, pale, thin as breath.

Mark Brandon, the young Englishman, is frequently at the bow at the same time. We watch together without conversing. Perhaps frost has formed in nodules over a stretch of refrozen lead, like a scatter of cornflowers. Or thin ice pressured by the wind has broken up and finger rafted. Heavier ice may have sheered in a neat staircase of fish-rib fractures. A great floe bursts apart with a run of dark cracks, like lightning, too fast to follow. In thick ice, a rough aquagreen block the size of a boxcar rolls over ahead of us as the ship backs away. We turn up into a sunlit lead in which whales laze, the smoke of their breath borne away in the breeze. The lead widens toward distant icebergs, still as entombed flowers. Brandon's hands rise up slowly from the bulwarks.

No afternoon is ever the same.

Terry Tempest Williams

The Erotic Landscape

from *Harper's*

A woman stands on her tiptoes, naked, holding draped fabric close to her body as it cascades over her breasts, down her belly and legs like water. A strand of pearls hangs down her back, her eyes are closed. She is at peace within her own erotic landscape.

This photograph taken at Studio d'Ora in Vienna, 1934, is the first image I see in Det Erotiske Museum in Copenhagen, Denmark. I take another step into the foyer and find myself confronted with a six-foot golden phallus mounted on a pedestal. I am tempted to touch it as I recall the bronze statues of women in museums around the world whose breasts and buttocks have been polished perfectly by the hands of men, but I refrain.

A visitor of this museum in Copenhagen could wander through four floors of exhibits ranging from a solitary Greek vase, circa 530 B.C., depicting Pan chasing Echo, to a wax tableau of Fanny Hill, 1749, to a prostitute's room reconstructed from a Danish police report in 1839.

Spiraling up to the fourth floor (you may choose to descend at this point to the Aphrodite Cafe for coffee and pastries), the Erotic Tabernacle provides the climax of this museum experience as the visitor is assaulted with twelve television screens, four across and three down, which together create a montage of pornography from 1920 through 1990, complete with the soundtrack from Pink Floyd's "The Wall."

As I watch these images of men and women simultaneously moving from one position to the next, I wonder about our notion of the Erotic—why it is so often aligned with the pornographic, the limited view of the voyeur watching the act of intercourse without any interest in the relationship itself.

I wonder what walls we have constructed to keep our true erotic nature tamed. And I am curious why we continue to distance ourselves from natural sources.

What are we afraid of?

There is an image of a woman in the desert, her back arched as her hands lift her body up from black rocks. Naked. She spreads her legs over a boulder etched by the Ancient Ones; a line of white lightning zigzags from her mons pubis. She is perfectly in place, engaged, ecstatic, and wild. This is Judy Dater's photograph, "Self-Portrait with Petroglyph."

To be in relation to everything around us, above us, below us, earth, sky, bones, blood, and flesh, is to begin to see the world whole, even holy. But the world we frequently surrender to defies our participation and seduces us into believing our only place in nature is as spectator, onlooker. A society of individuals who only observe a landscape behind the lens of a camera or the window of an automobile without entering in is perhaps no different than the person who obtains sexual gratification from looking at the sexual actions or organs of others.

The golden phallus I did not touch—in the end, did not touch me. It became a stump, a severance of the body I could not feel.

Eroticism, being in relation, calls the inner life into play. No longer numb, we feel the magnetic pull of our bodies toward something stronger, more vital than simply ourselves. Arousal becomes a dance with longing. We form a secret partnership with possibility.

I recall a day in the slickrock country of southern Utah, where I was camped inside a small canyon. Before dawn, coyotes yipped, yapped, and sang. It was a chorus of young desert dogs.

The sun rose as did I. There is a silence to creation. I stood and faced east, stretched upward, stretched down, pressed my hands together and bowed.

I knelt on the sand still marked by the patter of rain and lit my tiny stove, which purred like my cat at home. I boiled water for tea, slowly poured it into my earthen cup, then dipped the rose hip tea bag in and out, in and out, until the water turned pink. My morning ritual was complete as I wrapped my hands around the warmth of my cup and drank.

Not far, an old juniper stood in the clearing, deeply rooted and gnarled. I had never seen such a knowledgeable tree. Perhaps it was the silver sheen of its shredded bark that reminded me of my grandmother, her windblown hair the desert, her weathered face, the way she held me as a child. I wanted to climb into the arms of this tree.

With both hands on one of its strongest boughs, I pulled myself up and lifted my right leg over the branch so I was straddling it. I then leaned back into the body of the juniper and brought my knees up to my chest. I nestled in. I was hidden, perfectly shaded from the heat. I had forgotten what it felt like to really be held.

Hours passed, who knows how long, the angle of sunlight shifted. I realized something had passed between us by the change in my countenance, the slowing of my pulse and the softness of my eyes as though I was awakening from a desert trance. The lace-like evergreen canopy brushed my hair.

I finally inched my way down, wrapping my hands around its trunk. Feet on earth. I took out my water bottle and saturated the roots. I left the desert in a state of wetness.

The Erotic Museum in Copenhagen opened on June 26, 1992. It closed on September 2, 1993, because of financial difficulties. Over 100,000 visitors from around the world had paid admission to see erotica on display.

"The erotic has often been misnamed by men and used against women," says Audre Lorde in *Uses of the Erotic*. "It has been made into the confused, the trivial, the psychotic, the plasticized sensation. For this reason, we have turned away from the exploration and consideration of the erotic as a source of power and information, confusing it with the pornographic. But pornography is a direct denial of the power of the erotic, for it represents the suppression of true feeling. Pornography emphasizes sensation without feeling."

Without feeling. Perhaps these two words are the key, the only way we can begin to turn our understanding toward our abuse of each other and our abuse of the land. Could it be that what we fear most is our capacity to feel and so we annihilate symbolically and physically that which is beautiful and tender, anything that dares us to consider our creative selves? The erotic world is silenced, reduced to a collection of objects we can curate and control, be it a vase, a woman, or wilderness. Our lives become a piece in the puzzle of pornography as we "go through the motions" of daily intercourse without any engagement of the soul.

A group of friends gather in the desert, call it a pilgrimage, at the confluence of the Little Colorado and the Colorado River in the Grand Canyon. It is high noon in June, hot, very hot. They walk upstream, men and women, moving against the current of the turquoise water. Nothing but deep joy can be imagined. Their arms fan the air as they teeter on unstable stones, white stones in the river. They are searching for mud with the consistency of chocolate mousse and find it, delicious pale mud, perfect for bathing. They take off their clothes and sink to their waists, turn, roll over and wallow in pleasure. Their skins are slippery with clay. They rub each other's bodies—arms, shoulders, backs, torsos, even their faces are painted in mud and they become the animals they are. Blue eyes. Green eyes. Brown eyes being masks. In the heat, lying on ledges, they bake until they crack like terra cotta. For hours, they dream the life of lizards.

In time, they submerge themselves in the Little Colorado, diving deep and surfacing freshly human, skins sparkling, glistening, cold and refreshed. Nothing can contain their exuberance but the river. They allow themselves to be swept away—floating on bellies, head-first; backs, feet-first; laughing, contemplating, an unspoken hunger quelled.

D. H. Lawrence writes, "There exists only two great modes of life—the religious and the sexual." Eroticism bridges them both.

Ole Ege is the man behind the Erotic Museum in Denmark. It was his vision of eroticism he wanted to institutionalize. It is his collection that now resides in storage somewhere in Copenhagen. He still dreams of reopening its doors.

Standing on the sidewalk next to the red banners that advertise the museum, I watched each object, each exhibit, each wax figure being carried out of the white building and loaded inside two Volvo moving vans on Besterbrogade 31, minutes away from Tivoli Gardens, where the harlequins danced.

In spite of the museum's closure and whatever the shortcomings of the exhibits may have been, I believe Ole Ege's vision of the erotic life can be celebrated.

"Denmark has been liberated sexually for twenty-five years," he said. "But we are not yet liberated in our minds. It is a matter of individual morality how one conceives this subject. For me, eroticism relates to all the highest and finest things of life. Every couple on earth participates in this confirmation of the creation, the urge we have to share ourselves, to make each other whole."

The idea that governed an erotic museum and the ideal behind an erotic life may never find a perfect marriage or resolution. Here lies our dilemma as human beings: Nothing exists in isolation. We need a context for Eros, not a pedestal, not a video screen. The lightning we witness crack and charge a night sky in the desert is the same electricity we feel in ourselves whenever we dare to touch flesh, rock, body, and earth. We must take our love outdoors where reciprocity replaces voyeurism. We can choose to photograph a tree or we can sit in its arms where we are participating in wild nature, even our own.

The woman in the desert stands and extends her arms. Rumi speaks, "Let the beauty of what we love be what we do. There are hundreds of ways to kneel and kiss the ground."

John Haines

Shadows and Vistas

First publication

There are shadows over the land. They come out of the ground, from the dust and the tumbled bones of the earth . . .
from *The Stars, the Snow, the Fire*

I begin with "Shadows" as a way of speaking. Laurens van der Post, in *The Lost World of the Kalahari,* acknowledges that he believes in ghosts, in the spirit of the life that the land once held but which cannot be found any longer. Van der Post was looking for the Bushman, who for him signified a lost Africa, one that he had been told about as a boy; but all he could find of it was the changed land itself and a few sites where decades before the Bushman had camped and hunted. According to an old African of his household, from whom he had learned much, the Bushman disappeared because *he would not be tamed.*

I recall an afternoon in October many years ago, when I stood on the edge of that high overlook near Maclaren Summit in the Alaska Range and gazed down onto the wide sweep of the Maclaren River Basin. The cold, late afternoon sun came through broken clouds, and the tundra below me was patched with sunlight. The river, a thin, silvery-blue thread, twisted through the subdued autumn coloration of the land, stretching far up into the dark and gloomy hills on which the first light snow had fallen.

I was entirely alone at that moment; no traffic disturbed the gravel road a few yards behind me. The land before me seemed incredibly vast and empty. But it was not empty. Far below me, a few scattered caribou were feeding in the meadows of the river basin, their brown, white-maned forms dispersed among the bogs and ponds, moving slowly upriver toward the mountains. They were the first individuals of a herd that would appear later.

I felt as if I were looking down on a landscape elementary to our being, and that nothing had occurred to change it since the last of the continental ice melted from the earth, and the first grasses and shrubs began to grow; and very slowly the animals moved north into the newly restored land, finding their way, feeding on the fresh, undisturbed forage for the first time.

That image has remained with me as one sure glimpse into our past. Even the road that crossed the river on a tiny bridge in the distance did not break the continuity of the feeling I had then. It was all part of an essential vista, a sheer sense of the land in its original presence. On that afternoon, when the guns of the hunters along the road were silent and no cars passed, I easily slipped back a thousand years into a twilight approaching winter; a dusk in which I and a few others, following the game herds upriver, would find meat, fire and shelter.

That was well over thirty years ago, when the tundra life along the Denali road was still fairly abundant. I have looked over that same view a number of times since, but I have not seen the caribou feeding as they were then. And yet I know that their ghosts are there, that the land contains them and refuses in some mysterious way to give them up, though to the surface view the land appears to be empty.

It is not simply nostalgia, I think, that compels me to believe that this vista, its possibility, needs to be kept. We need it as a kind of model of life, whose images we are bound in some way to resurrect and imitate, even when the original has been destroyed. It is not so much a matter of saving a species, a particular herd and its habitat, but of saving something essential of life and ourselves. And not only our immediate selves, you and I, but those others who were here before us and will come after us, and whose land and nature we have so easily confiscated and misused to our longstanding peril.

It is foolish to believe that we erase life by killing it off, by driving into extinction the remaining game, by paving over the grazing grounds, cutting the forests, and pretending to ourselves that it did not matter after all. Too bad, we say, but let's get on with the business of things. Vanquished in one place, life springs back in another, as at the present time, in spite of all sophistication in transport and communication, coyotes are barking in the Los Angeles suburbs, and as all the killed and vanished life, animal and people, continues in one way or another to haunt us and question our wasting passage through the world.

As a friend of mine remarked to me some years ago, when in the course of conversation we both remarked on the great physical presence of Kluane Lake in the Yukon: "That place," she exclaimed, "really has spirit!" It does indeed.

And what does that mean? That places, lands, regions, watersheds, etc., all have a life, a felt quality of their own, which we can call *spirit,* and we cannot kill that spirit without destroying something in ourselves. A degraded land inevitably produces a degraded people. It is in fact ourselves we are destroying, a possibility of life that once gone will be a long time returning. I say "a long time" and not that it will never come back, because I do not hold with the view that we have the power to destroy life on earth forever. That notion is a part of our problem, a part of our arrogance and self-bemusement. We have got it backwards. Life has the power to destroy *us,* and to do so with our connivance, using our own misaligned means and purposes. A few degrees of climate change, a few more inches of topsoil lost, and our descendants may read the record for themselves.

Is it destined to be a law with us, an iron and withering rule, that anything that cannot be tamed, domesticated and put to use, shall die? A river, a patch of woodland, a wolf, a small tribe of hunting people? And all the while we preserve a few wretched specimens in a zoo, a controlled park or reservation, or as a collection of images on film, part of an ever-growing catalogue of fossil life.

You can kill off the original inhabitants, most of the world's wildlife, and still live on the land. But I doubt that we can live fully on that land accompanied only by crowds of consumers like ourselves and a few hybrid domesticated animals turned into producing machines. A sure poverty will follow us, an inner desolation to match the devastation without. And having rid the earth of wilderness, of wild things generally, we will look to outer space, to other planets, to find their replacements there.

Today, most of us are familiar with a continuing effort to save some part of a wild heritage, to rethink our lives in relation to the land we drive and park on and from which we draw what certainty we have. And we know the forces assembled in opposition to this effort: there is no need to name or rank them, they all flock under the flag of an ever more questionable progress and enterprise, whose hidden name is poverty.

On the occasion of a visit to New England in the 1930s, T. S. Eliot wrote the following:

> My local feelings were stirred very sadly by my first view of New England, on arriving from Montreal, and journeying all day through the beautiful desolate country of Vermont. These hills had once, I suppose, been covered with primeval forest; the forest was razed to make sheep pasture for the English settlers; now the sheep are gone, and most of the descendants of the settlers; and a new forest appeared blazing with the melancholy glory of October maple and beech and birch scattered among the evergreens; and after this process of scarlet and gold and purple wilderness you descend to the sordor of the half-dead milltowns of southern New Hampshire and Massachusetts. It is not necessarily those lands which are most fertile

> or most favored in climate that seem to me the happiest, but those in which a long struggle of adaptation between man and his environment has brought out the best qualities of both; in which the landscape has been moulded by numerous generations of one race, and in which the landscape has in turn moulded the race to its own character. And those New England mountains seemed to me to give evidence of a human success so meager and transitory as to be more desperate than the desert.*

Certainly, Eliot's description and the feeling it evokes could with a little effort be transferred to many an Alaskan urban landscape, be it Mountain View, North Pole, Soldotna, or one of those lost highway settlements in which it seems as if all the unwanted debris and waste of American life had somehow blown there to settle into an impervious drift composed of tarpaper, crushed plastic, ripped shingles and foundered hopes. I suppose there are few more unreal and depressing prospects than some of the housing sites, the outlying developed properties in Anchorage and Fairbanks. And what is unreal will sooner or later disappear, the transitory inspiration of a people come to plunder and leave. Van der Post, in another of his books, remarks on the physical fact of Africa as being by far the most exciting thing about that continent. And for him a definite sadness lay in the fact that it had not yet produced the people and the towns worthy of it. By comparison with its physical self, everything else was drab and commonplace.

We who have learned to call this north country home are only at the beginning of a struggle of adaptation between ourselves and the land, and if the evidence so far seems pretty meager, there's a long road yet to travel. The prospect of an Alaska in which a million or so people are on the prowl with guns, snowmachines, airboats and four-wheelers, is not only terrifying, it is finally unacceptable. An environmental ethic, believed in, practiced and enforced, is not just

* T. S. Eliot, *After Strange Gods* (London: Faber & Faber, 1934).

an alternative, it is the only one, though another name for it may be self-restraint. And it is sometimes possible to sense, behind all the noise and confrontation, a genuine urge toward a real satisfaction, a sane kind of plenitude, a fullness of spirit and being.

And we are all in it together, poet and plumber, even those so far unconscious people out there on the peripheries; and especially those in the halls of academe—our humanists, who surely ought to care but who seem often not to. Mired in their coursework, busily teaching (but what are they teaching?), satisfied to draw their salaries, to save for retirement, to drink the water, breathe the air and burn the fuel, without a whisper of protest or encouragement.

You may ask what these remarks of mine have to do with immediate politics and practical tasks—the issues, the problems that many of you understand as well or better than I do. And I have no ready answer, no claim that poetic imagery, the personal mythologies of which a writer is sometimes the master, can solve anything. And yet without that dimension of imagination, the instilled power to think and to visualize that poetry, for example, nourishes in us, the solutions, the resolved difficulties seem bound to lack a necessary human element.

So it is a matter of language also, of words common and uncommon, that with something of their original freshness and power have the ability to restore a much-needed sense of reality and reveal to us a few essential things with clarity and concreteness.

Not long ago I saw a marsh hawk, a harrier, hunting the Tanana River islands below Richardson, the first spring arrival of its kind. And that bird was, in a vivid way, rather like a ghost with its grey and white plumage slanting in the spring sunlight as it hovered and sailed over the winter-brown willows and frost-seared grasses. A real spirit, if you like, come back to claim its territory, as it or its ancestors have returned to those flats and adjacent meadows for far longer than our race has existed or can easily imagine. A small but definite image to end on, and returning me halfway to that glimpse into the Maclaren

River Basin I described earlier, haunted as I am by its persistent contours, and by what seems sometimes destined to become a vanished hope on earth.

> And to think, from this diminished perspective in time, from this long vista of empty light and deepening shade, that so small and refined a creature could fill an uncertain niche in the world; and that its absence would leave, not just a momentary gap in nature, but a lack in one's own existence, one less possibility of being.
>
> As if we were to look out on a cherished landscape, hoping to see on the distant, wrinkled plain, among the cloud-shadows passing over its face, groups of animals feeding and resting; and in the air above them a compact flock of waterfowl swiftly winging its way to a farther pond; and higher still, a watchful hawk on the wind. To look, straining one's eyesight, noting each detail of lake, meadow and bog; and to find nothing, nothing alive and moving. Only the wind and the distance, the silence of a vast, creatureless earth.*

* John Haines, "Shadows," from *The Stars, the Snow, the Fire* (St. Paul, Minn.: Graywolf Press, 1989), pp. 178–179.

Susan Brownmiller

Flying to Vietnam

from *Audubon*

Travelers should strike out into the unknown even within the context of the unfamiliar. With that in mind, while I was in Vietnam last November, I left Saigon for the Mekong Delta. A cryptic reference in something I'd read offered a promising destination: a bird reserve in the reedy marshland of Dong Thap province that was supposedly a short drive from Cao Lanh.

Who had set up a sanctuary in the delta, and how they had done it, were intriguing questions for me and my travel companion—and for Tuyen, our guide, who was looking for new tourist attractions. Our driver, Thanh, a sobersided realist who during the war had worked for "You-said" (USAID, the U.S. Agency for International Development), said that the road past Cao Lanh was unpaved and frequently flooded.

Of all the world's rivers that resonate with romance, conquest, fertile plains, warfare, human migration, and suffering, few command more respect than the Mekong, as it flows for 2,600 miles from the Tibetan highlands through Cambodia and Vietnam to the South China Sea. Laboring peasants turned the alluvial soil of the delta into Vietnam's rice bowl. The patchwork of tributaries, canals, dikes, and irrigation ditches is home to one-quarter of the country's people and sustenance to an additional 25 percent, who rely on its crops, its fisheries, and increasingly, its offshore oil.

During the Vietnam War—to them, the American War—the delta was a Vietcong stronghold, targeted for pacification, search-and-destroy operations, tons of napalm and chemical defoliants, and barbed-wire enclaves called strategic hamlets, which were ours during the day, theirs at night. More recently, refugees from Cambodia and the Khmer Rouge settled in the recovering region, for which no doubt they felt some affinity. On maps drawn before the 18th century, much of the watery land belonged to the Cambodian kingdom.

The sun was shining on the rice fields as we drove along at a leisurely pace, stopping now and again to observe the age-old rhythms of life along the Mekong, where three crops of grain can be harvested a year. We reached the river port of Cao Lanh by lunchtime, staggered by the size of the Soviet-style memorial that was inscribed, typically, THE FATHERLAND WILL NOT FORGET YOU.

After lunch we set off again for the bird reserve. By now it was past 2:00 P.M., and the road beyond Cao Lanh was not only unpaved but badly rutted as it stretched toward infinity, lined on both sides with thatch-and-wood houses, sometimes on stilts with a rickety little bridge of logs and branches spanning a muddy stream. On it went: a never-ending village of wall-to-wall humanity with peasants tending to mats of rice drying on the roadside, chickens crossing the path, children playing, women preparing a meal, shirtless men in green army pants, a water buffalo in harness, a cart loaded with pigs, a lactating dog, teams of bicycles, a roaring scooter, a lumbering, freshly painted DeSoto bus bearing the legend DONG THAP, a modest stand selling cigarettes and soda.

When Tuyen would inquire how far to the bird reserve, the answer was always "twenty kilometers on." Once it was "seven kilometers," and we visibly brightened, but then it was "twenty kilometers" again.

It was dark when we reached Tam Nong, a lively settlement in a New Economic Zone, and learned that the bird reserve was across the bridge. We had traveled more than 80 kilometers from Cao Lanh. (We didn't know that it would have been quicker and easier to travel the route by boat.)

Approaching a lighted, substantial house, I groggily wondered if they'd have to take us in. The reserve's director, who greeted us in his pajamas, seemed to be having the same thought. "This happens all the time," he said with a shrug.

The name of the reserve, we learned, was Tram Chim, which means "bird swamp." Tuyen introduced me as an American writer. The director beamed and said something I heard as "Audubon."

"Ah, yes, Audubon," I beamed back.

"You know this name?" asked Tuyen. "The director says he came here four years ago to help set up the sanctuary." That didn't seem right, but I was in no mood to quibble.

We were offered tea after we agreed to return to the nearby town for the night. At 6:00 A.M., if we wished, we could go out in a launch and see Tram Chim, or at least a portion of its 45,000 acres. Before we departed for the evening, we were taken to an exhibition room that solved part of the mystery. The name that I had heard was Archibald, not Audubon. Posters of the International Crane Foundation and a picture of cofounder George Archibald were on the wall.

After a restless night in the Tam Nong motel (at some point the karaoke music did stop; at 3:00 A.M. I crawled out of the mosquito netting and figured out how to turn off the refrigeration unit), we were ready for the birds.

This was not crane season at the Tram Chim Reserve. The sarus crane—a five-foot-tall, redheaded bird—arrives in late December and stays through April, while the painted stork comes by for a shorter visit. But during our three hours in the launch, guided by an earnest young man named Thieng, we saw black drongos, common kingfishers, purple herons, gray herons, great egrets, black-shouldered kites, lapwings, swallows, cormorants, and a purple swamp hen.

Thieng carried a dog-eared copy of *A Guide to the Birds of Thailand* for reference. He had been on the job for six months; we were his first tourists. Thirty guards, he told us, are hired during crane season to keep local villagers from poaching. We paid $15, plus a tip, for our excursion. Thanh—serious Thanh who seldom smiled—turned out to be our best birder. " 'Before the war I saw many birds, even near Saigon. But today! I didn't know we had such a place in Vietnam," he told me.

Eight days later I was ushered into the New York City apartment of Mrs. Jackson Burke, a friend and patron of the International Crane Foundation. Still in pursuit of the story behind the Tram Chim Reserve, I had been lucky enough to catch George Archibald where he had temporarily alighted.

A puckish fellow in glasses who was suffering from a bad case of jet lag when I met him, Archibald has a rare talent for feeling equally at home in the Vietnamese hinterlands and in a magnificent Park Avenue apartment, as long as the conversation revolves around cranes. A silver coffee service and four abandoned demitasse cups on a drawing-room table let me know that I had pulled him away rather sooner than expected from a most convivial luncheon.

Archibald is a Canadian who grew up on a farm in Nova Scotia and now calls Baraboo, Wisconsin, home. "Everybody realized that I was a bit different," he sighed as he settled into a silk sofa. "My first memories in life are of following ducks around on my hands and knees." After completing his undergraduate work, he enrolled at Cornell University in 1968, where a kindred soul in the department of ecology proposed that he study cranes. The idea struck him like a revelation. "There were birds and there were cranes, like there were apes and men," he said with passion.

Cornell in the late '60s was a hotbed of radical foment, a center of the antiwar movement. "Oh, it was a *terrible* time," Archibald recalled with a visceral shudder. "I wasn't involved with any of it—Vietnam, the political scene, the drug scene. I found it all very frightening. I just stayed with my birds on an abandoned mink farm the university let me use."

With Ron Sauey, a Cornell friend whose family had a farm in Baraboo, Archibald set up the International Crane Foundation (ICF) in 1972 and built a Noah's Ark—or more formally, a species bank—of rare cranes from around the world. The birds were housed in pens and compounds and bred by artificial insemination. By 1979 the ICF had attracted the attention of the Smithsonian Institution and had raised enough money from private sources to purchase its own tract of land in Baraboo near the Sauey place.

Today 205 acres of Wisconsin farmland house a permanent crane installation, and the ICF's annual budget of $1.5 million supports a full-time staff of 22 that flies to Iran, Russia, India, Pakistan, China, Japan, Thailand, Korea, Vietnam, and Cambodia in pursuit of the universally revered but often endangered crane.

In 1988 Archibald landed in Vietnam, with German ornithologists from the Brehm Fund for International Conservation of Birds, to help the sarus crane in the Plain of Reeds, in Dong Thap province—and as it happened, the painted stork, the greater adjutant, the Bengal florican, and the black-faced spoonbill, which made a reappearance after the crane habitat began to recover.

Symbolic to the Vietnamese of long life, wealth, and happiness, a leggy crane standing on the broad back of a turtle is a revered motif in Buddhist pagodas and temples. The real-life population of cranes in Dong Thap had been nearly destroyed during the war. Intent on denying the Vietcong their protective forest cover, the U.S. military command had cut huge drainage channels through the Plain of Reeds. As the wetlands dried out, unnatural fires—ignited in part by napalm—denuded the landscape. Helicopters swooped down on the big birds for fun, bored G.I.s emptied their rifles at them in "mad minutes," and hungry villagers killed them for food. The dried marshland in the area of Tram Chim was spared chemical defoliation, but the parched earth turned abnormally acid.

Now the birds were up against fresh, peacetime dangers. A human population explosion was affecting the environment with new settlements and expanding rice agriculture; and the government was launching a reforestation program, planting melaleuca trees (a freshwater mangrove) for medicinal oils and timber for houses. "Well," Archibald said, "we thought part of that land would make a *wonderful* nature reserve."

Luckily for the cranes, the governor of Dong Thap province, a former Vietcong commander known by his pseudonym, Muoi Nhe, had been having similar thoughts. Vietnam's leading environmentalist, Professor Vo Quy of the University of Hanoi, an ornithologist by profession, was also vitally interested in the project.

"In many ways, the Vietnamese are ahead of us in understanding environmental issues," Jeb Barzen of the ICF, a former duck biologist, told me in a later interview. "They are much more linked to the land than we are."

Remembering the beautiful area of Tram Chim from his childhood, Muoi Nhe had done what he could to restore a portion to its former state. It wasn't feasible to plug the American-made drainage ditches that slashed across the Plain of Reeds, because they had become important waterways for the people, vital to the transportation of fertilizer, rice, and other produce in the recovering delta. But the former Vietcong commander could and did construct a network of dikes around Tram Chim to hold back the floodwaters from the ditches during the heavy inundations of the June-to-October rainy season. The dikes were in place by 1984, four years before the western scientists arrived.

When the team of international scientists completed their studies, they determined that more elaborate measures were needed to encourage returning wildlife. A protracted period of negotiations ensued. The Vietnamese were worried that the foreign scientists' strictly environmental concerns would interfere with the country's needs for fish, melaleuca, and rice. "Ecosystem management and habitat fragmentation were new concepts for them," Barzen said. "Why should they believe our science?" Muoi Nhe was invited to Baraboo to share the American experience in wetland management.

The two sides reached a consensus in 1991. "This feels like the end of the second Paris peace conference," one of the Vietnamese scientists joked. The John D. and Catherine T. MacArthur Foundation ponied up money for sluice gates to control the water level at Tram Chim and offered additional funds for a small supervisory staff. The Vietnamese constructed a sturdy field house and exhibition hall. Tram Chim is expected soon to be a national park. Eco-tourism (what I was doing) is to be encouraged.

"Tram Chim is perfect for migrating cranes during the dry season, when the water level is low," Archibald explained. "They walk around very sociably, ankle-deep in water, digging tuberous sedges from the mud. But during their breeding season they live in Cambodia in solitary pairs, where they eat different things—a lot of insects and small fish." Protecting cranes in Vietnam, he concluded, would have to focus on Cambodia as well. So it was on to Phnom Penh.

Delicate international negotiations were old hat to Archibald by this time. In the mid-'70s he had mounted a media campaign to warn the Japanese that the red-crowned crane on the island of Hokkaido was in danger of extinction from development of the wetlands for dairy farming. The Japanese have a tradition of honoring cranes. Cranes figure prominently in their art, in their origami. "It was rather adversarial," he said. "They had thought the cranes were mating in Siberia, so it wasn't their problem. Imagine, a foreigner telling them what to do!"

The next stop was Korea. "I knew that red-crowned cranes and white-naped cranes wintered in the demilitarized zone between North and South Korea," Archibald explained. "The DMZ was the only place in Korea where any natural habitat was left—the rest had been ransacked by development." He frowned. "Now that North and South Korea are getting a little friendlier, there's talk about putting factories in those valleys. If that happens, the cranes are done for."

In 1976 Archibald went to Russia, intent on saving the Siberian crane despite a glacial response from Moscow. The former Soviet Union also honored cranes in the abstract as a symbol of life, peace, and renewal, as anyone who saw the 1957 Russian movie *The Cranes Are Flying* will recall. In an intricate set of maneuvers, captive Siberian cranes were artificially inseminated in Baraboo and the resulting eggs were sent to Siberia. At a propitious moment, the chicks were released into the Kunovat Nature Reserve.

From Russia it was a great leap forward to China, which turned out to have more crane species than anywhere else: red-crowned, white-naped, Siberian, hooded, Eurasian, demoiselle, black-necked, and sarus. "China didn't open to us until after the Cultural Revolution," Archibald wearily recounted. "From 1979 to 1988 I worked there two or three times a year. A huge investment of time, but very productive. They treasured cranes in China as metaphors of long life, but they didn't understand that cranes needed big marshes." Inspired by the ICF, the number of wetland reserves went from zero to 22.

In 1984, while he was scouting cranes in the Australian outback, Archibald learned via a hand-cranked telephone that he'd won a MacArthur grant, a five-year "genius" stipend. "I went back to the campfire," he said, "and all these aborigines were sitting around eating kangaroo. I wanted to tell somebody, but there was no way they were going to understand, so I just sat down with them and ate kangaroo."

Last year he rented a Cessna and flew over Tonle Sap, the great Cambodian lake that drains into the Mekong, where he saw hundreds of storks and pelicans and thousands of other birds. "Seventy-eight percent of Cambodia is still wild woods and swamps," he exulted. "They have more birds there than I ever saw in Thailand or

Vietnam." He promptly invited some Cambodians to Baraboo. "If their political situation ever becomes stable," he said, "they can take tourists to see the temples of Angkor *and* the birds. For the economy, that's hotels and meals and everything else."

The visionary in Archibald cannot be stopped. "Africa," he went on. "Our project for 1993. Africa has six kinds of cranes, about half a million square kilometers of inland wetlands . . . it's a whole ecosystem we're trying to save, for birds, fish, and people."

Pesky wars. Famine. Population growth. Development. And on the other side, cranes—and the fragile dream of reclaiming their natural habitat throughout the world. It is no wonder that Archibald has attracted a devoted following of patrons, or that he half-jokingly compares his work to the enormous scope of the United Nations.

"You really ought to come out to Baraboo," he said, exhausted.

David Rains Wallace

The Crowded Desert Islands

from *Manoa*

One of my adolescent fantasies was of being on a desert island, a small one with just a beach and a cliff. I'd live in a cave in the cliff and comb the beach. It wasn't a very imaginative fantasy. I had it on Sunday nights before I had to go back to another five days of junior high school, which explains its appeal.

The appeal became less urgent after I recovered from junior high, but I still liked the idea of desert islands. When I moved to California in my early twenties, I thought I might encounter such an island. Robert Louis Stevenson's *Treasure Island,* which my father read to me as a child, is supposed to be based on the California coast. I'd disliked Stevenson's Victorian longwindedness, but the island idea evidently had sunk in.

Living around San Francisco Bay, I developed a mild fixation on the Farallones, a cluster of islands twenty-seven miles west of the Golden Gate. They hovered on the fringe of my attention as they hovered on the western horizon. I'd see them as I hiked over a ridge at Point Reyes, sugarloaf shapes jutting from an otherwise empty Pacific, and feel a faint sense of frustration that I hadn't gotten closer, particularly since they were so near. They're really just an oceanward extension of Point Reyes, granite ridges that are being dragged northward from southern California's Transverse Ranges by sideways movement of crustal plates.

But it's not easy to get out into the cold, windy Pacific. I first came to California to visit a friend who had a salmon fishing boat, at Bodega Bay. When I arrived, the boat was broken, and all I ever got to do was to unsuccessfully help my friend try to fix it. The farthest out I got was on a rowboat on Tomales Bay, east of Point Reyes. After that, I was always involved with things inland, so that the Farallones just hovered. Crustal plates might have dragged them northwest to the Bering Sea, as far as I was concerned.

I finally visited the Farallones recently, when an Oceanic Society guide who was taking my nature-writing course gave me a ride on a whale-watching day trip. The trip was quite unlike my adolescent fantasy, which had revolved around solitude. Few experiences are less solitary than a whale-watching cruise. We never even set foot on the islands. Yet the desert islands actually proved more "imaginative"—in the sense of diverse, surprising, curious, lively—than fantasy.

A half-hour outside the Golden Gate, somebody said, "Look at the jellyfish." I glanced over the rail, expecting to see a few of the silvery little moon jellies that often get washed onto beaches. A few were drifting here and there, but below them floated an almost solid mass of golden-brown, furry-textured objects, each as large as a child. They were close enough to the surface to see in detail, but deep enough below to seem shadowy and mysterious, and extended in every direction—a mermaid's meadow of pelagic chrysanthemums.

My student, Mike Ezekiel, said they were lion's mane jellyfish, each a colony of tiny coelenterates that lives by straining microscopic plants and animals out of the water with structures on trailing filaments like poison darts. One hears a lot about how fertile California's offshore waters are from deep-ocean nutrient upwellings, but I'd never seen such graphic evidence of it. The big jellyfish had to be swimming in a virtual plankton soup to be so abundant.

Many things we passed seemed new to me, although I'd been living a few dozen miles from them for decades. I didn't recall ever seeing the shy little harbor porpoises that showed dorsal fins for an instant as they surfaced to breathe. I'd seen a lot of penguinlike common murres on shoreline rocks, but I was unfamiliar with the pigeon guillemots that flew out of the boat's way, the little Cassin's auklets that dived out of the way, and the tufted puffins that appeared to be wearing blond wigs. I'd seen red-necked phalaropes, but I hadn't seen these delicate shorebirds sitting on the deep sea swells like gulls. Mike Ezekiel said phalaropes like to follow blue whales and feed on the shrimplike krill the whales eat. He'd seen blues around the islands the day before.

We didn't encounter blue whales, but as we neared the main island we saw spouts, and then flukes as a whale dived. A pod of gray whales was feeding in the shallows, sucking up bottom mud and straining copepods and other small animals from it with the sievelike baleen in their mouths. Of course, we didn't see them doing this—all we saw was their tails as they dived, and their backs as they surfaced.

Despite this concealment, gray whales' pale, mottled bodies have a weighty solidity that seems unexpected in a medium that mainly produces amorphous things like jellyfish and seaweed. It's this substantiality that makes them so exciting to see, I think. But even the best photography can't convey their living bulk. When a whale surfaced, the passengers cheered as though for a scoring team, as though for a victory of form over matter.

As we passed the whales, I saw something stranger than the lion's mane jellyfish. A large circular object with one black eye floated a few yards in front of the boat. It might have been a giant, animated tea tray, something from *Through the Looking Glass.* As the prow approached it, the object suddenly brandished stubby fins and upended itself, then gave a lazy shake of an equally stubby tail and swam down out of sight. Mike Ezekiel had described it in one of his class essays: it was an ocean sunfish, a several-hundred-pound species that likes to sunbathe lying on its side on the ocean surface. I'd heard of them, but had assumed something so exotic lived only in the tropics. Ezekiel said they come to California's coast to eat the abundant jellyfish, although nobody knows how they get much nourishment from the watery jellyfish.

We steered past the islands into deeper water to look for more whales, and soon found some humpbacks. Although larger than the grays, they seemed less weighty and substantial, more a part of the amorphous offshore world. Their dark, slick backs made them hard to distinguish from the shifting swells, and they were harder to approach. They soon disappeared, probably diving deep for plankton swarms.

A swarm of sea birds rested on the water, a possible sign of schooling fish, and we headed that way. A herd of California sea lions appeared, perhaps also heading for the schooling fish. I hadn't seen sea lions swimming in a herd since my rowboat days in Tomales Bay, when a herd had surprised me by rearing up in the water at sunset and barking in unison as though performing a crepuscular ritual. Unlike the whales, the lions craned their necks and eyed us curiously. Some swam under the hull and surfaced on the other side. One group hung together timidly, probably juveniles still getting used to life on the water.

The lions departed as we turned back towards the islands, but a pod of black-and-white Dall's porpoises appeared and began riding our bow wave. A porpoise would surface just under the rail, glide alongside effortlessly as the wave pulled it, then veer off, to be replaced by another.

"It's like they're doing it to be friendly," a woman said. To me it seemed more like skateboarders attaching themselves to passing cars: exuberant daredeviltry.

As we approached the main island, the air filled with a fishy, ammoniac smell, then with screeching din and kelp flies—big, blackish flies that somehow managed to swarm annoyingly around our heads in spite of the sea winds. Aside from the empty houses of a former lighthouse station, birds and sea mammals covered every part of the island. Gulls, murres, and cormorants sprinkled the tan granite like salt and pepper, and hazed the island's outlines with their comings and goings. Seaside rocks appeared furred with blackish-brown moss, which turned into massed California sea lions when seen through binoculars. Lighter-brown patches were groups of larger Steller's sea lions.

One cove contained a litter of silvery, cigar-shaped objects, which binoculars resolved into basking elephant seals. They were so much larger individually than the sea lions that they confused the sense of scale. I remembered the first elephant seal I'd seen, a twenty-foot bull protruding from both ends of a sizable willow thicket at Año Nuevo rookery on the coast. It had been semihallucinatory to see something that big on land—it looked like something back-projected in a monster movie. Almost extinct when I first came to California, elephant bulls now roar up and down the Año Nuevo beach like dozens of wayward buses, confounding conventional notions of separation between monstrous sea life and manageable land life. They live very much like whales during the half of the year they spend on the high seas, diving a mile deep to feed on abyssal squid and fishes.

I'd have been nervous about landing a boat on the beach, where the elephant seals sprawled. They've been known to run over unwary visitors at Año Nuevo. The prospect of landing on the island seemed generally uninviting. Kelp flies, piles of maggoty guano, and attack by territorial gulls waited beyond the seals. Researchers doing field work on the Farallones have to wear protective clothing. The islands would have been more hospitable during the lighthouse days, when egg-collecting and seal-hunting had reduced breeding populations to a fraction, but I preferred the inaccessibility of their present incarnation as a national wildlife refuge. Thoreau wrote that we need some life pasturing freely where we never wander. I'd add that we need some life rampaging, shrieking, and stinking freely out there, too.

It was getting late, and the boat turned back. It had been a perfect August day, with a quiet sea and only light fog. I thought we'd seen everything. However, as we plowed back into the jellyfish meadow,

Mike Ezekiel shouted, "A turtle!" A dark spherical head and part of a ridged carapace protruded from the water a few yards off the bow. The turtle was probably five or six feet long, a leatherback, the largest sea-turtle species. Mike said they occasionally appear around the Farallones, probably to graze on jellyfish. Leatherbacks are less confined to tropical waters than other sea turtles because their great bulk reduces heat loss. I was still surprised to see a thousand-pound turtle in the waters off the Golden Gate.

I was even more surprised to see another leatherback about fifteen minutes later, long enough to be sure it wasn't the first. We got close enough to the second turtle to hear it breathe, and to see what looked like limpets and barnacles on its carapace. Both turtles had orange patches on their heads and pinkish skin on their throats, colors I hadn't expected on sea turtles. I wondered if they were epiphytic growths, like the limpets and barnacles.

The turtle reminded me of a picture in one of my favorite childhood books, Time-Life's *The World We Live In.* It was a painting of Mesozoic Era sea life, with plesiosaurs, ichthyosaurs, and mosasaurs disporting off a mountainous, palm-fringed coast. These toothy reptiles were thrilling, but what had struck me most had been an enormous, leathery carapaced turtle swimming under the exotic but extinct reptiles. I had seen living turtles, if not seagoing ones. "Why turtles were selected for survival on land and sea remains one of evolution's mysteries," the book said. That was in 1955, but it's still true. Sea turtles nest on desert islands. Maybe that has something to do with their survival.

Adele Ne Jame

Poems

First publication

Phosphorescence, North Shore, O'ahu

Like small pearls they arrive
but with a blue internal fire—; they persist
in emitting light with no sensible heat—
a bioluminescence I have not seen for years
and then only on the other side of the world—.
But here, tonight, they simply clutter
the dark shoreline, washed up like pebbles,
reckless as love, scatter light
and vanish—. A dissonance of dark
and light we are caught in so like
a Poulenc invocation I once heard someone
beautiful sing—. Abandoning
the kerosene lamp and with wet hands
I hurry to gather them up as best I can—
all light in a clump of sand, gambling
away their gifts like that until
finally, I give them up—,
slip them back into the water, suspended,
weightless and gone—. I think it is to come to this—

the full dark, naked and beyond loss—,
to remember the burning lights
of a hundred thousand candles set adrift
down a long river in Bangkok, perhaps,
to know, the mystic said, the heart
has only borrowed things to live with—
like the track of the moon on the water—,
gorgeous and dispersing—.

from *Hawaii Pacific Review*

The Wedding Feast

Photo 659: "Papuan husbands and wives live separately and see each other only during specially arranged occasions." Photo 680: "Papuan woman showing back scars sustained in love-making. Gashes are made with sharpened bamboo sticks. Dirt is rubbed into the wound which then becomes infected and eventually leaves a large raised scar. The scars are proudly exhibited as proof of the lover's passion."

Nash Ne Jame, *Natural History,* May 1938

He has come up the Flower River
for the wedding feast, traveled all night
in a dugout made from a single log.
He's listened all night to the sound of the paddle
sweeping the muddy water around him,
heard the impatient call of
the hornbill gathered in the wild palm,
his own heart beating.

Now he sees the moon spinning, her body
in the firelight, all that plumage
wrapped around her arms and bare waist.
Purple crown feathers drift into the fire
and the smell of boiled sago lingers on her skin.
He will look at the spinning moon
for as long as he can, for as long as he lies with her.
Under the wild palm, his heart beats fiercely
as she turns her back,
as he reaches out for the bamboo.

All day long she has carried sago
wrapped in banana leaves
from the forest past his kampong.
She has imagined him saying her name.
Still she keeps walking towards
the other women who wait gathered
around the boiling pot like forest birds.
And as she lowers her bundle into the hot dust,
the slashes on her back gleam
like jewels in the sun's glare.

from *Hawaii Pacific Review*

Dance of the Areca

for my father, Nash Ne Jame, 1897–1961

All day long this rain,
even the violets have darkened
and curled around themselves,
his heart quiet in its watery cavity.
And like a woman
whose body is smeared with white clay,
sitting and singing
for the dead one, I say to myself,
stay here. Only that.

And after a long time,
I become powerful in this work,
learn to take even the last
light from his eyes—his whole estate,
the thing not used up. Take the smell of
the pigfire from his hands,
take the New Guinea night dancing,
the feasting, his other life.
I swallow it like the thick juice
of the areca leaf called peace,
and become like the dark woman there
who, for the love of the dance,
rubbed her body with warmed fat. For him,
wore a diadem of plumes and beaks,
iridescent black and opal, the smooth
stone of the Flower River at her throat.

She who moved towards him with such grace,
those two pleasuring themselves
in another's honor. He told me this:
Once invited, you cannot refuse.
I would make a belief out of it.

And now, it's as if kneeling
before a platform of bones, like the Fuyughes,
who, after so much grieving,
chop them to pieces so that
the killing of the pigs may begin—
the night feasting, and with the sound of
bamboo cones pounding the earth,
the dance of the areca, mourners swaying
in the tranquil firelight, repeating
the names of the dead in the air.

from *Manoa*

A Bedouin's Dream

Hannah Rose walks the length of the beach,
a child, hair so white in the white light
the cabochon moonstones lashed around
her wrists go pale—and suddenly the heart
finds its walled garden and there, a torrent
of white jasmine, so that when I think of you
walking Manley Harbor in the failing light
the pines and palms side by side are no longer
a confusion and I am no longer
the one beside you as if I belonged there,
hands full of hours in this desert
I keep making—. Though
the scent of your back as we lay
close in the early morning is not unlike
this pungent air, the salt smell of
wet rocks where the pūpū kōlea cling
powerfully at low tide—. There is no
rescue from the desire and no retrieval, you said then,
the words like fish swimming out of your mouth—
when I was ten, my father's black bull,
wild in the night from a flood,
took the farmhouse porch, its hooves were
slipping in the mud and rising water,
its muscled flanks were rippling with power
but the terror showed in the eyes rolling
back in its head as it began battering
the kitchen door—fearless,

father brought him down with an ax—.
Alone now, every day I swim out farther
in the vacant-green ocean, each stroke
stronger, diving deeper
towards the bottom where everything is
undiminished—. Opening and opening
to that silence, the current
below the surface is a Bedouin's dream
you want to wrap your arms around—
the drifting medusae, the sea stars wound
in the watery light who shed an arm
and out of it know how to form
another perfect five-point replica—.
This water is endless, Rumi said. This salt
and blood, the mounting pressure against
the chest—. Finally bursting
through for air, I surface
and swim powerfully for shore—.

First publication

Saba and the Songs We Hear

The *Seraphina* anchored in the black
Caribbean light is a tautology
of beauty, you say, somehow trying
to measure it as we do—say—
the grieving of God's angel who stood
at the composer's grave failing
to leave. Stood there broken—
a vision that will not leave me—.
Or the power of Blake's angels still
in the trees, the hum of their wings
edged with pairs of eyes like jewels
as if that sound alone might carry us
away from a place like this, beautiful
but with no harbor—though the songs
we hear might only be some failure
we have not yet reached out for—.
Yet we carry our tin lamps up the thousand
steps of The Mountain, past a small cluster
of houses, backyard hurricane graves,
those barreled vaults of cement wedged
into the volcano's side holding the Saban dead
close to the living, and from the high wind
that would take everything here, hurl
even the long dead into the sea below us—.
And as we climb further up the steep
path of wet roots and palm break,
willing to forego a terrain less cruel

for the altitude, we say what we can:
the stone lit bench here
is worn and beautiful from the rain
as if it were the god of this place—.
And the small garden there—,
its gift of damp heat, its lush performance
of red against a dark jungle of trees,
the high twisting forest—. I say
last night, I read in a book love is
worth nothing until it has been tested
by its own defeat. You say, oh and the moon
is nearly lapis behind the tumbling stars,
the small complaint of rain—,
that Padre Pio battled demons all his life
and was washed, at last, by angels
in his cell—. After a long time,
we take up our lamps and the ground orchids
we've found for the empty vase
by our bed—, knowing nothing can save us
from what hourly we are making or unmaking—.

Doug Peacock

Walking Point in White Bear Country

from *Pacific Discovery*

A few years ago, I agreed to accompany a beluga whale expedition to the High Arctic—the Canadian island country west of Greenland. All this land was polar bear country and members of the expedition were understandably nervous. My job was to be the polar bear guy, to walk point in white bear country.

The pay wasn't much—the price of a plane ticket—but I figured I owed both my friends and the bears a bloodless trip with no casualties on either side. The problem was I didn't know much about polar bears. In fact, outside of the ethnographic and scientific literature, I knew next to nothing. I had seen a few distant polar bears out on the pack ice 20 years earlier but nothing since.

Brown and black bears were a different story: I had spent a good chunk—well over a decade—of my life living with grizzly bears and wanted to believe this experience would allow me a "quick study" of the white bear. After all, polar bear evolution probably followed the needs of a brown bear who wandered north 100,000 years ago and started hunting seals.

The brown and white bears, *Ursus arctos* and *Ursus maritimus,* share an adaptive intelligence. They are flexible with a knack for pioneering new habitats and situations, and both exhibit a cognitive complexity. Grizzly and polar bears are aware of their own track making. Grizzlies, for instance, may travel to denning sites only during a heavy snow, walk backwards carefully in their own tracks, suddenly leap off a trail onto a rock or behind a bush, or avoid leaving their paw prints in muddy areas.

One of the more disconcerting experiences in nature is to have a bear set up an ambush for you. This has happened to me twice with grizzlies. One April, I watched a big Yellowstone grizzly trace my showshoe tracks out of a clearing into the lodgepole forest; the bear was walking on top of the tracks I had made coming in. After waiting ten minutes, I started to follow the huge tracks, but it was almost dark and something made me stop short. A chill of premonition ran up my spine. I turned and quickly got out of the woods.

The next morning, I followed the prints out onto the crusted snow. The grizzly had followed my showshoe trail for nearly a hundred yards, then veered off to the right in a tight circle to an icy depression behind a large deadfall ten feet off my trail. There he had bedded behind a log that would conceal him, waiting for me. Had I gone further into the timber that night, I would most certainly have encountered the bear. The icy bed spoke of a long wait.

This was the second time I had known a grizzly to set up what looked like a deliberate ambush. Polar bears, I read, do it too. What it means, what the bear intends, I don't know; maybe it is only curiosity. Still, I had known a distinct if momentary perception of a malicious intelligence lurking behind that log.

So—to hedge my bets—before leaving for the North Country, I read everything about polar bears I could lay my hands on and started thinking seriously about the danger of white bears. The convoluted paths of this meditation tended to converge on the issue of fear of bears, my own fascination with animals that sometimes kill and eat humans, and why, from the human perspective, these seemingly expendable creatures lie so close to the origins of human consciousness and are central to our own survival.

In July 1991, my friend Doug Tompkins and I left from Vancouver in his Cessna 206 flying up the northwest coast of British Columbia towards the Queen Charlotte Islands, on the opposite corner of the continent from the High Arctic. This jaunt was a side trip. Our plan was to spend four days in the Queen Charlottes, then head east, taking a couple days to check out strategic uncut forests in the interior of British Columbia and Alberta. (Doug has devoted much of his life to acquiring and otherwise protecting virgin forest.) From Edmonton, we would load our gear on a commercial jet to Resolute on Cornwallis Island, pick up the latest information on where to find belugas, and head on out into white bear country.

What follows are excerpts from my trip journal.

July 19, 1991, Queen Charlotte Islands

Low scudding clouds shroud the rocky coastline, a gray indifference perched upon a dark and featureless ocean. A broad band of blue mussels, limpets, and horse barnacles runs along the shoreline—the tide level appears to be close to its lowest point. We are kayaking into the narrow east-west channel that cuts through the middle of the Queen Charlotte archipelago, timing our move to the rising tide, and hoping to reach the midpoint in time to ride the ebb tide down the other side. Beyond the slate landscape of sea and rock looms the muted green forest—fir, cedar, and Sitka spruce reaching up into the low clouds from an understory of alder and fern.

We make camp in a back bay and I follow the little creek up beyond the brackish water to fill my canteens with fresh water. Near the bank are several bear scats from last fall; berry scats from a very big bear. The locals told us that though there are no grizzlies on the islands, the black bears here grew huge.

Black bears are relatively harmless, but not polar bears or grizzlies. Most of the few experienced voices who have spent significant time with both grizzlies and polar bears consider the brown bear more dangerous. The American brown bear is aggressive in many situations: when wounded for example, or a mother with young, sudden close brushes, defending food, during the mating season, or being surprised on its day bed. Grizzlies may charge threateningly during any of these encounters, sometimes making good on the threat if people are very close or if they try to run away or climb a tree. Most grizzly bear maulings, especially those involving sows with cubs, are defensive accidents; if the person plays dead, the bear will often break off the attack.

Polar bears are generally considered by these people to be more tractable, less nervous, and even docile by comparison. The difference is that, while grizzlies are truly omnivorous and have diets that tend towards the vegetarian side of the table, the white bear is an effective predator and is largely carnivorous, and polar bear attacks on humans reflect this. About two-thirds of the deaths and injuries inflicted by white bears on man have been predatory, and uninterrupted polar bear attacks tend to result in the human victim being eaten.

July 20, 1991, Skidegate Channel

I am thinking about my choice of carrying a spear into polar bear country rather than the usual firearm. A friend forged the iron spearhead, knowing what I needed it for and how I intended to use it—as a pike, mounted on a stout wooden shaft of suitable length. The only time this defensive weapon would ever be used is at the conclusion of a bear charge. The theory was that you anchor the stern of the shaft on the ground and aim the tip of the spear towards the narrow chest of the white bear, who theoretically impales himself on his charge—if all goes according to plan. The odds, of course, are not in your favor.

My decision to carry a spear was made earlier in the spring, after considerable research and much reflection. The usual advice—law in some quarters—is to carry a big bore firearm for bear. Most of the "official" bear literature speaks of the necessity of guns for shooting charging grizzlies. I disagree. I have experienced dozens of close calls with grizzlies without resorting to guns and no bear has ever touched me. Eighty percent of the grizzly bears who charge are mothers with cubs who will stop short if you inoffensively stand your ground. So, short of shooting a bear that is actively chewing on you, it is never quite clear when to begin firing.

This argument about guns and bears lies perilously close to near-religious and cherished beliefs concerning the roots of dominion and masculinity in America. When is it acceptable to take another life in defense of your own life, your family, or your property? When do humans or other animals become true threats? We tend to fear all that is unknown, which in the so-called civilized world increasingly embraces much of the natural world.

Either you believe that a human life has more intrinsic value than that of a bear, or you don't. This is not the same as survival—for an individual or collectively as a species—which is different. If you think it is OK to blow away any bear you think might be threatening you, the discussion is over; otherwise, a firearm will get you into more trouble than it will get you out of. And I consider it unethical to voluntarily invade the homeland of polar bears only to blow them away. At the same time, I hate to be totally defenseless.

Carrying a spear resolves all these questions. I consider myself responsible for all my companions should an encounter with a white bear grow ominous. After all, that was what I agreed to do: walk point. The bedrock assumption, never discussed—that keeps my carrying the spear from being just a campy joke—is that the spear carrier must be willing to die.

July 21, 1991, Hecate Strait: Waiting Out Rain in the Tent

Last night I dreamed of white bears—a recurring image. The white bears of my dreams were grizzlies, not polar bears. They were alternately fascinating and terrifying and I spent much of my time breathless from fear, trying to scurry up trees and into rafters, staying just out of reach.

It is curious that in my dreams, the fearsome white bears often threaten me on the fringes of civilization, in cabins, outbuildings—human structures oddly out of place in the wilderness. At first, this seems a mere confusion of association. Yet—in reading the literature of polar bear assaults on humans—attacks often take place on the edges of industrial culture: out on the drilling rigs, the geological camps, scientific stations, or depredations upon displaced pods of eco-tourists or biologists. Thus reality lingers beneath the fear.

In Manitoba, a mistake of geography caused the voracious truck of commerce to plop a grain-exporting seaport on the site of an ancient migratory route of polar bears. Each fall, the bears, who are hungry, invade the town and feed at the dump. In 1983, a Churchill man closed a bar and walked down a street with his pockets full of scavenged meat from a burned-down hotel. A white bear caught him in the dark from behind, grabbed him by the head and shook him to death like a dog with a rat.

Other attacks have taken place further from civilization. During a midmorning of January 1975, on a drilling platform in Canada's Beaufort Sea, a worker was bending over cutting ice off a doorway, when a five-year-old male polar bear hit him without warning, a blow so sudden and silent that workers 20 feet away, inside, heard nothing. By the time the man was missed, the bear had dragged him a mile away and had stopped to eat him.

This is the typical pattern of contemporary polar bear attacks. A silent blow in the night of winter delivered from ambush with no warning, just outside the door of the camp, rig, outhouse. The attacks are predatory, the bear is often a young hungry male, and the human victim will be consumed as food if the attack is uninterrupted.

I try not to make too much of these coincidences; this fearsome mixing of wild beasts and human settlement seems a natural and metaphorical confusion of people who no longer maintain a bestiary apart from the barnyard, who fanatically fear the unnamed. Grizzly bear maulings near towns are somehow more terrifying than those set far apart in the wilderness, as is the notion of man-eating wolves roaming the streets of New York City. These are aberrations of association, I thought, caused by the poverty of our minds, the fear of everything beyond the steel barriers.

July 22, 1991, Flying Over Central Interior British Columbia

Below, snow cornices delineate the watershed of a lovely glacial valley, long white serpents of wind-driven snow hugging the ridges. Everything but the permanent snowfields and these remnant cornices have melted in the warm sunlight of late July. The plane climbs south, over a low divide. On a broad patch of cornice a small herd of mountain sheep escapes the hordes of insects by bedding on the snow. I lean out the window and see fresh bear tracks traveling along the snow cornice. The grizzly tracks veer sharply off to the left down into the head of another valley. It looks like the bear was traveling to another seasonal forage range.

Grizzly bears use well-traveled trails and traditional routes when moving from one section of their range to another, but they sometimes take shortcuts, too. I once tracked a grizzly who took advantage of a recent forest fire to take a shortcut to the next drainage. Polar bears may do this also, I read, out on the ice where there is open ice and soft spots. How do they know where they're heading if they've never been that way before? Taking the shortcut, for grizzlies or polar bears, is to go beyond memory. The animal must have some kind of map of the country tucked away in its consciousness.

Polar bears may travel astonishing distances; movements of 2,000 miles in a year have been recorded. But on the ice, with no apparent landmarks in an ever changing topography of ice and flows—how do they manage? This travel would be difficult enough in the mountains and forests, but to do so among the shifting flows and drifting ice goes beyond any science I could imagine.

July 23, 1991, Caribou Mountain, British Columbia: Doug's Cessna

Though I know that brown bear stalking, ambushing, or preying upon humans during the day is extremely rare, it isn't unknown. Five hundred miles to the north of our location, during the winter of 1970, a Doig River Indian went out following the tracks of a very large grizzly. He followed the tracks to a head-high mossy hummock, behind which the bear had circled, waiting to ambush the man. The male grizzly killed and partially devoured him.

It's difficult to assess the dangerousness of such encounters and—above all—impossible to generalize about bears. I don't think that every grizzly or polar bear lying in ambush intends to do you harm, but not for a second do I imagine that all these bears are just curious. This fresh though unsettling behavior by these sometimes predatory animals, creatures who are about our size or larger, resists easy classification.

July 24, 1991, Fraser River, British Columbia: Flying East

We are flying over moose country, caribou country, wolf country. I do not think the caribou fears the wolf, as humans so obsessively fear the shadows on the edge of their former world. The evolution of the caribou did not lead to escaping its fate as wolf meat but to an appropriate, timely offering. Among paired predators and prey, the progression over time is aimed not so much at how to avoid becoming a victim of predation as it is directed towards the suitable age and individual at the moment of truth. Even among our species, a good death is embracing the appropriate moment of dying. Certainly, there are times to rage against the dying of the light, but in the end, you have to wrap your arms around death.

Is there a vestigial fear of being killed and eaten by wild animals left over from our African roots, from our time on the savanna, or is it just another facet of the irrational fear of all creatures whose lives and habitats we no longer know? That cosmos surrounding our brain—the human mind itself—evolved from an ecology, a habitat whose remnants we sometimes call "the wilderness." What has evolved doesn't persist without sustaining the conditions of its genesis. Fear was appropriate when we hunted large mammals, but the vitality of that fear is lost in a world of crime, traffic, and video games. The stench of fear in war cannot replace the gift of life in a grizzly's charge; they smell different—I know this from experience. And—as the world sculpts caribou evolution or creates healthy moose—what today hones our organic intelligence that was born of hunting?

July 25, 1991, Canadian Rockies, Alberta: Last Day in Doug's Plane

Far ahead lie the High Plains of Alberta, Indian Country—Blood, Sarsi, and Piegan. Unlike the insular Europeans in their concrete tepees, the Plains Indians of the High Plains deliberately courted confrontations with grizzly bears during times of passage, vision quests, and wisdom seeking. You ferreted out the bear to get something, because if you weathered the encounter, you came away with wisdom. In this encounter, you offered up your whole life; all your talents and instincts focused on the moment. If you survived the appointment—and each time it was an open question—you walked away complete in soul and utterly alive. The confrontation was so intimately personal you sometimes never spoke of it again. To survive such an encounter was always a gift from the bear.

The Eskimos of old also deliberately sought out the white bear because the polar bear, like the grizzly, was "the one who gives power."

July 27, 1991, Boothia Peninsula: Commercial Jet to Resolute

Below on the pack ice are dark dots, probably ringed seals. The greatest interaction between animals may be among those who kill and eat one another: the lion and the zebra, the caribou and the wolf. Or the Eskimos and the polar bear, who alternated positions on the food chain, sometimes men eating bears, sometimes the other way around.

Of all animals who sometimes kill and eat humans, no species has as many strategies for success as the bear, especially the white bear. Not that they are designed to accomplish this purpose; on the contrary, all these animals know that stalking the upright ape involves considerable danger. The polar bear's strategies for human predation have mostly evolved around its chief prey animal, the ringed seal, a marine mammal with huge eyes and keen hearing. The white bear kills people the same way it kills the ringed seal; with bites or blows to the head or neck.

I wonder about the Eskimo hunter, crouched over his *aglu* for a seal, clinging to his spear in the dim or absent light of winter, listening for the hairy padded footsteps of the silent white bear.

July 31, 1991, 3:11 A.M. Cunningham Inlet, Somerset Island: Camped Above the Ice-free Waterway

A quarter mile to the south of my tent three immaculate white flecks are moving directly towards me across a contrasting canvas of brown and green tundra. They are bears. Through my binoculars I can see a mother polar bear and her two cubs. They will pass inland of my tent a hundred feet away near the foot of the bluff. I pick up my spear and head to a better vantage point, a hummock of bowhead whale bones, remnants of a thousand-year-old Thule sod house.

The white bear family ambles into a little ravine a hundred yards away, still heading my way. They move fluidly with unimaginable grace and beauty. Holding the eight-foot spear in my right hand, I grab a handful of lichen and moss with my left.

Like Antaeus, the giant of Greek mythology, invincible while touching the earth, I have to be on the ground, holding tight to the world, always sharing the land with wild animals who hold down the same living skin of earth with the fierce weight of their paws.

I await their passage.

Carolyn Kremers

Native Store

from *Indiana Review*

One afternoon in February, I watched my first musk ox butchering. Teddy John had gotten a bull out on the tundra "with only one shot," he said. He and a brother had hauled it home on a big wooden sled behind their snowmachine.

When I walked by their house after school, Teddy and his parents, Nicolas and Athena, were butchering the musk ox on the snow. Teddy's brother was helping. The brother seemed young—maybe twenty?—and very quiet. I had not seen him before. His face was covered with scars.

I stopped to watch. Nicolas nodded and Teddy smiled.

The musk ox had been skinned, and now everyone was working to cut off the legs. In the cold air, the carcass steamed. Athena did most of the cutting with an ulu, getting dark red blood all over her mukluks and her flowered parka, especially the fur-trimmed cuffs. Everybody's bare hands were covered with blood. Besides two ulus, they used two big butcher knives and an axe.

Everyone butchered and piled meat on the sled: four legs and then the carcass, hacked into pieces. Teddy and his father reached inside the abdomen up to their elbows and dragged out a sack of innards and organs, including the heart. The sack was as big as a brown paper grocery bag, only greenish-white. They set it on the snow and three dogs pounced on it, licking and tugging.

Teddy peeled the spinal column from the carcass and fed it to the biggest dog, which gobbled it almost whole. Then he scooped something dark and slimy into a bucket. The liver?

Every few minutes, the family wiped their hands with snow to clean off the blood. Nicolas sent Teddy indoors for a bow-saw and Athena asked him to fetch a small saucepan for scooping. Blood and bile.

When Athena lifted one of the musk ox legs onto the sled, the hoof caught in the front pocket of her parka and ripped the pocket half off. She laughed toothlessly. She joked in Yup'ik and chuckled almost the whole time I watched. I think she was delighted with the meat. She didn't seem to mind at all that her clothes were drenched with blood.

The musk ox head lay on the snow, a metal ring in its nose. The lower jaw had been broken off to send to the Department of Fish and Game in Bethel, as required by law. Half-closed wet brown eyes looked at me.

After almost an hour, the family finished piling all the meat on the sled. I stamped my feet, stiff and cold from standing still, and whirled my arms in windmills to thaw my hands. Athena smiled.

Teddy pulled the sled a few yards over to the food cache—grey boards—and unlocked the padlock. Then he and his father and brother (with the scalded face) piled the meat inside. It would freeze quickly there.

The parents gathered the tools from the blood-spattered snow and walked into the house without talking and without nodding goodbye. Nicolas, then Athena. At first, I thought they were tired. Or was it a moment of humility and respect that I saw in their hunched shoulders and downcast eyes? How many, many times they must have butchered animals.

The two brothers carried the shaggy brown hide to the family's steambath and hoisted it up on the roof to dry, and I walked on.

Nicolas John died of heart failure in the summer of 1989. He was seventy-six.

I have a few photographs of him Yup'ik dancing, crouched on his knees in front of three women dancers, his eyes closed, white ptarmigan tail feathers waving in his hands.

I used to see Nicolas in the Native Store, when I stopped there after school. He would be buying something small like a can of Coca-Cola or a tin of snuff. He wore comfortable wool shirts and red suspenders, and his large ears covered half the side of his head. Sometimes a stubble of whiskers bristled his weathered chin, but he had such a compact body and a wide-eyed look that he always reminded me of a boy.

In spring, when the wind let up and my favorite clerk, Natalia, propped the door open to let the sun stream in, Nicolas sat on a box across from the cash register counter, hands propped on his cane. He greeted all the people who came in: giggling children, hungry teenagers, busy mothers, men back from seal hunting, creaky elders. Everybody knew everybody and they all said hello.

Whenever Nicolas saw me—at the store or church or post office—he nodded, and sometimes he shook my hand. But during my first three months in Tununak, we never said more than hello, probably because I felt intimidated by him. Several people had told me that Nicolas was a spokesperson for the village and for Nelson Island. He was president of Tununak's I.R.A. Council, the organization that governed the village. The Council had been established by the Indian Reorganization Act, amended by Congress in 1936 to include Alaska Native villages. Sometimes Nicolas travelled to speak at meetings and to appear on radio and television in Bethel, Nome, Anchorage, even Seattle.

I had never lived in a place where elders were so respected, and I could not speak with most of them because I did not know Yup'ik. I had never been good at small talk, anyway, in English or otherwise.

Besides, Nicolas seemed different from my other male elder friends. Nicolas was more reserved, more intense. He wore a serious look instead of a smile. I knew I was that way, too, sometimes. Perhaps he thought the same of me.

One stormy afternoon in January, Nicolas surprised me. Maybe he had enjoyed the school Christmas program, when the elementary students sang songs and the junior high played guitars. Or maybe he just felt talkative that day. Not many people were in the store. Anyway, I was peering down inside the freezer, looking for some ice cream and reindeer meat, when Nicolas came over and shook my hand. Then he reached behind his big left ear, turned up his hearing-aid, and started talking. I had to listen carefully, since he was much shorter than I—at least a foot and a half—and he talked quietly.

"Too much to think about these days," Nicolas said, putting his small hand over his hearing-aid and shaking his head. "I go to meetings Outside and I don't know anybody there. I get lonely in those places. Do you know how old Anchorage is? Anchorage is very young. Anchorage begun in 1914, only one acre large then, one acre. Now it is very big, very big. But some Native villages is very old. But very small, not big like Anchorage.

"I use to love to read at the school about Pilgrims. I read and read that story of that first Thanksgiving. I loved that story. How the Indians shared with Pilgrims and Pilgrims were good, religious people. But then look what happen to the Indians later."

I nodded and tried to say something like I know what you mean, but Nicolas was coughing loudly. He cleared his throat and went on.

"I want to write books. I want to write many books, one after the other, about the land and sea. And our people and our spirits. And send them to Juneau and Anchorage and Canada and Washington and Seattle and the Lower Forty-Eight, so *kass'aqs* can really understand about us and what we think. I want all the books to be free. All the books will be free so everyone can read them."

Nicolas looked past me with bright brown eyes. "I don't like to tell *kass'aqs* what I think. They change it all around. Then they tell other people something different. So I am writing books. In Yup'ik. And they can translate."

He shifted his weight on his cane. I felt I ought to say something—what could I say about books?—but he went on.

"Do you know there is two kind of love? There is love that come from heart and mind . . ." He pointed to his heart and then to his head. "It is like God's love. It is sincere. It is true. And there is love that come only from mouth and is not real love." He pointed to his mouth. "The man that leave a woman after she have his baby only loves from mouth. Everyone must love everyone else, like their own brother or sister, their own father or mother. Love is what will save us. If there is love, then there is no stealing and lying and cheating."

Nicolas cleared his throat loudly again and gave me a quizzical look. "Even you had nothing to eat, you would not starve. You would not starve, because Native people would feed you and share with you. You would not starve, even you didn't have one penny. Some *kass'aqs* is good, some is bad. I don't trust the bad ones, 'specially not these days. 1991 is not far. Native people must be careful these days, very careful. 'Specially this year."

I knew what Nicolas meant. Since moving to Tununak the previous fall, I had heard much about the Alaska Native Claims Settlement Act, a piece of legislation I had not been aware of when I lived in Colorado. Passed into law in 1971, ANCSA grouped Alaska Natives into thirteen regional corporations and two hundred village corporations, including Tununak's TRC, the *Tununermiut Riniit* Corporation, Voices of the People of Tununak.

ANCSA represented a trade between Alaska Native people and the United States federal government. In exchange for giving up aboriginal claims to most of the State, Alaska Natives had been awarded 963 million dollars and forty-four million acres of land. The Act provided for a twenty-year waiting period, during which Natives were prohibited from selling their stock. The federal government hoped that Natives would become educated about the provisions of the law and that they would organize through the corporations and make informed decisions. In 1991, individual Alaska Natives as well as Alaska Native corporations would be able to sell their land if they wished.

Slowly, I had learned why many Native people, like Nicolas, were suspicious of ANCSA. Lawmakers had not realized that the heirarchical profit-based nature of the corporate structure was incompatible with Alaska Native traditions of consensus decision-making and of sharing property. Furthermore, Western ideas of land boundaries and of ownership of natural resources were incompatible with Alaska Native practices of hunting and gathering and with Native attitudes toward stewardship of the land and sea.

The people of the Yukon-Kuskokwim Delta had named their corporation *Calista.* The Worker. Calista represented fifty-seven villages in the Delta, about 16,500 people. It was the most subsistence-based population in Alaska.

Now Nicolas leaned closer to me on his cane and peered from under his eyebrows, right up into my eyes.

"All the problems is getting worser and worser," he said. "In old days, Native people did not use money. They did not have money, not even one cent. They had never had money because they had never needed it. They could get all the food from land and sea. Money is not needed, money is useless. Even if a *kass'aq* would give me millions or trillions of dollars, a whole pile of money," he traced a pile on top of the freezer with his brown hands, "I choose the land. The land is precious, the sea is precious. It is worth more than money. It can feed all the people. I am worried about the land and sea."

Before I could comment, Athena came up behind Nicolas in her navy blue parka. Without looking at me, she huddled against his shoulder like a bundled bird and said something in Yup'ik, her wrinkled face hidden by fur. I caught one English word, *snowmachine.*

Nicolas and Athena talked back and forth, and Nicolas seemed to make a decision. Athena nodded her small, scarfed head, then shuffled back up the aisle past jars of Smucker's grape jam and red cans of Pringle's potato chips.

"I go now," Nicolas said, turning down his hearing-aid.

I reached out to shake hands.

Tucking his cane under his arm, he took my white hand in both of his and held it. Then he hobbled away.

I looked down at the top of the freezer, where Nicolas had traced the pile of money. Then I stood a minute, staring at my boots. There was nobody else in the store.

Rick Bass

Creatures of the Dictator

from *Men's Journal*

We drive north from Bucharest, three Americans in a black Citroën crammed with backpacks and camping gear, in a country where we do not know the language, heading for Transylvania on the beautiful edge of spring and riding just behind the fall of Communism in Romania—so soon behind its wake that perhaps, underground, all the flesh has not even finished rotting off of Nicolae Ceauşescu's skull. Romania was the only Communist country to overthrow its regime with bloodshed, and I sense a bit of that capability—that irksome human affinity for applying steel to flesh, blade to bone—still lying latent in the centuries-old air outside. Only it isn't latent: It, the violence, has just been expressed, and the still-lingering echo of it, the *feel* of it, seems as recent as the upturned furrows of bare soil that are soaking in the spring fog and rains. Cherry orchards line the hilly roads, petals float everywhere like snowflakes. Old women walk to and from the spring fields carrying instruments of cutting and ripping and gouging: machetes and axes and sickles and scythes. They are beautiful old women, and I do not know where the men are. Ceauşescu and the *Securitate,* the secret police, killed tens of thousands of Romanian citizens, leaving an orphan population of 40,000. Over a quarter of the populace was either in jail or had a close relative behind bars at one time or another.

We don't see other cars, just horse-drawn carts which we swerve to miss, coming around blind corners in the little towns. Steaming horse turds, true navigational hazards, lie in mounds up and down the rain-slicked roads. White chickens run clucking in all directions at our approach, and we can barely take our eyes from the orchards, they're so beautiful in the mist. Ray, the photographer, is crammed into the back seat, making moaning noises as we pass orchard after orchard, churchyards, cemeteries, all that pretty-picture stuff. Sue, our guide—she was a Fulbright scholar here last year, but, upon returning to her cabin outside Fairbanks, Alaska, has forgotten nearly all of the Romanian words she learned except the two biggies, "thank you" and "please"—looks worried. She's concerned that we don't have a phone number for the man we've come looking for, Peter Weber, the only grizzly bear biologist in Romania. We have only a street name in the city of Mediaş. And we're not sure Weber knows we're coming. A friend of a friend—Joachim—was supposed to alert Weber to our arrival and ask if he'd take us up into the mountains—into grizzly country—but the phones haven't worked reliably in Romania for years, not since the December 1989 revolution.

The reason we want to go looking for grizzlies is that Romania has so many of them. About 12 times more than Montana, and Romania is only two-thirds the size of that state. And most of Romania's bears are concentrated in the North, in the Carpathian Mountains and Transylvanian Alps. It's estimated that there are more than 6,000 grizzlies up there, and if we can't find Weber, or if he's not willing to take us, then we're going to just park the car and start hiking until we see one.

The reason there are now so many grizzlies in Romania—back in the 1940s, for example, there were only about 900—is that Ceauşescu liked to shoot them, sometimes killing eight or nine in a day. He brought bears in from Poland, and had a very active captive-breeding and propagation program, raising scores of zoo bears and then turning them loose near his favorite "hunting" spot. He would bait the area with dead animals, horse meat and vegetables to keep the bears close, and each dusk when they came in to eat, he'd shoot the shit out of them. Then he would have his picture taken next to the carcass and, if the bear was large enough, apply to have his name entered in the record books. This practice ultimately led to a large overall population (though, like Communism, it was hell on individuals) because Ceauşescu forbade anyone else to kill a bear, even if it was raiding crops or livestock—although he'd allow wealthy foreigners to pay thousands of dollars for the privilege.

I've always believed that how you treat animals, and how you treat the land, is how you'll treat people. I've noticed that either you have lots of respect, have it in spades, or you generally don't have any at all.

Ceauşescu, obviously, did not have it; he just kept shooting. Blood just kept pouring into the soil. New bears kept springing up out of that soil. Of course, he's gone now—the bears outlasted him. It's new blood that's being turned over now, the old blood that's soaked into that soil being furrowed and spaded and chopped and graded, and there's a new government, new hope and it's springtime. Maybe this time it will all be different.

As we drive north toward the mountains, driving through the sinking, misty dusk, the cherry orchards grow more luminous until they seem to blaze in the gloom. The old women are still coming in from the fields, talking to one another, axes and sickles slung over their broad shoulders, and they're all dressed in red and black, vampire colors, the colors of blood and death, although we are not yet into vampire country.

It's so lonely to be in a foreign country, lost at night, not knowing the language, directions or anything; it's as if you cease to exist. All I want to do is get into Transylvania—the north-central part of Romania, just below the Hungarian and Ukranian borders—where the language of the woods and the bears, I feel sure, is universal.

We reach Sibiu after midnight and check into the Hotel Bulevard, in the center of that big city. It looms gray and prisonlike on the edge of a hill, but inside it is funky and musty in an elegant sort of way: huge high ceilings, chandeliers, worn red carpets, tarnished-brass art deco fixtures.

We drift into the cavernous dining room/ballroom, ravenous, bleary-eyed and overstimulated. The tables are set with immaculate white linens; it's as if we're two hours early for a wedding reception. Sue calls her friend Joachim to meet us there and fill us in on the agenda, if there is any. Over at the far end of the dining room—where, of course, there are no other diners—stands a huddle of cooks, waiters and waitresses, half-hiding behind the grand piano. They're watching us uneasily, and they're definitely refusing to wait on us.

We sit for five minutes until Ray goes over and politely harangues the work force. They grumble, but disperse to their stations. We have two hot American dollars burning holes in our pockets—dinner is about 75 cents each, and a bottle of wine is 50 cents—and we can order pork, or pork.

It's good pork, though; it's some of the best I've ever eaten. Romanian pigs range free through the countryside, like deer, and the pork loin, salted and peppered and cooked with a little butter, tastes like the finest, leanest venison. I could eat five pounds of it. The wine is delicious.

The grand clock on the high ceiling above us strikes 1 A.M. Joachim comes in through the big, glass double doors. He is a small, dapper, precise man with short dark hair and a trimmed beard—he looks a little Faustian. He doesn't mince words.

"They have killed a horse for you," he says when he sits down. He studies the menu. "It was not a very good horse. I told them not to buy one for over 250 U.S. dollars. It made the farmer very happy; it was an old horse. I'll have the pork."

It turns out Weber knows we're coming. But Joachim says he told Weber we'd be at his house bright and early in the morning, and that Weber would be able to spend three to four days with us in the mountains. That's why they killed the horse—to bring all the bears in.

Still, no one really knows where Weber lives. Never mind that we're supposed to be on his doorstep—wherever that is—in a few hours, in a city 50 kilometers away. Joachim bids us good night, slips mysteriously back out those double doors, disappears into the night, and we never see him again.

The dawn is not flattering to Sibiu. There are too many people, too many buildings, too much carbon in the air and too many lingering diesel clouds. Driving behind the large transport trucks, we breathe in so much diesel exhaust that we have to cover our mouths with napkins; and when we pull the napkins away, there are black circles outlined on them, lithographs of what's been strained out. God knows what went in.

It calls for whiskey—even if it's only 9 A.M. We've got a lot of it, from the airport customs shop in Frankfurt. Sue was going to give it to friends in Sibiu, but there isn't time for any of that. In the back seat, she starts mixing us drinks. We stop at a market and buy a two-liter bottle of some green glowing liquid, some Cactus Cooler-, Gatorade-looking fluid, and pour that into the mix. It's vile, like barium, but the scenery demands it. We pass through the factory town of Copşa Mică, where crude coal is processed alongside the river. Crumbling smokestacks spew plumes of ebony into the sky. The streets, the buildings, the dead trees are all cloaked in black, as are the people and the animals—the dogs, the cats—even the children. People are cruising down the sidewalks in grimy wooden wheelchairs—people without arms and legs. It's too much. I pass on the driving duties to Ray so that I can really slug down the medicine. I am crying. Just over the border, to the west, the Serbs and the Croats are killing each other, cutting one another into pieces, while up in the mountains, perhaps, the bears hide deeper in the forest and watch.

In Weber's bustling town of Mediaş, we drive around aimlessly for awhile, then park and get out to hunt for him on foot. We reel up and down the busy streets—it's Saturday, market day—in the bright sunlight, inquiring of everyone we meet how to find Weber. I, for one, am staggeringly drunk. We've written down Weber's name and address on a scrap of paper and are showing it to people, who keep pointing us in different directions, convoluted hand-chopping sequences of lefts and rights, so the effect, I think, is that we must gradually, in a spiraling fashion, be getting closer to Weber, but damn, are we lost. I'm not even sure where the car is. We reel down cobblestone alleyways, calling for Weber to come out and show himself.

It is gypsies who save us. They are coming up the steps of a dungeonlike place, a young boy and two women dressed in bright clothes and jewelry, and our paths intersect.

They can't understand a word we're saying, but their eyes show that they're concerned. I've been warned to watch out for the gypsies, and I remember that in the past some of them have not been particularly kind to bears. One gypsy tradition, I've read, involves training a bear to dance whenever music is played by forcing him out onto a red-hot sheet of metal. After a few such training sessions, the bear hops and moans and dances anytime it hears music, remembering the incredible pain. The gypsies then take such a dancing bear from town to town, and while the village folk gather in a circle applauding the bear, the gypsies pick their pockets.

But these gypsies look nice; they peer at our scrap of paper with genuine concern. They take us by the arm and lead us down the busy street, and then down an alleyway. They point to a big stockade gate, the kind that could protect a fortress during wartime. It has Weber's name on it, in tiny print, and his street number! The gypsies back away, pleased with our exuberance.

We pound on the door to the compound. It is a brilliant, blue-sky day, and the alley is swarming with people and bicycles. A wild, stocky, bearded, redheaded, *troll*-looking man throws open the gate and peers at us. He is dressed in hiking shorts with suspenders, and is wearing heavy boots with knee-high stockings held up by garters. He has on a long-sleeved wool shirt and one of those funny little Robin Hood caps with a feather stuck in it. He looks like he can yodel. It is Weber!

"We must go now, if we are to go," he says. I'd been told he didn't speak English, but he gets his message across fine: We're late and we're drunk.

Weber hurries us toward his garage, in which the world's smallest car is hidden—a small, brown job like the ones you see the clowns and poodles spilling out of in the circus. He rolls his eyes like a Chinese dragon when he sees all the gear we've brought. "We can take nothing," he says. "Sleeping bags okay. One pair of underwear. A toothbrush. Nothing else."

"My camera gear!" Ray cries, and Weber scowls, and says finally, "Okay."

Somehow we jam ourselves into the little shitbox. We rocket out of Weber's driveway like messengers in the King's employ. Anicka, Weber's beautiful girlfriend, slams the double gate shut behind us, throws the crossbar deadbolt in place. We're off for Transylvania: for the dark woods, the high mountains, the rushing rivers, the misty valleys.

The little car smashes and shakes over the potholed roads. Weber grins a mad grin and drives faster, as if to punish us for being late and for not knowing the correct foreign languages; in this case, German and Romanian. Along the way he points out places where he's had wrecks as he swerves around haywagons and blares his shrill little horn at bike riders. We're into the country now. "I was watching wolf up there," Weber says, pointing to the foothills—I want to look, but cannot turn my eyes away from an oncoming bicycle as Weber occupies the center of the turtlebacked, one-lane, rain-slicked road—"and *pow!!* I go off the road, roll car many times, break very much bones. A very heavy thing." He is still watching the foot-hills as the cyclist shouts and at the last second swerves his bike off the road and down the deep roadside drainage ditch.

American politeness precludes us from asking him to slow down.

He cuts a swath through village after village, and finally after we start to get up into some high valleys (which he pronounces as "wal-lys"), he begins to relax and grow more affable. He drops his speed to under 140 kilometers per hour. I've been trying feebly to converse with Weber, to compare notes about bears, science—but he won't have any of it. Everything I say, it seems, is incorrect or bad science. It's like he's on some superstrict kick to adhere *ferociously* to the scientific method. He's denying utterly, it seems, the individuality—the intelligence, spirit and soul—of grizzlies, and instead keeps talking about them as if they are bacteria in a petri dish. "If a bear lives or if it dies—to me, it makes no matter," he says. "As a scientist, I am interested only in"—he pauses, groping for the English—"social interactions within population."

It's classic Communism, I think smugly—and then I remember that Romania has more than 6,000 grizzlies while the entire grand old lower 48 has far less than a thousand. Still, it becomes my goal to try and get Weber to admit that, yes, he loves the bear.

I look out at the marvelous woods, the mixed conifer and oak-beech, hornbeam forests—the latter producing rich mast crops, so important to bears during the fall pre-denning period—and prepare not to see a bear. I know how secretive they are. In my valley in Montana, the population is down to about 10 individuals. In seven years of hiking almost every day, I've seen two. Dozens, hundreds of black bear—but only two grizzlies.

Their presence must be more visible in Romania, however. Evidently the frequency with which they come down into villages to steal pigs or chickens or sheep is high. I had read a recent account of a farmer who fought off a bear with a pitchfork. (For the most part, they don't have guns in the countryside, but most farms have four or so formidable dogs to scare off bears.) And Weber tells me about the case a few years ago of a schoolteacher who tried to take a shortcut through the woods. He says that he can take us to visit with "peoples who have good bear stories."

The people up in this part of Transylvania—the Harghita Mountains within the complex of the Carpathians—are direct descendants of the Magyars, wild mountain Hungarian stock who still view this area as Hungary, not Romania. All they speak—all they *acknowledge*—is Hungarian. But that's okay, Weber knows that language, too.

Everywhere I went in Romania, people would fill me in on what ethnic groups to avoid: how the mountain people were different from the village people, were different from the coastal (Black Sea) inhabitants, were different from the flatlanders . . . how the gypsies were horrible people, and how, above all, the terrible, blood-lusting Magyars were the worst. All this ethnic tension in a country two-thirds the size of Montana.

Transylvanians, especially, have a history of hiding out in the dark forests, battling back invasions by the Daco-Roman/Vlachs, the Ottoman Turks, the Russian steppe rabble-rousers and just about anyone else who carried a sword. (It was Vlad Ţepeş—also known as Vlad the Impaler—who saved the region from the Turks in the 1400s, spearing his enemies' heads on iron spikes and providing the legendary basis for Count Dracula.) Then in 1952 came the Communist Gheorghiu-Dej, practicing a nationalistic isolationism; and lastly, in 1965, the dictator Ceauşescu, the son of an abusive father, and the blood continued to flow.

Everywhere we went there seemed to be a kind of frightened, hesitant, half-passive, half-aggressive sense of waiting for the other shoe to drop, waiting for the vaporous combustion of latent hate to flash into being again. You would think that having just pulled together to overthrow Communism there would be a glowing national harmony, but that kind of community feeling seems to exist only within the borders of individual villages. On the face of it, Romania is now a democracy, but political scientists question how much power the government will ultimately return to the people. The new leader, Ion Iliescu, is considered by many to be nothing more than a "Communist retread" who, to preserve his own power, may have little interest in pulling the country out of its blood cycle.

What I think is that there are too many people over there, more than what is biologically sane for the social dynamics and evolution of our species, and that individuals within the human populations do not have enough space, and cliques are a defensive response. Small bands gather closer and closer together because there is nowhere else to go.

Weber, pointedly apolitical, sees this same thing happening to the high bear populations. He says that can be fixed by shooting some of them.

He is grim-faced and unapologetic. Now an official at the Municipal Museum in Mediaş, Weber used to be Ceauşescu's biologist; he was there, I guess, while the dictator squeezed off the rounds. And his government still sells permits to shoot the bears—up to 300 a year—charging wealthy Germans and other foreigners up to $20,000 a kill.

This money, Weber explains, is used to help the forest.

But his explanation sounds feeble, and I think he knows it.

We'll be staying in a log cabin along a creek, high in the little valley of Varság. Weber insists that I am mispronouncing it.

"Voar-shawwgg," he says, wagging his thick finger.

"Voar-shawwgg," I say, and he grimaces, shaking his head. Weber is flirting with Sue—telling us, in broken English, about the superiority of males over "ze femuls." And he's talking about feces, too—calling them "fay-cees." Talking about ze wally of voar-shawwgg.

Good biologists know that people are the largest factor in any animal's life, and, like a good biologist, Weber knows almost everyone in the little village (population 1,200) of Varság. They don't hesitate to tell him what the bears are up to, how many pigs they've taken in the last week.

We stop at an ancient stone farmhouse with a brook trickling past it. There's a water wheel outside the kitchen window. The barn is made of hand-hewn spruce logs. There's a wooden gate around the farmhouse. It's neat as a pin: All the wood is split and stacked perfectly, and even the barnyard animals—the chickens, the sheep and the dogs—appear to have a preciseness to them. A small old man who looks like he could be running a dry cleaners in New York comes out and hails Weber with affection.

The farmer's name is Ferencz Szabó, and he has plenty of bear stories. One grizzly in particular likes to play a game with Szabó's stock: The bear hides up in the woods, watches and waits until he and his dogs head into the fields with the sheep each morning. As soon as they're a few hundred yards from the cabin, the bear will run down the hill, jump the fence, grab a young pig and then run back into the woods with it.

Such stories are common in Varság—there is no one who does not have a bear story—but there doesn't seem to be any real loathing on the part of the villagers when they talk about them. When I ask Szabó through Weber how he feels about there being so many bears in the woods, his face grows thoughtful. He says something serious to Weber. Szabó compares it—the bear's occasional depredations—to the nature of humans. "Sometimes we go into the bear's woods to take his berries," he says. "It is only fair that sometimes he comes and takes a sheep or a pig. As long as we do not take too many berries, and he does not take too many sheep, it is fair."

We ask Szabó about Ceauşescu; what it was like in the days when he came here to kill things. I listen closely as Weber translates, and notice that he does not use Ceauşescu's name. (Romanians generally refer to him only as "the dictator," or, sarcastically, "our leader," and I don't know whether this was a subtle, psychological way of disempowering his violent memory or an after-effect of the days when it was dangerous even to say his name, when there were spies everywhere.)

Szabó points to the table where we're sitting. "He came through here in his limousine once," Weber translates. "He came in with his bodyguards and sat right there and asked if Szabó had seen any animals.

"Szabó told him there had been a stag feeding on his neighbor's field. Ceauşescu finished his drink, got up from the table and left with his bodyguards, got back in his limousine and drove off.

"About three minutes later, Szabó heard a gun—*piff! poof!*—go off three times." Weber shrugs.

Szabó says something. Weber stares back at him for a second but Szabó's old face looks firm.

"He says," Weber interprets for us, "that Ceauşescu was a small man with a big gun."

On our way out the gate, Szabó's dogs come trotting over to investigate. They're friendly but tough-looking, with nails driven through their leather collars, points sticking out to create spiked collars.

"For their fights with the wolves," Weber explains. "Sometimes the wolves come out of the woods and try to kill the dogs and eat the sheep."

The next morning we cook a fine Romanian meal on the woodstove. The cabin fills with smoke. More wild pork loin, bacon, fried eggs, potatoes, pancakes and thick Turkish coffee. Weber makes hash browns. It reminds me of Montana.

Except that I'm a little puzzled by the way Weber allows all the odors to get in his clothes—especially the bacon. How are we going to sneak up on wild grizzlies when we smell so strongly? They can smell an elk carcass at a distance of at least seven miles; how are we going to get Ray and his cameras, for example, within 100 yards?

Instead of bears, what we sneak up on that day is a wonderful old woman called Giza-nèni, and her tiny, wiry husband, Feri-bácsi. They're on the hillside raking and burning leaves from their sloping field. They rake them with a wooden tool they made themselves, load them into a huge straw basket they wove themselves and carry them down to one of the smoldering leaf fires, smiling all the while.

Giza-nèni and Feri-bácsi, the terrible old bloodsucking Magyars, put down their rakes and baskets, seize us by the arms and escort us down the hill into their yard. We wade through chickens and dogs, past an old horse, and they all but force us into their tiny home. We feel hugely guilty, arriving at midday like this—it's the spring planting season, and here we are, coming in unannounced, robbing them of their hand-to-mouth worktime—but Giza-nèni is glowing like an angel, and Weber makes signals with his eyes and face that we are *not* to hurt her feelings, that we are to abide by her wishes *precisely.*

Giza-nèni stands up on a stool—she's well under five feet tall—and pulls down her fancy shot glasses and a dusty, two-gallon glass jug of what appears to be gasoline. Its contents glow orange as she carries the jug with reverence over to our table, passing through shafts of sunlight and woodsmoke. Weber, standing in the open doorway, grins like a wolf. So does Feri-bácsi, and I know what is expected of us.

Giza-nèni pours each of us a glass and motions to us to down it. "*Pálínka,*" she says and points out the one tiny, dusty window toward the peach blossoms floating on the hill below. In the golden sunlight, I can see the fumes rising from the glass, as when you're filling your car at the gas station. "*Sa-vee-vi-shen,*" Giza-nèni says, or something like that—she clasps both hands to her bosom and smiles at us—"From the *heart,*" Weber translates—and it is time to face the music.

It is hot and vile and it hurts. It makes us cry and shiver and wretch and jump up and down in our seats. Weber and Feri-bácsi are laughing. Giza-nèni watches us with a concerned look, as if it would crush her heart were we to say we didn't like it.

"Good," I try to say, but the word doesn't come out; the lining of my esophagus is gone.

But Giza-nèni knows what I'm trying to say. She smiles and pours us all another round, even though we have not gotten down more than perhaps an eyedropper-full. Feri-bácsi laughs, shakes his head, gets up and goes out to water the animals. Finally, Weber saves us, grabbing us by the collars and pulling us from the *pálínka* table, which delights Giza-nèni to no end. She is blowing kisses and calling out *sa-vee-vi-shen* as Weber hauls us away.

Farther back in the mountains, even among the smaller villages, there is an autumn sport in which the men, after a bit of *pálínka,* roll up their trousers and wade barefoot into the icy stream, looking for trout. They sneak up on the trout, which they see resting behind a boulder, slip their hands slowly under the trout's great white belly and begin to tickle it, almost as lightly as the water-current itself, until the fish becomes strangely paralyzed—but only for a moment or two—and the fishermen are able to snatch the great fish up, clutch it to their chests with both arms and stumble back to shore to the cheers of the villagers, the winner being the one with the largest fish.

And not far from here, up in the high Alps, there is a monastery where monks raise Lipizzaner stallions. I picture the monks in their robes the color of dried blood, barefooted or perhaps in sandals, riding the great animals in lunges through the fresh powder to wear them down, to gentle them. Then monks sitting around sipping tea, each in his room alone, talking to *Cristos,* while down in the cities below, in the flatlands, Ceauşescu and the Securitate were laying the corpses out in long rows to be photographed, cutting the fetuses out of pregnant women.

We fall asleep to the sound of wolves howling at the full moon.

When morning arrives, Sue and Ray go through the village on foot, while Weber takes me to talk to people who've had bear experiences. The people are friendlier than any I've ever seen. We stroll down a dirt lane and pass a cheerful old woman who's casting seeds into her rich, black, fresh-turned furrows. She's dressed in blue and green—many houses here have these colors throughout—and she puts down her metal bucket of seed, and comes running across the field, waving to us to stop walking. It turns out she wants me to be her guest, to stay in her home for however long I'm in Varság and she wants me and Weber to come in for a meal—is it lunchtime?—*right now.*

We tell her no, but thank you very much (*"Ko-sho-nem"*), and leave her standing there in the field looking mournful.

The bear stories are relatively tame: more tales of pig-thieving, a lamb every now and then. But nothing like you'd expect—not with 6,000 of them roaming the mountains.

That night, as we eat the stew Weber has prepared, I try to steer the conversation back to bears. But Weber has still got that wall up. "Why do you study the bear, then?" I ask. "Surely there have been moments when you've felt the bear's magic, a hugeness of spirit, a kind of grace?"

Weber is as stiff as a board. He chooses his words carefully, as if someone is listening just outside the door. "What I like about this job," he says slowly, "is that it allows me opportunity to be out-of-doors. To go into the woods.

"I am only bear biologist in Romania," he says. "Only one." He looks away. "It is a good job."

And so I back off. It's so easy to be an eco-warrior in the States. But I wish to hell we had 6,000 grizzlies, big trout to tickle and monks on stallions in the high snowy mountains.

"This is good stew," I tell Weber, ladling out seconds. "What is it?"

"Oh," Weber says, smiling. "I thought you recognized the taste. You are eating grizzly bear."

All three of us stop eating and freeze, and Weber laughs.

The next day we stroll through the woods—Weber shows us a couple of bear dens—and wander through the village. Then, later in the afternoon, Weber takes us to see the bears.

It's a bigger deal than I'd realized; I'm still thinking in American terms, where the wildlife does not belong to anyone but the forest itself. Here, however, the grizzlies are like 10- and 20-thousand-dollar bills roaming the forest.

We meet the local game warden and his wife, who is wearing an ermine stole and jewelry. The game warden is one of the darkest, most frightening people I've ever seen. He is not intimidating physically—he looks like the actor Burt Young, with a five o'clock shadow—but he appears to have a heartlessness to him that strikes me as dangerous.

We ride in a big limousine into the woods. Neither the warden nor his wife will look at us. I feel badly for Weber, who's in the middle. The warden and Weber are chatting, but it is serious chat—I get the sense that Weber is defending us. The wife, the ice queen, stares out the window at the passing countryside, which is still barren and bleak higher in the forest, still only on the edge of spring. I get the feeling that it was better for her in the old days, when there was *real* power, power fueled by the fear of others, fear of the government, and that she is angry now; that her lot in life—the warden's wife!—has been reduced such that she is now having to ride in the back seat with three American journalists.

We ride quietly down red-clay roads, across meadows, past giant beech trees and into the dark forest. The limousine crosses a wooden footbridge—a beautiful brook rushes beneath us—and then we park and get out at the base of a little knoll. Another car is already parked there. The dusk is gathering fast; I want to linger, to walk by that brook, but Weber hurries us up the steep flight of steps to the little cottage at the top of the knoll.

As we climb the steps, Weber explains that this was Ceauşescu's main hunting cabin. "He was a small man, and not in good shape," Weber whispers. "He had trouble climbing these steps. They had to build this handrail for him."

It's chilling, even macabre, to be walking in his footsteps. Fog begins to rise from the Transylvanian woods, from the dark firs. Steam rises from the creek. No one would ever find us back here.

We step inside the little two-room hunting cabin. The ceiling is low. It's cold at first, but the warden's wife—who is now suddenly excited—busies herself lighting a fire in the woodstove, and sweeping the carpet with a straw broom. She seems at least ten, fifteen years younger. Two young Czech women have also come to see the bears. They're distant relatives of the warden's wife.

We move into the front room, which has two beds in it, and little windows that you slide open to shoot through. There's a clearing at the top of the knoll where bears often appear. There are feeding troughs, and a big, heavy apparatus, a cage with iron bars. "Is that for the really bad shots?" I ask. "Do they lock a bear in there for the people to shoot at, to keep the bear from running away?" I ask, and Weber looks embarrassed for both of us.

"They put the *bait* in there," he explains. "It keeps them from pulling the bait off into the woods."

Where is the horse? Our horse?

It didn't exactly work out, Weber says, and I'm not sure what he means by that, but I'm greatly relieved and I tell him so.

I tell him something else, too: "It feels *bad* being here." My heart is splitting, and I'm whispering to him not like a guest or a fellow scientist, but as a fellow lover of the woods: For I'm convinced he is one, too, even if he can't show it.

Weber looks uncomfortable, edges away from me, squints out the window. I turn and see that the game warden is sitting on one of the beds in the far corner, hidden in the shadows, studying me.

The two young women are giggling; they've brought video cameras. They're hogging the seats in front of the little windows. I feel an incredibly black depression, and I do not try to fight it. I walk back into the rear half of Ceauşescu's little sin parlor, which houses a big double bed decorated with cheap, red-tassel fringe like a backwoods whorehouse, and examine the gun cabinet and the pantry with all the expensive liquors and canned goods. Anchovies, for Chrissakes, in bear country.

The sin parlor is getting hot from all the people, I feel like I'm roasting in hell. I step onto the back porch, into the cold spring evening air, and look at the tops of the dark forest beyond. *This is no way to kill bears,* I think. I'm not even as upset about the fact that the bears are being shot, for once, as I am about the method; the incredible steps that have been taken to avoid an engagement with nature. We could be anywhere, I think—it doesn't have to be in Romania, at the edge of the old, crumbling Communist empire. We could be at a game farm in California, Texas or Illinois, in a hunting blind—a shooting gallery—set up for some rich industrialist to come and do their thing. I've seen plenty of it: The alligator "hunts" by jetboat, where the $3,000 fee includes a pair of boots made from your very own gator. The pathetic need to kill, to erase the large, the grand and the magnificent—to kill and bury it. How terrifying, this example of how the far ends of Communism and Capitalism meet in a circle.

In a while, the warden's wife pours shots of vodka into little jiggers and carries them around on a silver serving tray. Everyone accepts a drink with great bonhomie, but I refuse mine. This troubles her, but it's the only way I have of making sure they all know exactly what I think, that I can no more accept her liquor than I could shoot one of those tragic bears.

Then people jump up from the beds as if electrified, bumping their heads on the low ceiling, and hissing and whispering as four bears come gliding in from out of the dusk.

They are huge, and they are so close. Their claws, their muscles, their giant heads—all of them. They're right in front of us; you could almost kill one with a javelin. Everyone's scrambling around to see—the two Czech women elbowing to the front, and cackling like hens—"Sssh!" Weber cautions, and the game warden and his wife stand back, like proprietors, and watch us watch the bears.

Their movements are identical to those of Montana's grizzlies, 10,000 miles away—the tiniest nuances, the pauses and head swings, the way they *move.* Watching them there on the knoll, I know that they all come from the same spirit, deep within the core of the earth: molten wildness, muscled beauty.

I am almost unable to look at the bears—it feels pornographic. I concentrate on watching Weber. Between 1979 and 1981, he spent over 3,000 hours watching bears from this blind, hidden in the sin parlor, but still he leans forward quickly, lips moving, mumbling to himself; as if this is the first bear he has ever seen.

He loves the grizzlies.

I peek under one of the Czech women's underarms and see that a huge bear, with a head the size of a tractor tire, is standing over the feed, swinging his head left and right, looking and sniffing for the whereabouts of other bears and for the possibility of a trap.

"We have to keep feeding them or they will stop coming," Weber says.

"Is that a male?" I ask.

Weber turns and looks at me crossly. "Why do you ask that?"

"Because of his coloring," I say, "and the size of his head. Back home, the darker grizzlies are males, more often than not, and their heads are sometimes larger."

"Yes," says Weber. "It is a male."

More bears come out of the gloom: a forest of bears, a village of bears. Weber's excited, talking fast, pointing out subtle body movements that indicate where each bear lies in the social hierarchy.

"We call that one Money," he says, pointing to the largest one, weighing, I'd guess, close to 600 pounds.

"How much would it cost to shoot that one?" Ray asks.

"About 20,000 dollars," says Weber, watching the animal through binoculars. "He would be a trophy."

Ceauşescu and his wife, Elena, are dead. Yet his name is still in all the record books of Asia and Europe, not just for killing the biggest and most bears, but also wild boars, stags—anything.

And people.

They say that when they executed him, on Christmas Day in 1989, more than 300 soldiers volunteered to be on the firing squad; that they began shooting as soon as they saw him.

They say . . .

I feel as if I have sinned against my nature by even drawing this close to such a spectacle. I feel as if I am as guilty as Ceauşescu himself, or any of the old party bosses—being in the sin parlor and spying on those bears, those bears who are waiting to be shot. I feel like it's worse, for me, because I love the bears and the woods, wildness and freedom, and Ceauşescu probably hated these things. I cannot get away from there quickly enough.

That night, by lantern light, and downing that wine, Weber and I go over it again. *Say it, Peter: You love the bears. What they're doing up there on that knoll is wrong.*

He won't admit it. But—after about the fifth or sixth glass of wine, after Ray and Sue have gone to bed—he suddenly stops defending the operation and the money it brings in to a bankrupt government and admits that he has an idea, something he's been thinking over.

It turns out Weber doesn't like the foreigners coming in and shooting "his" bears like that (*piff! poof!*) after all. Weber would like to see some kind of rule in place where a person could still pay $20,000 to kill a bear, but would have to spend a week or two in the woods first, learning a little bit about the bears and the forest. Maybe even doing a little physical labor that would somehow benefit the bear. Erosion protection, or something like that.

Weber sighs. It would never work, he says—people who have and spend that kind of money don't generally like to do physical labor—and besides, he, Weber, is just one man.

It's Weber's goal to someday come to the United States and learn how to do telemetry tracking of animals—how to use radio collars to study movements of individual bears. His government won't buy even one collar-and-radio. I don't have the heart to tell him that in the States, biologists are moving away from a reliance on radio collars, since the individual's movements may not be entirely natural (while being chased by trackers, for instance). I don't tell him that biologists in the U.S. are trying to rely more on habitat protection for the overall population rather than just hounding a few individuals.

His goal is to go to Alaska and study those grizzlies and learn about radio tracking, he says, and for me, the grand, spoiled inquisitor, I guess that's enough. It says the same thing. *I love the bears.* It just says it in a different kind of woods code, a different language.

I have hundreds of memories from Verság, the valley of bears, the friendliest valley I've ever visited; from the dark, spooky mountains of Transylvania that seem like a second home, a place of comfort:

A hawk's wing in the carpenter's shop, used for brushing away wood shavings. Giza-nèni's girlish kicks and her bright dress. The high, short beds in the cabins, high off the ground, because at night as the cabin cooled, that's where cold air settled, close to the floor.

Woodcutters of all ages: boys, men and old men, standing on the side of the road with axes, tying up ricks of firewood to sell for a few fractions of a cent. Strong arms and backs from a lifetime of endless chopping at the edge of the dark forest, the American myth—that no forest, no wilderness, is endless—not yet revealed to them.

Walking through the ancient hillside cemetery in the rain, looking for the grave of the schoolteacher, the one who got it from the bear, when there were so many thousands who got it from the hands of their fellow man, the hands of Ceauşescu.

Watching the bears feed at that trough outside Ceauşescu's sin parlor, so far back in the woods, where so many bears had been shot, and wondering what the culture of bears had to say about the history of such a violent place; wondering if they could smell all the blood that must have leached through the soil there, wondering if the bears, like any intelligent being, could feel the still-lingering echoes of terror bouncing around on that strange knoll. Wondering if they know that Ceauşescu's gone. Wondering if the Romanians know it, *really* know it. I think that they do.

Weber showed me the stump of an apple tree in Feri-bácsi's yard. He explained to me that the bears loved the apples from this tree more than any other, and kept coming into his yard to get them, and kept making trouble. This went on for a few years, and so finally Feri-bácsi cut down the apple tree and made a beautiful picture frame out of the wood. The bears moved someplace else. And I see then what I have always suspected: It doesn't take any real patriotism or courage to kill a bear. It takes patriotism—love of the homeland—to let them live. To think of ways that will allow them to live. And to just plain *think,* rather than merely react, like sheep, like mindless masses with no concept of free thought.

Versúg showed this to me.

Thousands of countrymen butchered over a quarter of a century, and I get all hot and bothered about a few bears?

But that's exactly where it all began—the domination and oppression of the voiceless, of the supposedly "lesser" beings: the bears and the wolves, the forests and the rivers, the gypsies and "ze femuls." It is out there in the woods, I think, where it all went wrong first, and I believe that is one of the ways and one of the places where we must learn, all over again, how to do it right: how to remember the quaint ancient notions of tolerance, freedom and respect.

We say our goodbyes to Weber, thank him again and again for his hospitality. We leave Transylvania, home of wolves, bears and vampires, and return to America, the bloody continent, where there are very few bears, very few wild things whatsoever, except for our own lonely species.

Brenda Peterson

Animal Allies

from *Orion*

"My imaginary friend really lived once," the teenage girl began, head bent, her fingers twisting her long red hair. She stood in the circle of other adolescents gathered in my Seattle Arts and Lectures storytelling class at the summer Seattle Academy. Here were kids from all over the city—every color and class, all strangers one to another. Over the next two weeks we would become a fierce tribe, telling our own and our tribe's story. Our first assignment was to introduce our imaginary friends from childhood. This shy fourteen-year-old girl, Sarah, had struck me on the first day because she always sat next to me, as if under my wing, and though her freckles and stylish clothes suggested she was a popular girl, her demeanor showed the detachment of someone deeply preoccupied. She never met my eye, nor did she join in the first few days of storytelling when the ten boys and four girls were regaling one another with futuristic characters called Shiva and Darshon, Masters of the Universe. So far the story lines we'd imagined were more Pac-Man than drama. After the first two days I counted a legion of characters killed off in intergalactic battle. The settings for all these stories portrayed the earth as an environmental wasteland, a ruined shell hardly shelter to anything animal or human. One of the girls called herself Nero the White Wolf and wandered the blackened tundra howling her powerful despair; another girl was a unicorn whose horn always told the truth. All the stories were full of plagues and nuclear wars—even though this is the generation that has witnessed the fall of the Berlin Wall, the end of the Cold War. Their imaginations have been shaped by a childhood story line that anticipates the end of this world.

After three days of stories set on an earth besieged by disease and barren of nature, I made a rule: No more characters or animals could die this first week. I asked if someone might imagine a living world, one that survives even our species.

It was on this third day of group storytelling that Sarah jumped into the circle and told her story:

"My imaginary friend is called Angel now because she's in heaven, but her real name was Katie," Sarah began. "She was my best friend from fourth to tenth grade. She had freckles like me and brown hair and more boyfriends—sometimes five at a time—because Katie said, 'I *like* to be confused!' She was a real sister too and we used to say we'd be friends for life. . . ." Sarah stopped, gave me a furtive glance and then gulped in a great breath of air like someone drowning, about to go down. Her eyes fixed inward, her voice dropped to a monotone. "Then one day last year, Katie and I were walking home from school and a red sports car came up behind us. Someone yelled, 'Hey, Katie!' She turned . . . and he blew her head off. A bullet grazed my skull, too, and I blacked out. When I woke up, Katie was gone, dead forever." Sarah stopped, stared down at her feet and murmured in that same terrible monotone, "Cops never found her murderer, case is closed."

All the kids shifted and took a deep breath, although Sarah herself was barely breathing at all. "Let's take some time to write," I told the kids and put on a cello concerto for them to listen to while they wrote. As they did their assignment, the kids glanced over surreptitiously at Sarah, who sat staring at her hands in her lap.

I did not know what to do with her story; she had offered it to a group of kids she had known but three days. It explained her self-imposed exile during lunch hours and while waiting for the bus. All I knew was that she'd brought this most important story of her life into the circle of storytellers and it could not be ignored as if *she* were a case to be closed. This story lived in her, would define and shape her young life. Because she had given it to us, we needed to witness and receive—and perhaps tell it back to her in the ancient tradition of tribal call and response.

"Listen," I told the group as the cello faded and they looked up from their work. "We're going to talk story the way they used to long ago when people sat around at night in circles just like this one. That was a time when we still listened to animals and trees and didn't think ourselves so alone in this world. Now we're going to carry out jungle justice and find Katie's killer. We'll call him before our tribe. All right? Who wants to begin the story?"

All the Shivas and Darshons and Masters of the Universe volunteered to be heroes on this quest. Nero the White Wolf asked to be a scout. Unicorn, with her truth-saying horn, was declared judge. Another character joined the hunt: Fish, whose translucent belly was a shining "soul mirror" that could reveal one's true nature to anyone who looked into it.

A fierce commander of this hunt was Rat, whose army of computerized comrades could read brain waves and call down lightning lasers as weapons. Rat began the questioning and performed the early detective work. Katie, speaking from beyond the earth, as Sarah put it, gave us other facts. We learned that two weeks before Katie's murder, one of her boyfriends was shot outside a restaurant by a man in the same red car—another drive-by death. So Sarah had not only seen her best friend killed at her side, but she had also walked out into a parking lot to find Katie leaning over her boyfriend's body. For Sarah, it had been two murders by age thirteen.

With the help of our myriad computer-character legions we determined that the murderer was a man named Carlos, a drug lord who used local gangs to deal cocaine. At a party Carlos has misinterpreted Katie's videotaping her friends dancing as witnessing a big drug deal. For that, Rat said, "This dude decides Katie's got to go down. So yo, man, he offs her without a second thought."

Bad dude, indeed, this Carlos. And who was going to play Carlos now that all the tribe knew his crime? I took on the role, and as I told my story I felt my face hardening into a contempt that carried me far away from these young pursuers, deep into the Amazon jungle where Rat and his own computer armies couldn't follow, where all their space-age equipment had to be shed until there was only hand-to-hand simple fate.

In the Amazon, the kids changed without effort, in an easy shape-shifting to their animal selves. Suddenly there were no more Masters of the Universe with intergalactic weapons—there was instead Jaguar and Snake, Fish and Pink Dolphin. There was powerful claw and all-knowing serpent, there was Fish who could grow big and small, and a dolphin whose sonar saw past the skin. We were now a tribe of animals, pawing, running, invisible in our jungle, eyes shining in the night, seeing Carlos as he canoed the mighty river, laughing because he did not know he had animals tracking him.

All through the story, I'd kept my eye on Sarah who played the role of her dead friend. The detachment I'd first seen in her was in fact the deadness Sarah carried, the violence that had hollowed her out inside, the friend who haunted her imagination. But now her face was alive, responding to each animal's report of tracking Carlos. She hung on the words, looking suddenly very young, like a small girl eagerly awaiting her turn to enter the circling jump rope.

"I'm getting away from you," I said, snarling as I'd imagined Carlos would. I paddled my canoe and gave a harsh laugh, "I'll escape, easy!"

"No!" Sarah shouted. "Let *me* tell it!"

"Tell it!" her tribe shouted.

"Well, Carlos only thinks he's escaping," Sarah smiled, waving her hands. "He's escaped from so many he's harmed before. But I call out 'FISH!' And Fish comes. He swims alongside the canoe and grows bigger, bigger until at last Carlos turns and sees this HUGE river monster swimming right alongside him and that man is afraid because suddenly Fish turns his belly up to Carlos's face. Fish forces him to look into that soul mirror. Carlos *sees* everyone he's ever killed and all the people who loved them and got left behind. And Carlos sees Katie and me and what he's done to us. He sees everything and he knows his soul is black. And he really doesn't want to die now because he knows then he'll stare into his soul mirror forever. But Fish makes him keep looking until Carlos starts screaming he's sorry, he's so sorry. Then . . . Fish *eats* him!"

The animals roared and cawed and congratulated Sarah for calling Fish to mirror a murderer's soul before taking jungle justice. Class had ended, but no one wanted to leave. We wanted to stay in our jungle, stay within our animals—and so we did. I asked them to close their eyes and call their animals to accompany them home. I told them that some South American tribes believe that when you are born, an animal is born with you. This animal protects and lives alongside you even if it's far away in an Amazon jungle—it came into the world at the same time you did. And, I told them, it dies with you to guide you back into the spirit world.

The kids decided to go home and make animal masks, returning the next day wearing the faces of their chosen animal. When they came into class the next day it was as if we never left the Amazon. Someone dimmed the lights, there were drawings everywhere of jaguars and chimps and snakes. Elaborate masks had replaced the Masters of the Universe who began this tribal journey. We sat behind our masks in a circle with the lights low and there was an acute, alert energy running between us, as eyes met behind animal faces.

I realize that I, who grew up in the forest wild, who first memorized the earth with my hands, have every reason to feel this familiar animal resonance. But many of these teenagers have barely been in the woods; in fact, many inner city kids are *afraid* of nature. They would not willingly sign up for an Outward Bound program or backpacking trek; they don't think about recycling in a world they believe already ruined and in their imaginations abandoned for intergalactic nomad futures. These kids are not environmentalists who worry about saving nature. And yet, when imagining an Amazon forest too thick for weapons to penetrate, too primitive for their futuristic Pac-Man battles, they return instinctively to their animal selves. These are animals they have only seen in zoos or on television, yet there is a profound identification, an ease of inhabiting another species that portends great hope for our own species's survival. Not because nature is "out there" to be saved or sanctioned, but because nature is *in* them. The ancient, green world has never left us though we have long ago left the forest.

What happens when we call upon our inner landscape to connect with the living rainforests still left in the natural world? I believe our imagination can be as mutually nurturing as an umbilical cord between our bodies and the planet. As we told our Amazon stories over the next week of class, gathered in a circle of animal masks, we could feel the rainforest growing in that sterile classroom. Lights low, surrounded by serpents, the jaguar clan, the elephants, I'd as often hear growls, hisses, and howls as words. Between this little classroom and the vast Amazon rainforest stretched a fine thread of story that grew thicker each day, capable of carrying our jungle meditations.

When Elephant stood in the circle and said simply, "My kind are dying out," there was outrage from the other animals.

"We'll stop those poachers!" cried Rat and Chimp. "We'll call Jaguar clan to protect you." And they did.

This protection is of a kind that reaches the other side of the world. Children's imagination is a primal force, just as strong as lobbying efforts and boycotts and endangered species acts. When children claim another species as not only their imaginary friend, but also as the animal within them—their ally—doesn't that change the outer world?

This class believes it to be so. They may be young, but their memories and alliances with the animals are very old. By telling their own animal stories they are practicing ecology at its most profound and healing level. Story as ecology—it's so simple, something we've forgotten. In our environmental wars the emphasis has been on saving species, not *becoming* them. We've fallen into an environmental fundamentalism that calls down hellfire and brimstone on the evil polluters and self-righteously struts about protecting other species as if we are gods who can save their souls.

But the animals' souls are not in our hands. Only our own souls are within our ken. It is our own spiritual relationship to animals that must evolve. Any change begins with imagining ourselves in a new way. And who has preserved their imaginations as a natural resource most deeply? Not adults, who so often have strip-mined their dreams and imagination for material dross. Those who sit behind the wheel of a Jaguar have probably forgotten the wild, black cat that first ran with them as children. Imagination is relegated to nighttime dreams, which are then dismissed in favor of "the real world." But children, like some adults, know that the real world stretches farther than what we can see—that's why they shift easily between visions of our tribal past and our future worlds. The limits of the adult world are there for these teenagers, but they still have a foot in the vast inner magic of childhood. It is this magical connection I called upon when I asked the kids to do the Dance of the Animals.

The day of the big dance I awoke with a sharp pain at my right eye. Seems my Siamese, who has always slept draped around my head, had stretched and his claw caught the corner of my eye. In the mirror I saw a two-inch scratch streaking from my eye like jungle make-up or a primitive face-painting. "The mark of the wildcat," the kids pronounced it when I walked into the dimly lit room to be met by a circle of familiar creatures. Never in ten years had my Siamese scratched my face. I took it as a sign that the dance began in his animal dream.

I put on my cobra mask and hissed a greeting to Chimp, Rat, Jaguar, and Unicorn. Keen eyes tracked me from behind colorful masks.

I held up my rain stick which was also our talking stick and called the creatures one by one into the circle. "Sister Snake!" I called. "Begin the dance!"

Slowly, in rhythm to the deep, bell-like beat of my Northwest Native drum, each animal entered the circle and soon the dance sounded like this: Boom, step, twirl, and slither and stalk and snarl and chirp and caw, caw. Glide, glow, growl, and whistle and howl and shriek and trill and hiss, hiss. Each dance was distinct—from the undulating serpent on his belly, to the dainty high hoofing of Unicorn, from the syncopated stomps of Chimp on all-fours to Rat's covert jitterbug behind the stalking half-dark Jaguar. We danced, and the humid, lush jungle filled this room.

In that story line stretching between us and the Amazon, we connected with those animals and their spirits. And in return, we were complete—with animals as soul mirrors. We remembered who we were, by allowing the animals inside us to survive.

The dance is not over as long as we have our animal partners. When the kids left our last class, they still wore their masks fiercely. I was told that even on the bus they stayed deep in their animal character. I like to imagine those strong, young animals out there now in this wider jungle. I believe that Rat will survive the inner-city gangs; that Chimp will find his characteristic comedy even as his parents deal with divorce; I hope that Unicorn will always remember her mystical truth-telling horn. And as for Sarah who joined the Jaguar clan, elected as the first girl-leader over much mutinous boy-growling—Sarah knows the darkness she stalks and the nightmares that stalk her. She has animal eyes to see, to find even a murderer. Taking her catlike, graceful leave, she handed me a poem she'd written; it said "Now I can see in the dark" and was signed "Jaguar—Future Poet."

John Gierarch

Scotland

from *Dances with Trout*

For once it was exactly as I'd pictured it, which is something a fisherman doesn't get to say very often. There were real castles and slate-roofed stone cottages scattered around a green river valley, ghillies in knee-high breeches and leather vests, a water bailiff in a deer-stalker cap who slept days and only ventured out in the gloaming when poachers were about. Hundreds of pheasants strolled the fields and roosted in the oak forests where the deer live, waiting for the driven shoots in the fall.

We dressed in jackets and ties for dinner, drank the good whiskey they don't export to America and, of course, our party of five fished hard for six days and caught one fish among us.

We were fly-fishing for Atlantic salmon on a private river in Scotland in late June—a good river at a pretty good time of year, by all accounts—but this was what everyone had told me to expect. "Even if you do everything right, you might not catch one. *You've got to understand that,*" they said, or words to that effect.

The thing about Atlantic salmon is, once they've run out of the sea and into their home rivers to spawn, they don't feed. As always, there's a logical reason for that. If these big salmon came into the rivers hungry, they'd eat up all the salmon parr from the previous year's spawn and wipe out the whole next generation of fish. Perfectly logical, when you think about it.

So a salmon comes into a river carrying enough nutrients in its tissues to last it many months, its digestive system ceases to work and physical changes occur in the fish's hypothalamus that bring on what Lee Wulff called "a loss of appetite or nausea." This is not the moodiness you sometimes see in trout; these fish really don't eat, so they're really not supposed to bite.

This is something a fisherman has to think hard about and get firmly in mind.

Hugh Falkus, in his inch-and-a-half-thick, three-pound *Salmon Fishing: A Practical Guide,* says, "What is surprising is not that salmon are hard to catch, but that any are caught at all." Every salmon-fishing book I've ever peeked into has said something like that, usually right near the beginning so you won't get the wrong idea. This has been known to work, but you've gotta understand that it's not *supposed* to work, okay?

I'd never fished for Atlantic salmon before and in the end it was the very unlikelihood of catching one—the exciting weirdness of that—that finally attracted me to it, or at least that's what I thought. Looking back on it now, I realize I didn't believe I'd actually get skunked. I thought I'd experience the epitome of sport everyone talks about, work hard, confront frustration and otherwise take my lumps, but I also thought I'd eventually catch a fish.

I should have known better, because the sport is lousy with stories not just of blank days but of entire blank seasons. A man in Scotland told me he'd caught five salmon the first time he'd fished for them (that's unheard of and it cost him a fortune in scotch at the pub afterward) and then he didn't catch another fish for three years.

Once a story like that is told among salmon anglers, everyone else trots out *their* story. It's a form of competition, the winner being the guy who went the longest without a fish, but still didn't give up.

When I said okay, sure, it's just that I couldn't remember the last time I'd fished for six days straight without so much as a strike, I was told, "A bad week is nothing, lad, nothing a'tall."

The river had been held privately for the last six hundred years—the whole river, not just a piece of it—but an English company had recently bought the fishing rights from the estate and was offering them for sale on a time-share basis: one week in perpetuity for seventy thousand pounds, or about twice that many American dollars. There were six of us altogether: five American writers—Tom, Scott, Don, Clive and me—plus Laine, Clive's photographer (although Laine might have said that Clive was *his* writer). Some of us were magazine staffers, some were on assignment and others were freelancing, but that was the story: time shares on a salmon river in Scotland, a cultural hybrid of an idea that was supposed to make Americans dive for their checkbooks.

Since only five rods were allowed on a beat, Laine couldn't fish, but he said he wouldn't have even if he could. He thought fishing was insane. He hated the boredom, couldn't stand getting wet or cold and didn't care much for fish anyway, except maybe kippers. Turning to Clive he said, "Remember when I covered that sea trout story with you? Night after miserable night in the freezing rain, in a leaky boat, not even the paltry excitement of catching a fish, and having to put up with you the whole time."

But, he added to the rest of us, as a professional photographer he could, and would, take pictures of anything, and they'd be damned good, too.

We began downstream at the Downie beat. Our ghillie, Matthew, put me on The Breaches pool and asked to see my flies. I had a single box of brand-new wets: Copper Killers, Thunder and Lightnings, Undertakers and General Practitioners that a man who'd fished Scotland had recommended, plus a brace each of Jock Scotts and Green Highlanders for local color.

"Did you tie these?" asked Matthew.

"No, I bought them."

"In America?"

"Yeah, from a place called Hunter's."

"Well," he said, "they're terribly pretty," as if prettiness was a nice enough touch, but it wasn't going to make any difference.

He broke off my tippet and retied it—because no guide anywhere likes *your* knots—then selected a small General Practitioner on a double hook and tied that on for me, too. There's no reason in the world for an Atlantic salmon in a river to bite any fly, but among the people who fish for them this way there's still something that clicks, making one pattern look better than another.

Laine was photographing all this: the American fisherman being instructed by the Scottish ghillie with Croiche Wood as a backdrop and good morning light. He hated to get wet, but to achieve the right angle he had waded into the river up to his shins in tennis shoes.

There are subtleties to Atlantic salmon fishing (there must be, there have been so many thick, ponderous books written about it), but when you don't know what you're doing, you do what you're told. In this case, you "work the water."

You start at the top of a pool, make a quartering downstream cast, fish it out, take a step downstream and do it again. The fly is fished on an across and downstream swing, so you end up covering the entire pool in what would look, in an illustration, like a series of sickle-moon-shaped stripes about two feet apart.

At the bottom of the pool you get out, walk back to the top and start again. You're fishing with a floating line, so your unweighted wet fly swims very shallowly, within an inch or two of the surface. Of course the salmon usually lie much deeper than that so, as unlikely as these fish are to bite in the first place, they have to make the full commitment and move for the fly. It seems like an outside chance, but that's how a gentleman fishes.

I asked if maybe a guy shouldn't concentrate on places where salmon would likely be lying. "Yes," said the ghillie, "that would be all right."

"So where do you suppose that would be?" I asked.

"Oh," he said, making a gesture that seemed to include the whole pool, "all through there."

You think the ghillie should have more to tell you about this, but he doesn't, or at least you assume he doesn't because you don't see much of him. I had assumed the ghillie was there to be helpful, like an American guide, but then I was from out of town.

I fished down the pool, letting the fly hang in the current for a minute or so at the end of each swing because sometimes a salmon chases it and hits it when it stops. I fished through the pool maybe five times. On the third or fourth pass two men on horseback trotted into a clearing on the far bank and sat watching me. I waved, but they didn't wave back. That was the most exciting thing that happened all morning.

A friend of mine said he'd been salmon fishing once and had actually enjoyed the mindless, repetitive nature of it. He didn't mention whether he'd caught a fish or not, which means he didn't. He also said he can spot the Atlantic salmon story in which the writer got skunked by the first paragraph. "It's all about the castles, cottages, ghillies and deer forests," he said.

We were staying at the Cruvies House, a large cottage on the river at the bottom of the Falls beat, complete with a tile-floored fishermen's changing room and a heated drying closet for waders and rain gear. The river side of the dining room had a line of French doors looking out on the cruvies themselves—a set of V-shaped stone dams with cribs used for netting salmon in the old days. The old days in this case dated back to the 1400s.

Lunch was served at the hut on whatever beat we happened to be fishing, but we ate breakfast and dinner in that room overlooking the river, usually with Dick, who was president of the company that owned the fishing rights.

Dick was charming, quick with a joke, always in charge in an evenhanded, British way and, he said, a student of all things American, even to doing most of his riding on a western saddle. He gently instructed us in the ways of salmon fishing—more the etiquette than the technique, although some of us were weak on both—and occasionally corrected our speech.

When the subject of priests came up, someone asked, "What do you mean by a 'priest'?"

Tom said, "In this context, it's a little weighted club you use to bonk a salmon on the head to kill it."

"I wouldn't put it quite that way," Dick said.

"Why not?"

"Because here 'bonking' means 'screwing.' "

He also tried to explain cricket, but gave it up when I said I didn't even understand baseball.

These dinners were at least three courses, prepared and served by Jane, who is probably the best fancy meat and potatoes cook I've ever met. She was self-employed, working sometimes for Dick and sometimes for other parties of salmon fishers who rented cottages in the valley. She was the best cook in the county, she said, and these rich folk, being used to the best of everything, often bid against each other for her services.

One day I got to talking with one of these guys, a wealthy sport who was a tenant on half a dozen of the country's best salmon and sea trout rivers, and who seemed to stop fishing only long enough to do a little driven grouse and pheasant shooting. He seemed like a nice man—if nothing else, he was spending his money right—but he also gave off a certain air that's hard to describe: almost as if he thought he could have you beheaded if the mood struck him. Anyway, he'd told Dick he wanted to meet some of these American writers who were such hard-core fishermen they weren't even stopping for tea.

He asked me about the Frying Pan River in Colorado, which he'd heard about.

"Now, when you go over there and camp for a week," he said, "do you bring your own cook from home or do you engage someone locally?"

I had to tell him that, as far as I knew, there was no one like Jane in Colorado. He winced slightly when he heard the name. She was cooking for us that week, which apparently meant he and his party were getting by on cold porridge, stale bread and cheap wine in bottles with screw caps.

I liked Jane immediately—we all did—and not just for the great food she put out. She was a genuine wild Highlander who pointedly took no crap from anyone, addressed no one as "mister," liked to refer to us as boys, her boss included—although she was younger than most of us—did not engage in false modesty and managed the kind of dignity that allowed her to serve meals without seeming like a waitress. She made you want to hang out in the kitchen, even though (or maybe because) that seemed to be frowned upon.

Jane could do a great impression of a midwestern American accent, complete with appropriate dialogue ("Hey, Bob, get a load of this here church"). She said, "You can always spot Americans by their wide arses and small heads." She also happened to be pretty: willowy, but not anorectic-looking like a model.

I noticed right off that Scott was hanging out in the kitchen more than the rest of us, but I thought maybe he just had a domestic streak and was pumping her for recipes.

I think that cottage is the most comfortable place I've ever stayed while fishing. We each had our own big, homey, high-ceilinged room with a huge bed, down comforters and a private bath (with English plumbing, but then nothing's perfect). My room looked out on the river, and since the nights were only chilly, I slept with the windows open. We put in long days fishing, drank some and ate large meals, but I still think it was the river that put me away each night. The sound of it hissing through the cruvies had the same effect as morphine.

Laine seemed happy enough for a day or two. We fished methodically and he took pictures. Fishermen casting, or wading, or tying on a fly while standing conveniently in front of an ancient churchyard. He'd pose you carefully one minute and then tell you to just do whatever it was you were doing the next.

At first he'd be saying, 'Yes! Great! Perfect!" all the time he was shooting, but then he started muttering things like, "No," "No good," or "Nope, not weird enough."

"Not weird enough?" I asked.

"Any idiot can take a picture of a man fishing," he said. "Anyway, the magazine likes weird photos. That's why they hired me. And by the way," he added, "is someone going to catch a fish soon?"

Don did catch a fish the next day when we rotated up to the Falls beat. It was about eleven o'clock in the evening, just dusk that far north, and he was casting to a salmon that had boiled several times more or less in the same spot. Tom said, "Now that's a taking fish," and Don had started down the bank saying, "Let's see."

A "taker" is the salmon everyone is looking for. It's the one fish in God knows how many that, for reasons of its own, will take your fly. This may have to do with habit or the memory of feeding, aggression, curiosity, playfulness, the fish's freshness from the sea, time of day, time of the most recent tide, weather, water conditions, fly pattern, a defective hypothalamus or some combination thereof. It's a mystery but, since it ultimately has to do with sex, the odd moodiness of it also seems vaguely familiar. One thing is clear: A taking fish is defined after the fact. As Matthew told me, "A taker is the one you caught, if you catch one."

"How do you know that's a taker?" I asked Tom.

"Just a guess," he said.

And then Don caught the fish, a lovely fourteen pounder. It was what they call a "bright fish," fresh from the ocean with sea lice still on it and shiny as a chrome bumper. We all ran down to watch him land it and take some photos, even though the light was almost gone. All of us except Scott, that is. He hadn't come out with us after dinner. In fact, it seemed as if he vanished about the time Jane went home.

Come to think of it, Laine wasn't there either. Earlier that day he'd begun mumbling about taking a different approach and needing some props. No one had seen him since.

It turns out that Laine had driven into the nearest town and, after hours of haggling, had rented an ornate old grandfather clock from the suspicious owner of an antique shop. When we came in that night it was lying in pieces in the front hall.

"What's it for?" Dick asked at breakfast the next day.

"I don't know exactly," Laine said, "but, you know, it's about time shares, so I felt I needed a large clock."

Dick nodded thoughtfully. There *was* a certain logic to it.

We were late getting on the water that day because it took an hour or more to drag out Don's salmon and pose it and him in every way any of us could think of. Then someone else would have to pose with it so Don could get some shots. After all, it was his fish. And then you'd have to do everything both with and without the ghillie, who would have been happy to get done with this foolishness and get on the water. "This is a good deal of excitement over one fish," he said.

Laine followed us around for another day and a half, taking candid shots, posing each of us in turn at the scenic Back of the Castle Pool, fooling with fill-in flashes and reflectors and generally waiting for someone else to catch a fish.

It seemed as if all of us fishermen were waiting for the same thing. That's what it feels like: the repetitive, almost hypnotic cast, drift, step; cast, drift, step. You're not so much fishing as you are waiting for a fish.

Of course as writers we had other things to think about. Presumably Don had at least the germ of his story, but what about the rest of us? Fishing with fishing writers is strange enough anyway, but when almost everyone is getting skunked and searching for a new angle, the conversation can get pretty weird. You'll make some idle comment like, "Well, it's a pretty spot anyway, with those castle towers poking up above the trees," and someone will say, "Yeah, man, there's your lead."

Scott seemed to be sublimely above all this, taking the lack of fish philosophically, but he *was* under some strain. In the evenings he'd say he was bushed and was going to turn in early. Then in the morning we'd come down to find him in the kitchen chatting quietly with Jane as she cooked breakfast. But it was all just a little bit *too* discreet, and peeking into his room was too much of a temptation for some of us. Sure enough, the bed hadn't been slept in, not that it was any of our business, of course.

Then later, out on the river, Scott would turn up missing again, only to be found curled up in the tall grass sleeping like a baby. When he'd get caught at it he'd say something like, "Gee, this salmon fishing is more strenuous than I thought."

One day Laine and some of the others decided to photograph one of the great lunches we were having catered at the fishing huts. (The angle everyone seemed to be working on now had more to do with cuisine than fishing.) We hauled the table outside—for natural light and the river as a background—and Laine, Tom and Don began arranging food, wine, wicker picnic baskets, two-handed fly rods and Dick into the perfect *Gourmet Magazine*–style composition.

Of course no two photographers think alike, so there was some disagreement about what should go where. I didn't have an opinion, so I was standing off to the side, out of the way. Scott sidled up beside me and asked, quietly, "Ever hear the expression, 'high-speed goat fuck'?"

I said, "No, but I like it."

Someone commented that the only thing missing was a salmon, at which point Matthew jumped into his little pickup with the dog kennels in the back and roared off down a dirt road. I thought he'd gone to the cottage to get Don's fish, but instead he came back in ten minutes with a nice grilse (young salmon) of about seven or eight pounds. The fish was so fresh that, although he'd killed it, it was still twitching.

Someone said, "Perfect!" but I thought, Wait a minute, if the ghillie knows where a fish can be caught that easily, shouldn't he be putting one of us on it? One of us like me, maybe?

It was just an idle thought. The grilse did complete the photograph and Dick, who'd been standing at the head of the table holding a glass of wine and wearing a frozen smile, seemed relieved to finally hear the shutters clicking.

"May I drink this now?' " he asked.

On the fifth day we trudged back to the hut on the Home beat for lunch and Dick, who looked a little confused, said that before we sat down to eat, Laine would like to see us all up at the cruvies, in waders, with our rods.

We drove up to the house, and when we got out of the van I heard bagpipes. They were faint, but unmistakable.

"Scott," I said, "do you hear pipes?"

"Yeah, I do," he answered sleepily, "but I wasn't gonna say anything."

It seems that the same day Laine had rented the clock, he'd also engaged the services of a piper; an authentic Highlander in a kilt, bearskin hat, dagger in his boot, the whole catastrophe. By the time we arrived Laine had the clock sitting in a shallow riffle out in the river with a battery of lights and reflectors trained on it. Don's salmon had been resurrected and was lying on the bank. It was a couple of days old now; its eyes were glazed, its jaw was locked open and it was starting to look pretty dead.

The piper was standing back in the trees to keep out of the light drizzle. He was playing his heart out because, as near as he could figure, that's what he'd been hired to do.

I've always loved the sound of bagpipes—played well, they make me want to either cry or fight—but I noticed Matthew cringing every time the guy launched into another tune.

"Don't you like this stuff?" I asked.

"Well," he said, "a little of it goes a long way, doesn't it?"

I thought, of course: punk rock, spiked hair, pale girls dressed in leather. Our immediate surroundings notwithstanding, this is still the twentieth century.

Over the next two hours, in a steady light rain, Laine posed every possible combination of one grandfather clock, one piper, one dead fish, five fishermen and one bored ghillie with a long-handled landing net. He was the only one not wearing rain gear and he was soaked to the skin.

"This is it!" he kept shouting. "Time! Salmon! Scotland!" Then he'd rush to adjust some small detail. "What time should the clock say?" he asked of no one in particular. I guess we were watching genius at work.

Dick was a little puzzled by all this, but he wasn't shocked. Over the last few days you could see him slowly getting used to us. We asked some impertinent questions, but then we were writers. Sometimes our language was a little rough, especially after a few drinks, and we seemed to prefer the company of the help instead of the rich sports, but then we were Americans.

I didn't think Dick cared about Scott "taking up with the cook," as he put it, until we rotated back up to the Falls beat on the last day and Scott wasn't there because he'd disappeared with Jane again. Dick didn't say much, but he was clearly scandalized, so I asked, "Does this really bother you?"

"Who's bonking who isn't my business," he said, "but one simply *does not* give up a salmon beat."

As near as I can tell from the little bit of reading I've done, fly-fishing for Atlantic salmon is based on the premise that anything that can happen will, eventually. There are many theories on when, where and on what fly pattern salmon will bite, but, by all accounts, no theory produces fish often enough to be proven true.

Even the experts speak in italics. There *should* be a fresh run off this last tide; this fly *should* work in this pool, if only because it has, off and on, for generations. When salmon aren't caught—which is most of the time—these people take a kind of sly comfort in the fact that, given the circumstances, you really ought not to be able to catch them at all. Meanwhile, the accommodations are posh, the food is good, the booze flows freely and there's the general feeling that things are as they should be.

This would seem like an expensive snipe hunt except that you see fish. Some are boiling and porpoising, others are jumping to dislodge sea lice. Jumpers won't bite, they said, and that was the only statement about salmon I heard that wasn't followed by several contradictory footnotes.

You put yourself through this because some fishermen say catching an Atlantic salmon on a fly is as good as sex, even though you know in your heart it isn't. I agree with a friend of mine who says that if fishing is really like sex, then he's doing one of them wrong. Still, there do seem to be similarities.

For one thing—as the salmon fishers tell it—either you catch a fish way too soon, before you're fully able to appreciate it, or you have to wait much longer than you think you should have to, so that when you finally hook and land one the elation is tempered by a profound sense of relief.

And, of course, repeated failures don't lead you to the logical conclusion; they only whet your appetite.

Back at the cottage in the evenings, the more experienced salmon fishers—Clive, Dick and Tom—would hold forth. The river flowed by just outside the French doors. It was clear but, because all its water had first filtered through peat in the Highlands, it was slightly whiskey-colored in the deep pools. The way to catch salmon, they said, is to keep your fly in the river and be of good cheer. They didn't seem to understand it either, but they still appeared to possess a kind of wisdom.

It reminded me of when I was a kid and some grown man would decide to take me aside and give me the kindly lecture on women. He'd fall into this vague, humorous mode, trying not to let on that, although he had considerably more experience than I did, he still didn't know what the hell he was talking about.

Apparently, the genuine salmon fisher takes pride in his acquired tastes, strength of character, fine sense of irony and apparent craziness, which he and a few other aficionados know isn't really craziness but, well, something else entirely. As a trout fisherman, I used to think I understood that, but salmon types look down on us trouters as dilettantes. I mean, we catch what I now think of as quite a few fish. Small ones by comparison, but fish nonetheless.

We fished for six days and took Sunday off, not because we were tired or discouraged, but because it's illegal to fish for salmon on Sunday. I asked why, but no one knew. It's just always been that way. We took the rented van and, with Dick as guide, drove up into the Highlands to look around. All of us except Scott, of course. By now, no one had to wonder where Scott had gone.

I kept dozing off in the backseat. When you've fished long and hard and it's become obvious that you're not going to catch anything, it's a relief to finally stop and let it all sink in. As it sank in, I tended to lose consciousness.

On the flight over, Tom had gone into that old salmon-fishing refrain: *You've gotta understand you might not catch one,* and I'd said, maybe a little impatiently, that I understood that. "You understand it intellectually," he said, "but if you really *don't* catch one, there's a hump you'll have to get over."

Right. I could see that now. You have to learn to see yourself not catching fish as if from a great theoretical height.

I also realized that I liked it and that I'd probably do it again, and then again if I had to, until I finally hooked and landed one of the damned things. To prove something, to be able to say I'd done it and because I knew it would be beautiful somehow; not like sex, of course, but in a way so weird that that's the only fair comparison. I also knew that this is how a life can be ruined by sport, and just as I was dozing off I had a vision of myself on a street corner with a tin cup and a sign reading, "NEVER COULD CATCH AN ATLANTIC SALMON ON A FLY ROD—PLEASE HELP."

The next morning, Dick drove Don and me to the airport at Inverness. Clive and Laine had left early, and Tom was staying on for a day and then heading to Russia, where there were bigger, dumber salmon that hadn't seen six hundred years' worth of flies. We could only guess at Scott's whereabouts. He hadn't been seen for at least a day and a half.

Dick was in a good mood. He said he'd enjoyed having us. "There was a lot of laughter this week," he said, "much more than usual. To be honest, some of the people who fish here are a little stuffy."

Then he asked, "Do you think we'll see Scott at the airport?"

There was some shrugging and throat clearing, and I thought, Would *I* be at the airport?

Dick drove on quietly for a minute and then said, "Well, if he turns up in the next few days, I'll see if I can find a little job for him."

(Author's note: Five months later, in Virginia City, Montana, Scott and Jane were married.)

Cindy Van Dover

Octopus's Garden

First publication

I was twenty-nine when I first looked over the rim of the Grand Canyon. Though my visit to the great hole was brief, the experience marked me, settled into my being. It became, I am certain, a subconscious part of what defines me and the way that I look at the world. Don't get me wrong. I don't mean to say it was some sort of religious experience that changed my life. But it did add a dimension to my sense of the natural world that had been missing. The aurora borealis was like that, too. I recall being a free spirit, exploring the autumnal woods of northern Maine with my backpack and dog, where I chanced upon a fortnight's display of light beams dancing through the midnight skies. I was mesmerized. And I wondered at my naivety; how could I have lived so long in ignorance of the aurora? It is a fundamental. Like the Canyon, the aurora is so magnificent, so awesome, that it seems to be a part of the very soul of nature, an elusive soul that defies description and is not to be captured in any image.

There is another place, a vast expanse of places, really, that rivals the grandeur and mystery and phantasm of a Grand Canyon or an aurora borealis. But you can't go there, you can't see it for yourself. I've been, though. I go all the time. To the bottom of the sea, to the Octopus's Garden.

I was drawn to the seafloor by science, securing my do from MIT by studying the ecology of some of its more exc interesting denizens. But the deep sea is a compelling pla being a passenger on an occasional dive to the seafloor didn't satisfy. So I became one of three pilots of *Alvin,* the premier deep-diving submersible in the world. For more than a year I was pilot-in-command, carrying two other scientists to explore and experiment on the seafloor.

Getting there is a study in understatement. Though the technological feat seems akin to sending a man into orbit about the earth, the three-man submersible *Alvin,* operated by Woods Hole Oceanographic Institution, dives up to two miles below the surface of the sea, day in and day out, following a routine that is stunningly anticlimactic. There is no countdown, no army of personnel to supervise the launch or recovery. Even the audience of curious scientists diminishes to naught after they have watched one or two launches; thereafter, they gather to watch only when the seas have built to a height they think might challenge the skills of the operators. The submersible and ship's crews pride themselves on making the whole operation seem effortless. Though seemingly casual, the operations are highly choreographed yet responsive, with flexibility borne of the legacy of maritime improvisation.

There is no real boundary to the part of the planet I think of as the deep sea. Technically, it is defined as oceanic depths greater than a few hundred meters. In my mind, the deep sea encompasses the depths of the open ocean beyond where daylight penetrates. Beyond where the sun at noon becomes twilight, beyond darkness, into utter black.

It is a silent world. I have set the submersible on the seabed and systematically shut down all of the systems. We call it "going dead boat." Silence and darkness are immediate and ultimate, surrounding and pervasive. I feel the silence more than hear it; it feels cold, oppressive, alien. My voice in the silence sounds thin and nervous, insignificant. Never am I more conscious of the tons of water that overlie me. Only when I return power to the boat does my pulse return to normal.

You have heard that the seafloor is a desert, a vast and uniform wasteland, all but devoid of life. Textbooks on the shelf in my laboratory say so. But I know it is not true. Life on the seafloor is often unusual and diverse, more the stuff of science fiction; life is occasionally abundant, sometimes spectacularly so. Granted, in many places the diversity and wealth of life is only to be appreciated through a microscope and painstaking identification of the plethora of small worms and mollusks and crustaceans captured in the soft muds of cores taken from the abyssal plains. Dr. Fred Grassle of Rutgers University, guru of deep-sea diversity, figures that the variety of life per acre of abyssal seafloor vies with the richness of life forms in an equal amount of tropical rain forest.

As on land, local topography plays an important role in affecting the distribution of organisms. Exploring the summits of submarine mountains, I have encountered inverse "timberlines": only the peaks were populated by stands of shrublike corals. The corals feed passively on bits of organic material suspended in the water: only at the peaks is the current fast enough to supply food that sustains the corals.

In other places, controls on the distribution of animals are less obvious. We have worked the submarine basins off the coast of California. On the soft mud bottom of San Nicholas Basin, red shrimp, jumbo-sized, are the most abundant and ubiquitous of the large animals. When strong winds forced us to move our dive operation north and east a few miles to the lee of Santa Cruz Island, we dove in Santa Cruz Basin. There, elegant sea pens populate the mud bottom, their fleshy bodies creamy yellow, their plumes white and frilly. They are everywhere, a meadow of sea pens, all oriented into the current, ready to snatch small bits of life and debris passing by in the sluggish bottom current. Their spacing was regular, a telltale mark that the flow field around each one defines the optimum spacing of neighbors. Why do two adjacent basins support such contrasting life forms?

There are other wonders. I have encountered herds of sea cucumbers. Picture your garden bed of cucumbers, a very large patch of them, a bumper crop. Take away the vines and expose the cukes, all lined up in one direction. This gets close to what I saw. Of course, deep-sea cucumbers are not vegetable, but animal; they are related to sea stars, though not as aesthetically appealing. As I drove over the herd with the submersible, they rolled out of the way like tumbleweed before the wind. That's because they are neutrally buoyant, made up almost entirely of water. I could actually see through them, except for the pentium of long bands of white muscle that run the length of their bodies at intervals. I don't know why they aggregate as they do, though food or sex are two likely explanations. How fast they move across the seafloor, how long they stay together as a group, what effect they have on the sediment and the animals living in it are all unknowns.

The seafloor is rich in visual textures. Where the ocean crust is young, lava flows dominate the landscape. The lavas pool and ripple and swirl in frozen motion; pillows of lava with elephant-hide skins drape the slopes of submarine mountains like icing runs down the side of a cake. Stilled lavas are torn, ripped apart, prelude and aftermath of the violent birth of new seafloor. I have driven into fissures cut deep into lavas, deep beyond seeing, and followed them until their steep-sided walls begin to close in on either side. Exposed in the cuts are the histories of eruptions, flows built upon flows. Each flow shows as a discrete unit, the events and the passage of time marked by layered differences in form and color. Elsewhere, emptied ponds of lava with walls marked by bathtub rings are features common in the central valleys of submarine mountain ranges, but not found in any terrestrial environment. The bathtub rings are presumed to be lithic signatures of repeated filling and drainback of lava. Where particularly fluid lavas fill a depression, the surface exposed to seawater cools and solidifies, forming a solid rind an inch or two thick. The underlying molten lava drains back into the crust. The roof, now unsupported, collapses, leaving behind a level mark that rings the depression. Later, lava again fills the depression, again a crust is formed, the lava drains, the roof collapses and another mark rings the emptied pond. Over and over the cycle repeats itself until a hundred or more rings accumulate. These collapse features can be extensive, big enough for the submersible to explore. I work in them often and all but take them for granted, though few people have ever seen them.

The lavas, their distribution and form and composition and age, provide clues to the dynamics and mechanisms of the geological processes that create the seafloor. They are the cache that geologists seek and must be carefully plucked from the seafloor. Sometimes the lavas are hard and dense, broken, but in place and easy to pick up with the manipulator. Other times the lavas are intractable and must be left attached to the planet. More often, the lavas are glassy and brittle, easily shattered as the manipulator's jaws close upon them. Then I have to call on experience and patience to secure a sample for science. Once *Alvin* is back on deck, I always go to the basket to touch the rocks I've collected, to match my tactile sense with the visual image of a rock type. Rocks brought to the surface don't look so extraordinary; in fact, to an untrained eye they look pretty much alike. But each is labeled and catalogued, chipped, cut, powdered, assayed and probed. Once the rocks are grouped into mineralogical classes, the scientists can begin to decipher the sequence of events that led to their formation.

Animals retrieved from the seafloor attract the most attention on the ship. I have seen knots of sea spiders come back alive and squirming in the bottom of the collection box; I have reached for slimy sea anemones that slipped out of my hand like soap; I have felt sorry for the ugly fish, all wrinkled and squinty-eyed. Each one is carried off to the laboratory for observation, description and experimentation. A single animal may be dissected down to organs and tissues, which are then parceled out like gold dust to waiting biologists.

David Petersen

"Blood, Hair, and the Ground Tore Up"

from *Ghost Grizzlies*

In mid-September of 1993, just after returning from two weeks of grizzly chasing in Glacier National Park, I got a call from a friend in the San Juan Grizzly Project. Story was, in late June of 1993, some fellow from Santa Fe had hiked through a high back corner of a nineteen-thousand-acre private ranch down along the Colorado/New Mexico border south of Pagosa Springs, and claims to have observed a sow grizzly with one cub, feeding on an open tundra slope in the vicinity of a place we'll call Grizzly Lake.

Grizzly Lake, the maps told me, is a deep glacial tarn in the center of a huge glacial bowl just below timberline. Our anonymous grizzly observer, it was said, was a "working field biologist who knows his bears." He also knew he was trespassing on stringently posted private land. His fear of being chastised or worse for that, along with concern that if "the authorities" got wind of his sighting they would coerce him into revealing the exact location and "come bulling in to mess things up," were his professed motives for refusing to go public.

Everyone these days wants to think they've seen a grizzly in the

San Juans. And too, this was fourth-hand information, and anonymous at that.

But then, maybe the observer *was* a working field biologist who knows his bears. And even on paper the place looks intriguing, sitting as it does just below timberline and walled in on west, north and east by raggedy cliffs and peaks like bear's teeth, on the south by a fifty-mile slope of national forest. Hike a few minutes up from Grizzly Lake and you're onto the tundra, a little ways down and you're into the subalpine forest. And no livestock grazing nowhere. A seemingly perfect grizzly hide-out.

Moreover, a bear dig into a marmot tunnel and a marmot skull discovered in 1981 by Colorado Division of Wildlife biologists and confirmed as grizzly spoor, was within sight and earshot of Grizzly Lake. Then, in 1990, a local game warden found an extensive marmot dig he felt sure was the work of a grizzly, and this only a fistful of miles southeast of Grizzly Lake.

Hooked, I phoned Dennis Schutz, foreman of the private ranch in question, whom by now I'd come to consider a solid friend. Yes, he said, he knew the place well and would be glad to take me up there. We could "pack light and ride hard" and be there in less than a day.

September 28, 1993: "Grizzly Lake," Colorado

After two hours of uphill riding, we enter the bottom of a broad avalanche chute spilling from a high cirque that Dennis says is always full of wildlife. Verifying that praise, our hoof-pounding arrival sends a dozen wapiti crashing up the left side of the little valley and a clot of mule deer bounding up the right. Three turkey vultures rise heavily from a copse of runted spruce beyond where the deer had been bedded, circle a couple of times for altitude and soar indolently away. On what had these feathered morticians been feeding? We decide to break for an early lunch and watch for a spell.

After twenty minutes, the vultures still haven't returned and our binoculars have revealed no hint of what they were scavenging, if anything. We debate strolling up the valley to investigate—imagining a bear kill—but it's a hell of a hump and the side-hill terrain is all broken and brushy and unsuitable for horses, so we opt to head on to Grizzly Lake.

Breaking out of the little valley midway up its port side, we steer onto what Dennis calls "the Devil's trail." The muddy elk path quickly verifies its name, crossing a greasy-slick talus close along a bone-crushing drop-off then winding up through crowded evergreens bristling with hat-grabbing, eye-poking, flesh-rending snag limbs. But this too finally passes, and the dark woods give way to a weird and lovely purgatory of dwarfed and misshapen trees the Germans named *krummholz,* or "crooked wood" . . . back to the Pleistocene.

Out on the tundra, we ride the swales between swells, skirting wide around a tiny, marsh-moated natural pond we'll dub Cub Lake. We round the next little knoll above the pond and suddenly I'm back at Granite Park in Glacier. Here in the lap of this hidden saddle, perched midway between *krummholz* and tundra, an entire little hillside appears to have been bear-dug.

Having just returned from studying grizzly digs in Glacier, I recognize here the distinctive pattern of grizzly meadow excavations for glacier lilies, alpine bistort and other sweet-rooted forbs. While other animals—including, rarely, black bears—also dig for roots, none save the grizzly has the inches-long claws and powerful shoulder musculature to rip out and turn over huge clods of earth . . . which is exactly what it appears has happened here, though not recently.

I lever my horse to a stop—he's pooped now and stands to dropped reins—climb from the saddle and drop to my knees to examine the digs. The excavations are roughly oval in shape, stair-stepping down a gentle, south-facing slope. The digs average a hundred square feet in area, are six inches to a foot deep with lots of big dirt clods still visible throughout. Complete revegetation and weathering of the sharper features prove these excavations are not this year's work. Beyond that, it's hard to say.

Dennis rides back, curious as to why I'm crawling around on all fours grinning like a dolt. I explain that just two weeks ago I examined and photographed dozens of grizzly digs at Glacier, a great many of which were identical to these in every way—size, shape, depth, clods, the stair-stepping down a gentle slope. Looking around, I see multitudes of alpine bistort—a favorite dig-for grizzly food. Unh-huh.

"Dennis," I say, trying to conceal my excitement, "I think these may be grizzly digs."

"How sure are you?"

Good question. I survey the geomorphology of the little saddle, ruling out water erosion as the excavator—no way; the digs are well up on the side-hill above the bottom of the swale, with no lateral run-off channels anywhere.

Nor are these choppy, vertical-edged dishes the work of geliflucion ("soil flow"), an almost-rare erosive phenomenon that occurs on alpine slopes where the surface soil is composed primarily of fine-ground gravel and other glacial debris (regolith), and underlain by a permafrost substrate. In spring, when the thawed surface layer becomes saturated with snow-melt, big teardrop blops of the liquefied regolith mass will sometimes break loose and flow with glacial sluggishness downslope, leaving a dished hollow above and a lumpy lip below. But here, the soil is soil, not regolith, and firmly anchored by plant roots. There is no permafrost. And finally, the sharp edges, lumpy clods and lack of a lower lip all deny that these depressions could be slumps. They are grizzly digs.

The troubling bit is—how old are they? Were they excavated in a recent summer, or could these depressions be the work of the last "confirmed" (that is, dead) Colorado grizzly, killed only a handful of miles from here back in 1979?

I take some pictures and we ride on, up and over the day's first crossing of the Divide. The alpine bowl that reveals itself on the far side is pintoed with alga-pinked swatches of last winter's snow. Across one of these icy remnants meanders the trail of some large animal. After switchbacking down a precarious talus to the bottom of the bowl, we invest in a brief side trip to check out the tracks, but they're old and badly melted and ultimately unidentifiable.

Down, down into the "crooked wood" again, and Dennis's dog Belle, who's been running circles around us all day, suddenly lines out for a patch of dwarf willow fifty yards ahead. As she squirts into the bottom of the clump, a lanky coyote, twice as big as Belle but probably weighing less, explodes out the top. Dennis whistles once, and good, always obedient Belle returns and falls in behind, tongue-lolling proud.

For the next long while, we sail our equine ships across a rolling sea of alpine tundra, reaching Grizzly Lake in late afternoon. There, we set immediately about preparing for the evening—unsaddling and brushing the horses, splitting wood for a fire, carrying water up from the lake, spreading ground cloth and bedrolls on the lumpy frost-heaved soil and the rest of the mundane but heartily satisfying camp-chore ritual.

That done, we strike out across the tundra on an evening hike, climbing toward a low spot on the northern rim of the Divide. Dennis says he wants to show me a certain "hole" that lies just beyond, where "something strange" happened a while back.

The elevation at Grizzly Lake is about eleven-five and up in every direction. Dennis lopes effortlessly ahead and I follow, lugging and chugging, very much affected by the altitude. What begins as a pleasant leg-stretch after a day in the saddle quickly degenerates into respiratory torture. Given a few days up here to acclimate, I'd be fine. But we don't have a few days, only two, so all I can do is keep lifting one leaden boot ahead of the other.

Onward and upward, past twelve grand and still climbing. A predictably cold alpine wind buffets this way and that, uncaring and real. I fetch my watch cap from my day pack and pull it like a sock down over my burning ears, wishing I'd brought gloves as well.

Finally I approach the rim, tripping over scree slabs that shift and slide and clank like terra-cotta shingles under my clumsy boots. Dennis is standing on a promontory just ahead, and when I join him the world shifts beneath me, my head goes into a spin and I have to sit down fast. Vertigo is unusual for me, having spent the best five years of my youth hanging in the sky on whirling rotors and an insincere prayer. But this is an unusually abrupt, windy and disorienting aerie, and I'm exhausted and a little altitude-punky.

When I regain my equilibrium, I butt-scoot up to the edge of the cliff and peer down some two hundred feet into a fairy-tale *rincón,* a high hidden bowl a half-mile across its corrugated bottom. Unlike the tundra we've just walked across, the parklike amphitheater below is still green with grasses and forbs, and glinting with silvery slivers of running water.

Across its middle, the undulant cirque is whiskered with subalpine spruce and fir. At the far end, where the bench holding the bowl cliffs off no telling how far down to who knows what, one tiny diamond of a tarn mirrors the late sun. On all sides, access to the *rincón* is hindered by steep talus slides or outright denied by cliffs. Forget horseback access. I check the map, find the place nameless and, with the reckless power of a god or a government cartographer, dub it Schutz's Hole.

After searching the hole for several minutes with binoculars—we see only one lonely-looking cow elk and a few flighty ravens—I settle back against a slab of rock cold as a tombstone to hear about the "something strange" that took place down there not quite four years ago.

It was September, 1989, and archery elk season was on. Old Charley Hughes had died, the ranch was in escrow and being hunted under the supervision of a professional outfitter. Dennis had hired on as an elk guide, and was shepherding a New Mexico bowhunter.

Early in the afternoon, while glassing from where Dennis and I now sit, the hunters trumpeted a couple of bugles down into the cirque and were answered by two bulls. It took them a good long while to find a way down, but when they did, they were rewarded by a distant glimpse of a seven-by-seven, or "imperial" bull—a rare huge monster even by local standards. It was while maneuvering toward the big deer, circling the inner curvature of the cirque in an attempt to sneak in close above him, that the two men stumbled onto the scene of the recent "bloody slaughter" of an elk.

This was a year prior to his running into a grizzly sow and three cubs at Willow Creek, over on the other side of the ranch, and grizzlies were the last thing on Dennis's mind. Yet, he tells me now, "The atmosphere down there reeked of violence. There had obviously been quite a battle. It was a full-grown elk—judging from the size of the hooves and bones, either a cow or a smaller bull that would have weighed maybe five hundred pounds—and it clearly had not died without a struggle. There was elk hair and blood all over the place and the ground was all torn up. A blood-smeared drag trail showed where the elk had been pulled maybe fifty feet from where it died to where it was eaten. The hide had been peeled off and was ripped to shreds, bones were scattered all around, most of the ribs had been bitten off and devoured and the skull was missing; we searched all over but never did find it; some scavenger had probably dragged it off, like they often do."

I have to chuckle, so closely does Dennis's colorful narration parallel Mark Twain's description of the scene of a ferocious dog fight, with "blood, hair, and the ground tore up."

"And three different spruce trees around the kill site," Dennis continues, "had been clawed about six feet up their trunks. The claw marks were thick and widely spaced and deep and several inches long and real fresh. It was one more element adding to the weird feel of the place. I didn't know what had killed and eaten that elk, but it was big and it liked its meat fresh . . . the blood hadn't even turned black on the grass and bones. Night was coming on, we were unarmed except for our bows and agreed to forget about the big bull and get the hell out of there. I haven't been back since."

I ask Dennis if it appeared the elk's remains had been covered with debris, as both cougars and bears will sometimes do between feeding sessions. He says no.

I ruminate the possibilities. It could have been a mountain lion; they take even the biggest bulls sometimes, though it's usually when deep snow gives the big-footed cats a leg up on the action. And though they roam everywhere, you don't expect to see cougars at timberline as late as the tail end of September, when most of the deer, their primary prey, have already migrated down. And not even a female lion with yearling cubs could consume an adult elk in one go, but would have covered the leftovers with debris to camouflage them from scavengers while resting nearby between feeds. Whether a 150-pound cat could drag a quarter-ton elk that far I'm not qualified to guess. As for the claw marks—assuming that whatever autographed the trees also killed the elk, of which Dennis is convinced—such high, deep, precise engravings are atypical of the catlike scratchings of pumas.

Black bear is more likely. A big blackie could certainly kill a medium-sized elk, if he could catch it. But black bears rarely try for any elk larger than a calf, unless of course the animal is injured or ill. And again, no black bear, not even a big boar or a sow with cubs, could eat that much flesh and bone all in one go, but would have covered the remains and napped near or even on top of the cache between feeds. And without seeing the claw marks, I can't even guess whether or not they were the work of a black bear—except to note that six feet up is awfully high for even a big blackie to stretch, and grizzlies are better known for territorial tree-marking than are blacks.

Might what Dennis is describing have been a grizzly kill? Certainly, it could have been—the long drag of a heavy carcass, the indications that an entire elk was consumed in a brief time and the claw-marked trees all hint at that likelihood. When a grizzly hunts elk, sometimes it's just a matter of one powerful slam-dunk and the prey goes down, spine smashed. Other times, especially when the elk is an antlered bull and the encounter takes place in the forest where the prey has trees to put between itself and its attacker, it can be a prolonged battle, though inevitably ending with the elk dead and "blood, hair, and the ground tore up." Finally, grizzlies are known to stalk and ambush rut-distracted and exhausted bulls (which the "slaughter" victim easily could have been) during September.

"I'd like to go down there tomorrow and poke around."

"Thought you might," Dennis says, grinning. "Matter of fact, I was counting on it."

The sun is about gone and the wind getting no warmer, so we withdraw from the edge of the abyss and trip back down the mountain to camp, home sweet atavistic home, where wait the proverbial cheery fire, chow and sleep.

Morning.

A hundred yards below camp, Grizzly Lake mirrors snowy peaks. Moby trout leap and roll, leaving rise-forms that grow concentrically outward, like well-lived lives. A small group of elk feed and play on a subalpine slope across the lake, a quarter-mile distant but brought detail-close by the optical magic of binoculars. After a while, the bull of the batch singles out what must be a sweet-smelling pre-ovulatory cow and chases her round and round a little clump of spruce, never quite catching up and she obviously not quite ready. After a few turns round the Maypole, the amorous bull gives up and pretends to graze, offering a classic display of displacement behavior.

Feeling ornery, I whistle a challenge bugle out across the lake and wait for the antlered Romeo's reaction. And wait. If he hears me, he's not sufficiently impressed to reply; I'm far too far away, I guess, to pose a threat to his sovereignty over the little harem. After a while, the boss cow leads the group off into the forest south of the lake, there (no doubt) to bed through midday and chew contemplative cud.

We eat a quick breakfast of cold muffins and hot coffee, pack lunches of fruit and pepper buffalo jerky, saddle up and ride out. As we're leaving, a camp robber glides in to rob our camp of any food or garbage that's been left unsecured; she'll be disappointed.

Rather than retrace our hike of last evening, which would bring us again to that windy aerie from which there is no way down but free-fall, we loop around and above the lake, riding close past where the several elk had been not so long ago. The bull's musky rut scent still perfumes the air; you can *smell* the lust in it. From the lake we climb toward the northeastern curvature of the Divide; Dennis says he knows a way down into his namesake hole from there.

Up this high, autumn is already dying into winter, with most of the wildlife long since moved down to lower climes, the grasses and sedges gone sere and a few aged asters and harried harebells about the only survivors of what must have been a resplendent alpine summer. Two hundred yards ahead, a big coyote works the scree like a street person checking trash bins—poking his long snoopy nose into every crevice, hunting picas, those yummy little "rock rabbits" of the alpine. Belle doesn't see him but the picas have the coyote spotted; their shrill, piping alarm cries electrify the cold morning air.

A hundred feet above the coyote, a red-tailed hawk spirals with deadly intent, big as a young eagle and every bit as beautiful, with a gleam of what I imagine to be hopeful anticipation flashing in obsidian eyes, looking to pick off a coyote-distracted pica. I tip my hat and wish all of them equal good luck. They'll need it.

The wind is in full fury when we reach the rim, and I'm amazed to see an occasional bright aspen or cottonwood leaf floating by *above* us, sylvan butterflies carried up two thousand vertical feet. One at a time, the adventurous leaves sail over the Divide, where they abruptly lose their lift and flutter down the far side, many to be snagged by the web-work boughs of altitude-stunted conifers, lending the blue-green little trees the festive look of Christmas.

From this remarkable vantage, we sit in our saddles for a while, watching coyote, hawk and picas and inspecting our back-trail, glassing the tundra slopes that funnel up and out from the lake, looking for bears and seeing nothing of the sort. But my steady mount Lurch is enjoying the break, munching grass the color of old gold, one long stem sticking a foot out the right side of his mouth, wobbling up and down as he chews, giving him the look of a contemplative country bumpkin.

An hour or so out of camp, we drop down off the wind-blasted hogback Divide and onto a narrow shelf above the east rim of Schutz's Hole. Here Dennis leads into a wind-sheltered alcove of big rocks and little trees, where we tie our horses and prepare to make the final descent on foot. What we're looking at is a near-vertical two-hundred-foot rubble of fractured sedimentary boulders, some as big as boxcars and all stained a luminescent lichen green—a formerly proud cliff face reduced by time and gravity to ten thousand angles of repose.

We pick our individual ways slowly down off the talus and onto a grassy bench. Remarkably, the vegetation down here is still verdant, while just a few hundred feet above, out on the tundra, it's pretty much gone beaver.

Moving parallel to the slope, we walk and walk, and after a while Dennis allows as how we may be in for a long search. "I came in a different way before," he explains.

We walk and walk some more, finding only a few scattered elk bones with tiny scraps of crusty red meat still clinging to the folds of their joints, far too fresh to have been lying naked on the ground for several years, and the scenery isn't looking exactly right to Dennis. So we drop down a few hundred yards to the next bench and resume our back-and-forth searching, passing in and out of dark fingers of trees, down and up knolls and lateral gullies, some steep and deep, others broad and shallow.

It's while crossing one of these dry, rocky, snow-melt ditches that I spot a patch of ground maybe four feet across and several inches deep that has been recently excavated, with several big clumps of turf neatly scooped out and flipped down-side up. So fresh is this dig that the vegetation growing on the inverted surfaces of the overturned clumps is still bright and alive, indicating that the greens couldn't have been lying inverted and hidden from the sun for more than a very few days. The soil in the dig, however, is dry, suggesting that it has been exposed to sun and air for at least a day.

In keeping with the inconclusive nature of all San Juan ghost grizzly spoor, there is no supporting evidence such as tracks or scat. Nor can we say for sure what the bear had been digging for, though the remains of a ground squirrel tunnel run through the dig area.

"Dennis," I say with feigned quietude, "this may be another grizzly dig. And a real fresh one at that."

"How sure are you?"

Again, it's a good question. It looks just like dozens of Glacier grizzly digs I've recently studied, and I sure can't imagine what else could have scooped out and turned over such big perfect clods as these.

To document the scene, we photograph each other holding big chunks of the earthy evidence.

When we move on, I find myself stepping more quietly and peering more intently into the shadowy woods ahead, stopping a lot to listen, even testing the breeze for any scent of . . . what? As always, even the *suspicion* that a grizzly *could* be lurking nearby snatches me back through ten thousand years of human evolution to a state of pure primitive alertness. This is the most, I realize, that Colorado has ever felt like Montana. My heart is pounding, and not from exertion.

On a knoll several hundred yards north of the dig, a certain fir tree, just one among many, stands out like a billboard, stopping me cold.

Years ago, a Navajo acquaintance and follower of the Native American Church was talking about hunting for sacred peyote cacti in the southwestern deserts. "She hides from you at first," he said. "But if you can find just one of her buttons, and if you sit down right there and eat it, you'll start seeing Peyote everywhere—she'll *reveal* herself to you."

Perhaps those old digs above Cub Lake were my first peyote button for this trip, guiding me on to the fresh dig just back down the way, and now to this . . . a deeply claw-scarred tree, exactly like those Dennis describes having seen around the site of that violent elk kill four years ago.

I whisper Dennis over for a consultation. No, he says, this isn't the place; it wasn't on a timbered knoll like this, but on a gently sloping bench just beyond a line of trees. And there were three marked trees, while here is but the one. And too, the claw slashes Dennis remembers were higher, "about eye level on me," while these come up to only my chest. "But the size and pattern," he says, "look real similar."

I take a small steel tape from my day pack and record the statistics: The three parallel gouges average about three inches long, are spaced nearly two inches apart, are incised a half-inch to three-quarters of an inch deep (in pretty hard bark and wood) and have a wide, gaping appearance, as if made by heavy claws, though some enlargement could well have occurred as the injured wood dried and shrank. The scars are, we reckon, at least two years old. I haul out the camera and record the evidence, to be analyzed later by those more in the know.

We search another hour before giving up for the day—Dennis wants to drop even farther down into the bowl and make another pass, but I'm thinking about the long climb back to the horses and cleverly weasel out, suggesting that what I'd really like to do is to return on another trip when we have more time, hang around camp for a couple of days to acclimate, *then* resume the search. To this plan Dennis readily agrees, and we start the long slow hump back up the boxcar talus to the dozing horses.

While riding back along the rim of the Divide, just as we attain a view of Grizzly Lake—far below, glowing like burnished pewter under the dying sun—Dennis spots a flash of something passing beneath his horse's hooves and calls back for me to check it out. We stop, I dismount, search around for a moment and pick up an arrowhead black and lustrous as obsidian, which it is. Half an inch wide, a couple long, delicately thin in profile, its cutting edges intricately serrated, its base unnotched. Perfect.

This is private land; finders-keepers. I hand the ancient treasure up to Dennis.

As we ride on, we ponder what manner of man might have fashioned and carried the delicate point all the long way up here—hunter? vision seeker?—and how it was lost. It's probably not Folsom, since Folsom artisans rarely used obsidian for small points; it tends to collapse under the rigors of primitive pressure flaking. Nor were their lithic skills so finely developed as this. More likely Ute or Apache. Probably Ute, "only" a few hundred years old.

How, I wonder, did the owner of this tiny ancient weapon perceive his grizzly neighbors?

Clarice Dickess

Learning to Breathe

First publication

To begin the Salute to the Sun, one must Stand Tall. Give attention to the feet where they touch the earth. Are the toes gripping? Relax them. Raise the chest and chin, line up the vertebrae in the spine. Let the arms hang at ease. The body rises up out of the floor with a firm base to the summit of the head. This is called Mountain Pose.

Climbing down Mount Crosson upset my stomach with fear. I had to lead, belayed from above. Standing tall made the snowy terrain below me drop out of sight, so I crouched. A sliding layer in the snowpack kept my crampons from gripping.

A few yards below and to the right, a horn of rock stood above the snow. An anchor. Once I reached it, I could sling my loop of webbing around it and fasten the rope to the webbing. Then, the anchor would stop a falling climber. A few steps above the rock my left foot kept sliding; I lost control. My cramped bowels loosened, and I felt a thick oozing of warmth in my crotch.

One day, during my high-school typing class, my friend Sandy and I started joking around. Stupid silly stuff. We started out by giggling behind our hands and ducking our heads to keep the teacher from scolding. He didn't. He even cracked a smile at us, against his will. So we started to chuckle openly. Before long, just the sight of each other became so funny Sandy and I laughed helplessly, loudly.

The teacher finally confronted us, though he was still smiling, but by that point I realized I couldn't stop. I felt the same wavery feeling within my solar plexus that I felt after I cried hard. I felt softer and more open all over my body.

My parents taught me how to swim and water-ski when I was five. I could slalom ski by the time I was eight. In those days, physical activity seemed as easy and natural as my breathing.

From Mountain, raise the arms in a smooth arc to the sky. Look up. Reach with the fingertips, stretch the body from the toes as far as it will go. Inhale slowly and deeply. Feel the muscles begin to let go.

I remember my father's face in anger. He would clench his teeth, hard, until a cord of muscle stood out at his clean jaw. He would work the muscles of his face, clenching and unclenching, a hollow in his cheek darkening and fading. He looked ready to explode from within.

Once, during a free period in grade school, I took out my knitting project and began drawing woolen loops through woolen loops. As my hands created the scarf, I began to cry. I set aside the knitting, leaned my head on my arms and sobbed. "What's wrong?" my teacher asked. "I don't know," I said, and continued to cry, sobs wracking my body as if someone else lived inside. I was taken to the nurse, who asked me, "What's wrong?" "I don't know," I told her. I tried hard to stop the foolish crying. The nurse must have thought I was crazy. She called my mother and spoke to her in low tones. I turned to the wall and tried to hide my uncontrollable tears. When my mother arrived, she asked me what was wrong. She smiled at me as if I was a silly girl. On the way home from school, I finally regained control. I didn't want to be silly.

Bend forward at the waist, exhaling. Hang the head and shoulders loosely as the fingers touch the floor. Relax. Allow gravity to exert a gentle pull. This is Standing Forward Bend.

When he had been drinking, Dad would explode. He would yell, waving his arms and pacing up and down the floor. The more he yelled the angrier he got. Somewhere inside him a stain spread, blotting his soul, its source a mystery.

When I started grade school, I began collapsing during recess when I ran or played, unable to breathe. Asthma, the doctor said. He pricked my back with needles to test what set me off. My mother put a dehumidifier in my bedroom and drove me to desensitization shots every week. We got rid of the family dog. On some sticky Connecticut nights, I struggled for air. Mom said she could hear me wheezing from across the hall.

I fell in love with Nadia Comaneci and gymnastics at the same time. I started off on a mattress downstairs. Accompanied by Carly Simon on the eight-track tape player, I ran and sprang and fell in a repeating cycle until one day I landed a handspring on my feet.

Even now, when I talk with my mother on the phone, she draws on her cigarette so hard I hear the slimy hiss of intake, a muffled hiccup, then the harsh blow from the bellows of her black lungs.

In middle school, I tried the uneven parallel bars for the first time. I learned to point my toes, keep my legs straight, stretch into full splits on the floor. Then I tried the lower bar. I swung and fell off until I could do a full hip circle around the bar, unaided. After another few months of practice, I could swing my hips off the top bar onto the bottom one, change my grip from the top to the bottom, and circle the lower bar with my hips, all in one fluid motion.

When the time came for the coaches to choose their teams, we all assumed I would be included. But halfway through my try-out routine, I grew tired. I started breathing hard. My lungs didn't want to expand. I didn't make the team because I fatigued too easily.

Inhale, bend at the knees, hands on the floor. Exhaling, jump the feet back into the Plank Position. Line up the spine and the legs and head. Breathe. Exhaling, slowly bend the elbows, lower into the Push-up Position. Pause. Breathe.

My mother is one of those smokers who talks with the cigarette in her mouth. The paper filter sticks to her lips, the cigarette bobs with "b" words, her eyes squinting against the smoke.

For my twenty-eighth birthday, I trained all summer so that I could run the eleven-mile leg of the Klondike Relay from Skagway to Whitehorse. That felt pretty good. For my twenty-ninth birthday, I gave myself the present of completing the hilly Equinox Marathon. I finished twentieth out of forty women.

I hate the sight of men in uniform. My father looked handsome in his blue airline pilot suit, all hard-edged creases and shiny buttons. My mother once told me that even when he came home very drunk, Dad always matched up his inseams and hung his pants in the closet when he undressed.

Exhaling, straighten the elbows and raise the head and chest into Upward Facing Dog. Keep the facial muscles relaxed. Relax the shoulders.

My first bad headache hit me when I was in my early teens. A dull ache at the back of my skull deepened to a pain hard enough to make me nauseous. My eyesight went next, wavy lines crossed my vision. Finally, my left hand and arm and half of my tongue tingled and turned numb.

I am told I look like my father. I have his face and hands.

The kids in my neighborhood challenged one another to see who could swim the farthest underwater before surfacing for air. I would suck big air into my lungs and dive, pumping hard with my legs. I imagined myself a torpedo. As the oxygen got used up, the water pressure squeezed my head. I waited until it felt like tiny blood vessels began to burst before I shot up into the air and gasped. The blood throbbed in my head. When the dizziness passed, my body felt hollow. I felt a strange sense of peace.

During my last two years of college, I took about twelve hours per week of ballet and jazz dance lessons.

My mother grinds her teeth in her sleep hard enough to loosen them and wear out the enamel.

My father was a chain smoker. When I was seventeen, he died of lung cancer.

From Up-Dog, inhale, bend the knees and elbows and raise the buttock-bones back and up into Down-Dog. Press the armpits and chest toward the floor. Keep the tailbone moving up and back, working the heels down onto the floor.

Dad thought I faked the headaches. My mother, an R.N., took me to a special doctor. He made me undress and stuck cold diodes on my chest and temples. He put me inside an enormous white tube that rotated around me like a kaleidoscope. EKG, EEG, CAT scan. My favorite doctor figured it out. He wore jeans and long hair. He was skinny and tall and homely. He talked to me more than my mom. He said I was having migraines. He said he saw these headaches in compulsive overachievers. He said to take aspirin and drink a Coke when I felt one coming on. I wished my mom had married someone like him.

I Eskimo-rolled my kayak back upright, unaided, during my first lesson in a pool. Out on the river, though, when I tipped over in the boat, I would rush the maneuver and end up swimming. When you're upside-down in a river, the sound and feel of water rushing around your head drowns all other sensations. I had to learn to expect that bullying push and cacophony. I learned to hold my breath long enough to get oriented, set up for the roll calmly, and burst through the surface with a firm hip snap.

Mom has tried to quit, but she doesn't have enough control over her body's dependence on nicotine. She knows I hate to breathe the stuff, even secondhand. She tries not to smoke inside when I visit. Last time I visited, she had gotten a little air machine to suck away her smoke.

Inhaling, from Down-Dog, jump the feet between the hands. Try to land quietly, gracefully.

I skied down the race hill in my blue instructor's uniform. I rode over a bump, my binding released, I fell and rolled. I'm late for teaching a lesson, I thought, and stood up too fast. I reeled and sat. Then I saw bright pink snow. The edge of my ski had slashed my knee open. A woman doctor sewed three layers of stitches in the ER. The fingers of her non-sewing hand made feather-light motions on my knee. The other hand arced the needle into the skin, tugged, and arced back up. The doctor's motions were precise, delicate, deliberate, like ballet.

The second time I went rock climbing in my mid-twenties, my friend Lon took me to Smith Rocks, in Oregon. I followed his lead up a crack. Technically, it was an easy climb. But right between my feet I could see the Crooked River winding hundreds of feet below. I hesitated, and got "singer" legs. I felt them vibrating faster than I could have made them do without the aid of adrenaline.

"Everything okay?" Lon called from his belay point above me, out of sight. "Yeah," I called. My voice wavered, too. Suddenly, my quaking body seemed funny to me. From a point around the pit of my stomach, I felt a welling of humor. I chuckled out loud and made it to the top of the pitch. When I reached Lon and got anchored to the rock, I hugged him. I wished I could express the feeling of love I felt for this person who had made this moment possible for me.

My mother is still given to heaving heavy sighs. She's usually not even aware she's doing it. Sometimes it's as extreme as pulling air in hard through her nostrils, then pushing the air back out, fast, through lips shaped as if to whistle. In a gentler version, when she's feeling content, she'll breathe in and accompany the outgoing air with a hum.

I turned nineteen before I started the journey toward awareness. Once during that year a healer friend of mine touched my back above the shoulder blades. The muscles instinctively recoiled into a rocklike defense.

"What are you carrying around in here, Clarice?" my friend asked. She tried to loosen the sinew by pressing her fingers into the reluctant flesh.

Exhaling, straighten the knees into Standing Forward Bend. Grasp the hands behind you and pull them up as far as they will go. Keep releasing in the hamstrings. Breathe.

My bubble of personal space has grown a little smaller over the years. Still, too many people that I either don't know or like well enough insist on standing toe to toe with me in conversation, breathing right into my face. Or they want to bump knees and elbows when we're sitting. I enjoy this now, if I like you. The more I like you, the more I enjoy it. But I still find myself backing away from people, quite literally. I bet it would be funny to watch—it's amazing how some don't get it, and will keep stepping forward when I back away.

The shots, growing older, and moving to Idaho's dry air tamed the asthma. In junior high I fell in love with field hockey and downhill skiing.

I buy the moisturizers marked for Sensitive Skin.

The migraines plagued me through high school. This will sound contrived, but I think I stopped getting them so much after Dad died.

Inhaling, smoothly raise the arms above the head in any gorgeous movement.

I fear I may still be regarded as "intense." As I interpret it, this means I forget how to relax and have fun, to laugh or sing or hum. I have always wanted to be able to sing well enough not to be embarrassed, but I only sing along with favorite songs when I'm alone. But I'm willing to shake loose on the dance floor when the music and the beer are good. I'll ski very close to the line of control.

I am a wood burner again. I moved to a cabin smaller in rent and size a month ago, and it heats with a tiny woodstove. I ordered a cord of wood, unsplit, from a number in the newspaper. "I owe you a hundred dollars, right?" I asked the man. "For you," he said, "ninety dollars, since you helped unload."

I have met my new neighbors while splitting the wood. They have stopped by and said to let them know if I need anything. I compete with myself, aiming for a specific spot with the axe, trying to improve my accuracy. I'm about three-quarters finished with the pile. Every time I hit just the right spot, the wood emits a sharp *crack!* and flies off the block, and I have to grin.

Now and then, after orgasm, I cry.

Exhaling, press the palms together overhead. Lower the hands slowly back to Home, Mountain.

Rick McIntyre

The Gift of a Wolf

from *The War Against the Wolf*

Recently, Manuel Iron Cloud, a Oglala Lakota and a co-worker at Big Bend National Park, and I had a conversation about wolves. I had been telling him about a wolf lecture tour I had just completed in Arizona, California, and Colorado.

Manuel, who has a habit of speaking openly about spiritual matters, asked a question that startled me: "Why are you doing all these things for wolves? Did they give you a vision?"

I thought for a minute and said, "Well no, but I once knew a wolf who gave me a gift and I've been trying to find ways of repaying him. The books and lectures I do on wolves are small installment payments on the debt I owe him."

After telling Manuel more about that wolf, he considered my story and commented, "I would say that the wolves did give you a vision." Since then, I've often thought about this statement and have come to agree that a gift can sometimes be the same thing as a vision.

Whenever I think about wolves I invariably visualize one particular wolf who belonged to the East Fork Pack in Alaska's Denali National Park. I first saw him in 1979. That initial glimpse was at a distance, perhaps half a mile, but it was close enough to recognize that something was seriously wrong with him. As he traveled across the tundra, he held his left front paw off the ground. His motion was limited to an awkward three-legged hop, rather than the graceful, effortless trot of a healthy wolf. At the time, I assumed he was an old wolf, well past his prime, and close to death. Obviously, a predator with such a severe disability could not survive long.

I eventually learned I was wrong on that assessment. The limping wolf lived on for another eight years. Not only did he survive, but he became the alpha male, the dominant breeding male of his pack. Despite his handicap, the other pack members deferred to him. When the whole pack was out on a hunt, the others periodically waited for the limping male to catch up. They gave him their allegiance and never withdrew it.

His paw never healed, but he somehow managed to adapt to his disability. Later in his life, he was briefly captured by Park Service biologists. To them, it appeared that the wolf had been caught in a steel trap when younger. The border of Denali National Park lies just a few miles north of his territory and wolf trapping is legal beyond that point. His left front foot must have stepped into the trap and, as he struggled to free himself, he likely yanked it loose. The price he paid for his freedom was the loss of part of that foot, a maiming that stayed with him until his death.

When he had to chase a caribou or a Dall sheep, the limping wolf would run on all fours. There was no chance of catching Denali's fleet game on just three legs. When running at top speed, he appeared to function like any normal wolf. Sometimes he caught his targeted prey, sometimes he failed. Either way, when the pursuit was over, he would collapse on the tundra in exhaustion and begin licking his paw, which would be bleeding profusely from its repeated contact with the rough, rocky ground. There were times when I saw him lick that foot for an entire hour.

Sometimes he ran on the maimed foot during pack activities that appeared to be play sessions. An observation I entered into my journal back in the spring of 1981 describes such an incident:

A patch of white, about a mile across the tundra, catches my eye. Looking through my binoculars, I see that it is a wolf. Its coloration—bright white fur—matches the markings of the East Fork alpha female. Hoping to watch her hunt, I set up my forty-five-power scope.

As I focus on her, I notice a second wolf stretched out fifty feet away. Looking over the nearby area, I find a total of five wolves. Except for the white female, all the other pack members are light gray in color. Soon they all get up and trot off to the east. I then see that the largest of the gray wolves has a pronounced limp in his front left leg. He holds his paw in the air and rarely puts his full weight on it. This is my old friend, the alpha male. He and his white female are almost certainly the parents of the other wolves.

As the pack travels, the limping male falls behind. At times he rushes forward on three legs and momentarily catches up. When he drops several hundred yards behind, the other pack members halt and patiently wait for him to reach them.

The wolves frequently stop to socialize. The white female, the mother, invariably is the center of attention. The younger wolves repeatedly come up to her and touch noses or roll on the ground under her. She, in turn, gives most of her attention to the limping male. The pack is in high spirits, like a group of kids on its way to play ball in a vacant lot.

The evening moves on and the pack rests. Suddenly all five wolves simultaneously sense or see something. Jumping up, they run off in close formation, shoulder to shoulder, to the west. The excitement causes the old male to ignore the pain in his crippled foot; he runs on all fours for the first time. One of the younger wolves runs faster than the others; it breaks away from the pack and sprints ahead.

The lead wolf is ten lengths ahead of the others when something new appears in the margin of my scope. The pack is chasing a grizzly bear! The bear is just a few lengths ahead of the first wolf, who is now seventy feet ahead of the pack. Surging forward, the lead wolf closes the gap to five feet. The grizzly looks back over its shoulder.

As both animals run, they momentarily lock eyes and communicate with each other in a way that no human can decipher. Whatever passes between them, it causes the wolf to end the chase. The bear continues on a short distance, stops, glances back, then calmly begins feeding on grass.

The wolf who led the charge trots back to its companions, and the pack immediately leaps into exuberant play. They wag tails, touch noses, playfully nip each other, run side by side, and roll on the ground. The wolf who played tag with the bear is the focus of the play. From a human perspective, it looks like a joyous congratulatory celebration. For fifteen minutes, the wolves give uninhibited expression to their emotions. Several hundred yards away, the grizzly eats its dinner in quiet dignity.

The extraordinary aspect of this incident is that the limping wolf endured the agony of running on his maimed foot simply for the joy of participating in the playful activities of his fellow pack members. The events of that evening taught me how important companionship and social involvement with its pack is to a wolf. For the limping wolf, it was worth the pain.

On another occasion, I watched the limping wolf and his mate, the alpha female of the East Fork Pack, hunting for caribou. I'll draw on my journal entry to describe the incident:

On this day, the alpha pair is traveling across a broad, flat valley when the female suddenly stops, sniffs the air, and catches sight of a herd of caribou bedded on the tundra. She and her mate, the limping wolf, immediately sprint toward them. The caribou see the charging wolves, jump up and easily outrun them. After chasing the herd a few hundred yards, the wolves give up, rest a bit, then continue on their rounds, looking for another opportunity. They find and test several other bands, but are unable to make any kills. As the limping wolf rests, he frequently licks his injured paw.

An hour later, they find another caribou herd and charge toward it. At first, it seems that these caribou are also going to escape, but then one young calf falls behind. Recognizing the opportunity, the female wolf shifts to top speed and closes in on the calf. Her mate, hindered by his lame paw, struggles to keep up.

The calf's mother has been running beside her offspring but now sees that the wolves have targeted it. She stays with the calf for a few more moments, then resigning herself to the hopelessness of the situation, distances herself from it.

With every stride, the female wolf gains on the calf. A few seconds later, just as it is about to be seized, the calf collapses, and the alpha female immediately kills it. The limping male joins his mate, and they feast on the carcass. This has been an easy kill, but it comes only after many failed attempts. The wolves have run far and worked hard for their meal.

From this observation, I learned how difficult it is for wolves to find a vulnerable target and make a kill. Based on my experiences in Alaska, I think an average, healthy caribou can run about ten miles per hour faster than the average wolf. To survive as an individual, and to feed its pups, a wolf must search long and hard for an individual caribou with a weakness that limits its running speed.

A later episode involving the limping wolf taught me about the role of dominance and submission in the politics of a wolf pack:

Late one afternoon, the limping wolf and a younger, slightly larger male member of his pack leave their den and travel upstream on the East Fork River, looking for game. The younger wolf is anxious to travel and quickly outdistances the old alpha male. Struggling to keep up, the old wolf limps along and occasionally uses his bad paw. As they walk, I notice that the two wolves have identical markings. The limping wolf has been the breeding male of his pack for many years now. This younger male is almost certainly his son.

I swing my spotting scope back to the den to check on activity. The alpha female, the limping male's mate, is playing with their pups. After the pups plop down for a nap, I turn back to the two adult males as they continue to hunt the upper regions of the river.

A few minutes later, the lead wolf sees something and charges forward, into a clump of willow. With great agility, he zig-zags back and forth through the brush, in hot pursuit of some unseen prey. Suddenly he stops, reaches down and comes up with a plump Arctic ground squirrel in his jaws.

The second wolf appears on the scene and approaches his companion. Since he faces away from me, I can't read his facial expressions, but it looks like he wants to take the squirrel away from his partner and eat it himself.

The first wolf drops the squirrel and instantly transforms himself into the terrifying image of a dominant wolf who is ready to fight to the death to defend his possessions. Even from my distant position, I can see his erect mane and snarling face. The other wolf immediately gives in. He tucks his tail under his stomach, lowers his body, and rolls on the ground under the dominant wolf. From that submissive pose, he watched the other wolf consume the squirrel.

As I watched the confrontation, a great wave of sadness overwhelmed me. I had just witnessed the limping wolf's loss of status to a younger and stronger wolf. I had never seen him submit to another adult wolf before, but he had clearly done so here. He would never again be the alpha male of his pack. Or so I thought.

When the squirrel was gone, the wolf who had caught it turned and walked away. Like a chastised puppy, the defeated wolf got up and unobtrusively followed him, maintaining a respectful distance between himself and the dominant animal.

It was then that I saw my mistake. The lead wolf, the one who had caught the squirrel, walked with a severe limp! I had misidentified the two animals. The limping alpha male still had the agility to capture a squirrel as it raced through a thick patch of brush, and he still had the ability to exert his dominance over a younger, and larger, wolf.

From this experience, I came to understand how an old wolf, one who is past his prime and suffering from a severe handicap, can still dominate other members of his pack. The limping wolf did this through an aggressive display and through the force of his personality. Never, in this case or during other observations, did I see him physically attack another pack member. He could control them in other ways, ways that avoided injuries. This incident taught me about the toughness needed by an alpha male as he leads his pack.

The encounter between the limping wolf and an adult wolf who was probably his son reminded me of an earlier observation at the East Fork Pack's den:

Standing completely still, the wolf stares straight ahead. With a slow, fluid motion, it lowers its body into a crouch, then charges forward at a dead run. The wolf races toward the center of a small meadow where an animal lies on the ground, seemingly asleep. On the far side of the meadow, three other pack members burst into view, sprinting toward the same target.

At the same instant, the four wolves strike their prey. Two grab his head while the others attack the flanks. Their victim jumps up and vigorously shakes his body, hurling the wolves from him. Each wolf hits the ground, scrambles to its feet, and flings itself back into the battle. In a moment, all four wolves reattach themselves to their quarry.

Their beleaguered prey, with great effort, again tries to dislodge his attackers. First one wolf, then all four are thrown off. The wolves pause to see what their prey will do. He stares back at his assailants, then slowly limps off a few dozen yards, lies down, and goes to sleep. Losing interest in the game, the wolves trot over to him, curl up, and doze off.

The four wolves are six-week-old pups and their intended prey was their father, the limping alpha male of the East Fork Pack. The pups used him to practice their stalking and attacking techniques. The adult willingly played the victim but walked off when the game grew too painful.

Through this incident, I learned of the gentleness of adult wolves toward pups. The alpha male had enough aggressive power to face down a younger and stronger wolf, but he also possessed the tenderness to let a gang of pups attack him.

The East Fork alpha male is the toughest animal I've ever known. The final act of his life showed that toughness:

One summer day, while on a solo hunt, the limping wolf finds a young bull moose. The bull outweighs him by four hundred pounds, but the wolf decides to take the big animal on by himself, challenging the moose to a fight to the death. Over the next thirty-six hours, he attacks the moose at least fourteen separate times. The moose fights back, stomping and kicking his attacker. The wolf's bad paw is hit during the counterattack and bleeds profusely.

Each attack weakens the moose. Near the end of the drawn-out battle, he wades out into a swift river channel. Jumping into the water, the wolf swims to his opponent. As they fight, the moose holds the alpha underwater and nearly drowns him. The wolf slips away to rest, then comes back for one last round. By this point, the wounds on the bull have taken their toll. Weak from loss of blood, the moose can't fight back any longer, and the wolf finishes him off.

After the moose dies, other East Fork pack members arrive and feed alongside their leader.

The limping wolf pays the ultimate price for his hard-fought victory. His injuries will slow him down considerably in the weeks ahead. Within a month he will disappear, and I will never see him again. The beta male, a wolf who is also a skilled hunter, will take over the alpha position. This male, like nearly all the other East Fork wolves, almost certainly was fathered by the limping wolf.

The wolf, during the eight years that I knew him, fought the good fight. His death was a good death, a fitting death for an alpha male. As was true of his entire life, he died a fighter.

I gradually came to realize that the limping wolf had given me a gift. His gift was to teach me what it means to be a wolf. He showed me the full spectrum of the life of an alpha wolf by allowing me to watch as he hunted, played with his pups, disciplined a fellow pack member, and pursued a grizzly bear just for the fun of it. Each incident he let me watch had a point, a lesson to learn, a truth to absorb. He was my teacher and mentor.

To me, he became the ultimate example of the warrior spirit of the wolf. He never quit, he relentlessly pursued his quest for personal survival and survival of his pack. No adversity, even a life-long problem with his maimed paw, could deter him. He continued on, despite the pain.

In many ways, he reminded me of the great outlaw wolves of the Old West. The Custer Wolf, Rags the Digger, and Lobo, King of the Currumpaw, like the limping East Fork wolf, never gave up in their arena of battle. They mounted personal guerilla campaigns against the forces that had decimated their race. They served as champions of their kind and carried out an effective resistance until the moments of their deaths.

This warrior spirit of the wolf was the reason the Wolf Nation survived all that our race did to it. They never quit or gave up. They died in huge numbers, they lost 99 percent of their original range in the Lower 48 states, but they survived to fight another day. Now they are back in many of their former homelands. Soon they will be back in other territories. From the perspective of the late twentieth century, we can look back at the War Against the Wolf and say that the wolves won.

Since the death of the limping wolf, other wolves have carried on his tradition and taught me truths about their race. The limping wolf's son and his fellow East Fork Pack members allowed me to observe them as they carried on after their leader's death. I eventually built up a total of about five hundred wolf observations in Denali, mainly East Fork wolves. The wolf packs of Glacier National Park allowed me to watch them as they continued their colonization of Montana.

While working on *A Society of Wolves,* I spent portions of two years studying a captive pack of wolves in Montana. I came to know Queenie, the alpha female, so well that she allowed me to closely watch as she nursed, cared for, and played with her pups. She even allowed me to crawl down into her den and experience the underground life of newborn wolf pups.

All these things were gifts from wolves, gifts that brought me further along in understanding their race.

In researching and tracking down selections for *The War Against the Wolf,* I was struck by the scheme common to Native American stories of wolves. Wolf characters are nearly always presented as elders, teachers, mentors, and benefactors. The Blackfeet stories "The Medicine Wolf" and "When Men and Animals Were Friendly," the Dena'ina narrative from Alaska, "Wolf Story," and many others, show wolves as kindred beings who willingly give gifts to humans. These gifts teach people how to relate to the natural and spiritual worlds and frequently save the lives of starving human beings. In return, all the wolves ask is respect and understanding, small payback for their extraordinary gifts.

Also common to Native wolf stories are human characters who

are willing to give the wolves the respect they desire. In response, the wolves give more of themselves to those individuals open to their gifts. Perhaps this is what Chief Dan George was thinking of, the willingness of wolves to relate to humans, when he gave this advice:

> If you talk to the animals they will talk with you
> and you will know each other.
> If you do not talk to them you will not know them,
> and what you do not know you will fear.
> What one fears one destroys.

Manuel Iron Cloud's grandmother taught him the same lesson about wolves. As a young boy, Manuel heard his grandmother tell the story of a conversation she had with a wolf during World War I. The grandmother's nephew had been wounded in battle in Europe and, as he lay bleeding in a forest, he saw wolves looking at him. With a respectful attitude, he asked that they come over. Glad to help, the wolves approached him. When they found that he would recover from his wounds, they howled out a message that was transmitted from wolf to wolf, from Europe to the Pine Ridge Indian Reservation in South Dakota. The South Dakota wolf told the grandmother that her nephew was wounded but was in good spirits and would survive.

In telling the story to young Manuel, she finished with these words, "So when you see a wolf don't be afraid of him, instead talk to him, he might have something to say to you."

During my most recent wolf lecture tour, I did several programs in partnership with Kent Weber of Mission: Wolf, a Colorado nonprofit operation that cares for unwanted captive-born wolves. I presented my slide show on wild wolves and then Kent explained the purpose of his organization. The climax of each event was the appearance of one of Kent's tame wolves. As the audience responded to the charismatic appeal of the wolf, Kent explained why wolves belong in the wild, not in cages in people's back yards.

After one of our joint appearances, Kent told me a startling story about the gift of a wolf. He often brings wolves to elementary schools and sometimes speaks to groups of kids as large as five hundred. In some cases, he will allow a tame wolf to run free in the auditorium. The wolf will circle the entire room several times, running at top speed. As the wolf runs, the school children go crazy with excitement.

Kent began to notice that when a wolf was allowed to run free in such situations, it would almost always pick one child to greet and make friends with. It usually was just one kid out of the several hundred in the auditorium. Curious as to why the wolves were picking out certain children, Kent began to ask teachers if there was anything special about the ones the wolves chose.

The teachers were astonished at the behavior of the wolves. They told Kent that the boys or girls selected by the wolves were always the worst outcasts in school, the kids everyone else picked on. The wolves had decided to make friends with those outcasts.

I've been around wolves for eighteen years, and have learned many things about them, but I am not certain why Kent's wolves behaved that way with those kids. If I had to guess, I would say that they may have sensed that those children weren't being taken care of as well as the other kids in the room. Wild and captive wolves love to take care of pups, their own or orphaned ones. Wolves automatically want to care for helpless, defenseless young creatures. Perhaps to the wolves, those kids were the equivalent of abandoned, orphaned pups, and they wanted to care for them.

Whatever the reasons for the wolves' behavior, I can imagine no greater gift, from a wolf to a person. Imagine what it must be like for a young child to be a total outcast in his or her school, to be picked on by all the other kids. Then imagine what it would be like to be sitting in a huge auditorium, surrounded by hundreds of people who don't like you, when a wolf is set free and races around the room, finally stopping beside you. At first, the wolf's approach would likely be interpreted as just one more unfair attack, but then the wolf clearly shows that he is friendly and greets and licks your face and hands.

Such an experience, such a gift, would change a child's life forever. Whatever unfair or negative things might later happen in their lives, they will never forget that once a wolf picked them, out of all the other kids in the entire school, to make friends.

Perhaps, like the wolf characters in the Native American stories, these wolves were trying to teach humans a lesson. To the outcast kids and to the rest of the student body the lesson was the same: reach out to people in distress and offer them your friendship.

I feel I owe the East Fork limping male, and the other wolves who have given me gifts, a tremendous debt. They freely gave of their lives to help me understand their race. I have vowed to repay the wolves by passing on their gift to others of my race.

With my wolf books and lectures, I try to teach other people what wolves are like and why they deserve our respect. I explain the horrendous things our country has done to the Nation of Wolves and try to show why we should restore them to suitable portions of their former ranges.

The best way I can repay the wolves for their gift is to help bring them back to places like Yellowstone National Park, Colorado, Arizona, New Mexico, Texas, and northern New England. If I can help wolves regain those old territories, I will be able to say that I've repaid part of the debt I owe them.

In the Oneida story *Who Speaks for Wolf,* as told by Paula Underwood, a Native man, known as Wolf's Brother, tries to repay his debt to wolves by getting his people to move their camp away from the home range of a community of wolves. Through a calm and reasoned approach, acting as a spokesman for his wolf brothers, he succeeds in resolving the conflict that had arisen between the Oneida Nation and the Wolf Nation.

I don't claim the honorary title of Wolf Brother. I haven't done enough to deserve it, but I do aspire to serve, like the Native man in the story, as a spokesman for the wolf. It's part of my debt to the wolves for the gifts they've given me.

Lyn Buckley

Poem

First publication

Elegy for Vincent

for Vincent Kight (1970–1994)

Like chairs left askew around a table
where a sumptuous meal has been served,
absence leaves its profound presence behind.
Have you noticed how, long afterward, in certain trees
that in the fall are most yellow, something
of summer's brightness seems trapped?
How a person far away can more frequently enter
your thoughts than he who is in the same room?
How a walk along the shore is marked by ordinary
things once impossibly lost? Although sometimes
the seas seem almost kind this way; seedpods
travel out from distant lands like miniature
caravels and dows; pregnant messengers,
they arrive: Yes there *is* possibility of another life.
Strange trees, poisonous plants, who could survive?
Many, rather, have thrown themselves back. In pieces,
sea things may remain intact; their sharp edges
smoothed over, glass and teeth and shells all

tumble together forming heaps of curios,
the same everywhere, really. Here the sea confuses me:
Is this you? A clam half small in my palm?

I know this is true: the world creates riotous
expectation in us. Can thousands of wild swans here
balance the extinction of crows on an island somewhere else?
This is nature's algebra, perhaps: one equals a million,
and God, knowing this, resides in arbitrary
places. In dragonflies, for instance.
If we are mud given breath, surely
they are the breathing jewels, peridots,
olivines, green diamonds on the wing, reflecting
ambient light and glowing within, double
our brilliance. Yet already unearthly,
they build no temples, no spiraling towers.
This is why we tell each other stories,
how the shipwrecked sailor was tossed
upon the beach entirely whole with only
his fingers and toes water wrinkled and
nothing else to mar his blond beauty. We like
to tell how, by human breath alone,
he was brought back. How although he'd forgotten
the name of his ship, his port of origin,
he took up life in that new place easily,
sitting down before a large table of steaming food.
And how when he thinks to comb, in the stark sunlight,
the ragged edge of that becalmed sea for a clue
to his own mystery, he will find
a perfect blue bottle containing a note,
with no inky illegible smears, but clear words.
And they will not be a call to revolution,
a plea for food or medicine, but will come
from his mother and his uncles.

Otherwise we have no way to exclaim:
Our children have played
amid brown recluses and black widows and *live*.
By explaining our good fortune to ourselves
and making plans for these things, being chosen,
escaping, we create everywhere,
in hundreds of languages, a din so like happiness
that the disinterested, universal hum is suppressed.
We can't bear a drowning sailor's indifference.

Yet sadly we have lost the language of portents.
When nothing worse happens, we forget
the crowd of black ants in the Dresden sugar bowl.
We joke, let this cup, let this saucer too, pass from me,
and never reckon how often they do.
What if we were not blind to that which is
averted? Wouldn't every moment the child survives
cast innocence and light into all
darkened pools, into all strangers' faces?
If only we could see, that when the child
returns from the woods unharmed,
all the diamondbacks are blessed.

In the end, I was never fully accustomed
to your presence. In my life you were always a little
like a humming bird in the house.
Sometimes, at night, I would mistake
your beating heart so near me for
the footsteps of someone prowling in the hall.
Your sounds in another room were often,
at first, anonymous. Then a reminder:
He *exists,* that little boy whose light skin
seems unable to contain all the sunny weather
he carries inside so it burns his cheeks,

dampens his curly hair, and contradicts his strange
dreams of fish swimming in the cellar.
Separation is one of attachment's conditions.
But now, in the same way that a short summer
and the hot tail ore of a passing comet
conjoin, this year, the fall of leaves and stars,
I grieve for you in the deaths of presidents
and blond boys who sing. That *must* be you
pumping gas into your Apache in Reno.
I see you in the desert, in the snow.
Lost, you are nowhere, and yet
I have found nowhere you are not.

Gerard Gormley

The Winged Whales

First publication

Part One (January–April)

In late December 1983 one of the arrivals on Silver Bank was a fifty-foot female whose back bore a series of parallel white scars inflicted by a boat propeller. She arrived in the company of two other whales. One was her sister, younger by two years, and her constant companion since the death of their mother three years earlier. The other was the scarred female's one-year-old son.

The scarred female was pregnant and near term. This was her second pregnancy. Her sister, now five, was entering estrus for the first time. Provided she accepted a male, she might conceive her first calf this winter.

As the three whales entered the bank's northwest passage, they saw a sight new to them since the last winter. On the northeast reef of Silver Bank lay the wreck of a small freighter. Listing to starboard some twenty degrees, stern awash and bow high and dry, the vessel appeared to have run onto the coral reef without ripping out her bottom.

The pregnant female led the way to the eastern central part of Silver Bank, between the great northeast coral reef and the many isolated coral heads some ten miles south. Here the calf to come would be sheltered from the northeast trade winds. Should the wind blow out of the northwest, the mother could move her calf into the lee of the southern reef. The chosen area would also keep the calf well away from the localities where the adult males did most of their singing, breaching and fighting.

That evening, barely twelve hours after reaching Silver Bank, the scarred female began labor. Escorted by her sister and son, she swam in a slow circle, arching her body as contractions occurred. Sometimes she swam on her back and lashed her tail against the water. Her labor continued for five hours, then the birth began.

Nine months ago the calf, then an embryo barely a foot long, had the rudimentary limbs and teeth that suggest that humpbacks evolved from toothed land mammals. Now fifteen feet long and weighing some 1,500 pounds, she had exchanged her limbs for flippers and flukes, and her teeth for three hundred to four hundred baleen plates on each side of her upper jaw. Her baleen, now one and a half inches long, would be more than thirty inches long by the time she stopped growing.

Light gray in color (adults range from black to charcoal gray), she was a perfectly formed humpback, all her senses fully developed. Lying doubled over with her tail positioned near the birth canal, she listened to the thud of her mother's heart and the great draughts of air coursing through her lungs. The powerful contractions frightened her. Life inside this fluid-filled sac had been a snug existence, but all that seemed to be changing.

During one great contraction, her sac burst and the fluid drained away. Then she felt herself being squeezed tailfirst into a tight passage. The birth lasted barely an hour, but to her it seemed endless. She felt her flukes enter a wet place cooler than her mother's body, then she felt the cool wetness rising along her body. At one point her umbilical cord became tautly stretched and cut off her blood supply. Just about the time she was becoming desperate for oxygen, the cord pulled free and her mother's blood restored her oxygen supply.

Moments later she emerged from her mother's body into a world not quite as dark as the one she had just left. With a puff of blood the placenta fell away and the umbilical cord parted cleanly at her body, leaving a foot-long tube of skin dangling from her navel. Her mother's bleeding quickly stopped.

Instinctively she swam to the surface. As soon as she felt the light cool passage of air against her nostrils, she opened them and took her first breath of air. For some time she wallowed clumsily at the surface, breathing deeply and exhaling hard to clear the fluid from her lungs. Her aunt supported the baby with her flipper. Born like all cetaceans, with her dorsal fin folded over and her flukes curled and flaccid to ease her passage through the birth canal, she could barely swim well enough to keep her blowhole above the waves. Within a few days, though, her flukes would flatten out and stiffen to provide full propulsion power, and her dorsal fin would straighten.

The scarred female expelled the afterbirth and floated at the surface to rest from her labors. The calf began to butt at various points along her side. The adult rolled over to expose her mammary slits. When the calf located the slits, the mother protruded her nipples and the calf grasped one teat between its tongue and the roof of its mouth. The mother then squirted a creamy white mixture as concentrated as condensed milk down the calf's throat. The nursing session lasted only a few seconds. The calf would nurse approximately forty times every twenty-four hours, drinking about three gallons each time.

Although the scarred female had gradually weaned her one-year-old son over the last few months they were on the northern feeding grounds, the sight of the baby feeding stirred fond memories, and he tried to nurse. The mother pushed him away with her flipper. When he insisted, she turned away and smacked him with her flukes. He would try again, more and more frequently as his hunger grew, but she would continue to refuse him, for her new calf needed all her milk.

Now that the calf was outside her mother, she could hear clearly the many sounds that had been partially masked by the adult's heart-beat and breathing. The sea was filled with the sounds of male hump-backs breaching and performing their long, complex songs.

The baby tried to float beside her mother to rest, but it was a case of swim or sink, for her blubber was too thin to buoy her up. On the higher-latitude feeding grounds she might have been able to float, but the density of tropical surface water is comparatively low.

Mother came to the baby's aid, supporting her on one of her sixteen-foot flippers.

Terns flew about in the darkness, vocalizing steadily. Sometimes, as baby and mother rolled in a swell, one eye cleared water and the little one could see the night sky filled with stars. She saw lights in the water all around her, too. Some were caused by two-inch marine worms, polychaetes, which swam in spirals and left highly persistent helical ribbons of blue-green bioluminescence as much as a foot long. The glowing trails looked like the tentacles of a Portuguese man-of-war. As the worms spiraled along just below the surface, smaller luminescent creatures resembling oversize copepods con-verged on them at high speed and attached themselves to the worms. Soon the worms and their apparent attackers were all around the calf, drifting on the current as they performed their brilliant intri-cate maneuvers, doubling back on themselves and forming complex glowing patterns that looked like galaxies of stars drifting away into the distance. For some minutes the display continued, then the water went black.

Despite the thunder of male humpbacks breaching, and their even louder songs—both of which she would find continued night and day—the calf managed to sleep.

She awoke to a burst of light on the eastern horizon. The light frightened her. She had thought the world to be a place of darkness. When a fiery ball began rising out of the sea, she dove and comforted herself at the teat. By the time she surfaced, the sun had risen.

The mother dove, then rose vertically and thrust her head high out of the water—a behavior called spyhopping. The baby tried to follow the mother's example, but with her flukes still curled she could not get enough thrust to keep her head above water. She could sense excitement in her mother. Not knowing how to interpret this, and as a result feeling fearful, she pressed against the big familiar body.

The mother was spyhopping because this enabled her to see along the surface with binocular vision. And all across the horizon from southwest to northwest, she could see male humpbacks breaching. Some executed spinning breaches, with flippers extended, usually landing on their sides and slapping the surface hard with one flipper. Others breached with their flippers close to the body, splashing down on their backs. Some even performed tail breaches, hurling the rear halves of their bodies into the air and landing on their sides. Sometimes, in lieu of breaching, males lob-tailed, raising their flukes high out of the water and striking the surface with great force and loud sound. Other times they lay on their sides and struck the surface hard with their flippers.

The mature males expended incredible amounts of energy. One of them breached once every thirty or forty seconds and totaled 130 consecutive breaches.

When not breaching or engaging in other physical displays, a male would go deep, hover head down at an angle of about forty-five degrees, and sing nonstop for anywhere from six to thirty minutes. These songs, which ranged from deep rumbling sounds to high-pitched squeals and squeaks, appeared not to attract females. On the contrary, they often attracted other males, at which point the singer usually ended his song and joined the group, sometimes to fight, though most fights occurred when two or more males vied for one female. Fights between mature males could be quite vicious. They rammed each other and struck tremendously hard blows with their flippers and flukes. Fighters were often left bruised and bleeding. Most lacerations were caused by the large barnacles that festoon humpbacks' heads, flukes and flippers.

It may be that the energy of the males' breaching and the length of time they can remain submerged, singing their complex songs, serve to tell females which males are strongest. But it is just as likely that breaching and singing are meant to intimidate other males.

Had the scarred female been in estrus, she would have visited the display grounds and made herself available, perhaps to a number of males. But she had a baby to raise and, unless the calf died, the mother would not enter estrus again for a year. She settled down into the water and nuzzled her baby.

As a rule the mature males restricted their breaching, singing and fighting to the deeper, more open parts of the bank, well away from the birthing areas. But one day three young bachelor bulls passed close enough to the scarred female's nursery group to taste the signs of estrus from her younger sister. The ensuing melee made it necessary for the scarred female to take her newborn calf into water so shallow that her belly frequently scraped bottom. Her son joined her, but when her sister tried to do so, she drove her away with full body blocks and flipper slaps. The young female fled, pursued by the three young males, and did not return for a week. When she did return, she was no longer secreting the taste of estrus. In a year or so, she might well be applying what she learned about motherhood by watching and helping her older sister.

A somber day. The sky to the east was slate gray. The sun, approaching zenith, shone through a gap in the clouds, its glare turning the sea silver. In this sparkling light a solitary whale was lob-tailing, thrusting ten to fifteen feet of its tail section out of the water, then slapping the surface with its flukes. The sound reverberated from the bottom like underwater thunder. Time and again the whale thrust its tail high, then smacked the surface with all its strength. When it tired of that, it floated on its side and slapped the water with one flipper. Then all at once the whale disappeared. Minutes later another song was added to the many being sung.

Not far from where the whale had been lob-tailing, the scarred female and her baby saw, riding at anchor, a large sailing vessel that frequented Silver Bank during the humpback calving season.

This vessel was R/V *Regina Maris,* a 144-foot barkentine operated by the Ocean Research and Education Society (ORES). During the day, weather permitting, the ORES people maneuvered their vessel cautiously among the coral heads and charted each one, meanwhile observing and photographing any whales they encountered. The ORES scientists were particularly interested in photographing the distinctive markings on the undersides of humpbacks' flukes, for these make it possible to identify individual whales and track their movements. But on Silver Bank the whales presented a problem. Rather than "fluking up" as they so often do on their northern feeding grounds, the humpbacks usually sounded on a forty-five-degree angle and scarcely showed the undersides of their flukes at all.

The reason for this is unclear, but a number of factors may cause the whales to make fewer steep dives. For one thing, the water on Silver Bank is much shallower than on the northerly feeding grounds. In depths only twice their body lengths, the whales would quickly hit bottom on steep dives.

Another possible cause is buoyancy. While on their wintering grounds, humpbacks show no signs of eating. Instead, they live on food reserves stored in their blubber. As they lose blubber they lose buoyancy, and so may be able to sound without the added push provided by the weight of vertically positioned tails. If this is so, we should find humpbacks showing less fluke when they first return to the higher latitudes, then showing more as their blubber is restored. This may be a subject worthy of study.

Another possible buoyancy factor—tropical seas are generally less saline than high-latitude waters. Lower salinity means lower density and lower buoyancy for the whales. Also, density is inversely proportional to temperature, so warm water is less dense than cold water.

Finally, the vertical dives and associated fluke displays so common in the higher latitudes may be associated with feeding. Humpbacks often appear to dive deep beneath prey schools, perhaps the better to see them silhouetted against the surface glow and to drive them to the surface with bubble clouds. Since humpbacks appear not to eat in the tropics, they may have less need to go deep in a hurry, and so do not "fluke up" as much.

Toward evening each day, the ORES people often anchored about a mile from the wreck, then shuttled over to the freighter in two inflatable boats to salvage things and take them back to the ship.

The barkentine had been a familiar sight to the scarred female during her last five stays on Silver Bank, and the people aboard had shown themselves to be benign, so one day she let her baby, then a month old, approach the ship. The calf went within fifty feet of the vessel and spyhopped to look it over. Her mother floated close behind her. The bond between mother and baby was very strong. If anyone or anything tried to harm her calf, she would fight to the death in its defense.

The baby saw a dozen or more persons lining the ship's rail. Others climbed aloft. Nearly everyone had a camera. One group launched an inflatable boat and motored slowly toward her. Seven persons equipped for snorkeling slipped over the side and approached her. More curious than fearful, she probably would have played with the swimmers, but her mother moved in and gently fended off the swimmers with her right flipper.

The scarred female's sister and son showed up—they often wandered off for days—and swam among the people for a time. Then a pair of male humpbacks appeared near the ship and began to breach, splashing down dangerously close to the swimmers, who got back into their inflatable boat and withdrew. The scarred female's sister and son followed them back to the ship. For nearly an hour the two males seemed to compete with each other, hurling themselves almost completely out of the water and reentering with thunderous splashes that sent waves coursing all the way to the ship.

Then several groups of from four to ten males each came along and dashed about near the ship, lob-tailing, flipper-slapping and fighting. At a touch of her mother's flipper, the baby turned and followed the adult away from the ship. The scarred female's sister and son remained near the ship.

Mother and baby spent the rest of the afternoon in shallow water near the coral reef. The sea was calm, barely a ripple to be seen. The sky was thick with clouds. As the sun approached the horizon, its light burned through the clouds and turned the sea bright copper.

The baby was growing rapidly on her mother's rich milk, gaining 100 to 150 pounds a day. Now two months old, she had already added about three feet to her length. So fast was her growth that she shed a layer of skin daily.

When they were on the move, the baby usually swam just above her mother. This protected her from the occasional large oceanic shark that happened onto the bank. Swimming above her mother also made it easier for her to surface for air, which she had to do every three or four minutes, while her mother could easily remain submerged for ten to fifteen minutes.

Sometimes she swam beside her mother, but whatever her position, she always swam close enough to be carried along by the adult's pressure field. This way she could move effortlessly, saving energy and investing it in growth. And by swimming close, she could also stay in touch with her mother. Touching was very important to mother and calf. The adult often caressed the youngster with her flipper. They were nearly always in physical contact, if only with the tip of a flipper.

Swimming with slow facile grace near the surface, their bodies dappled by sunlight, they presented a beautiful sight. Symmetry in motion.

During rest periods the mother often hovered at a depth of about forty feet, while the calf napped near the surface so that she could more easily rise to breathe. Sometimes, when her mother hovered closer to the surface, the calf rested underneath her chin.

Whenever the adult dozed at the surface, the baby amused herself by rolling over her mother's back, splashing and blowing, rubbing against her, and slapping her with flippers or flukes. It seemed unlikely that the mother could get any rest this way, but never once did she push her baby away or do anything that might discourage its playfulness. And the calf was extremely playful now, often breaching, lob-tailing or slapping the surface with her flippers. When she and her mother spent any time near another cow and calf, she and the other calf played together under the watchful eyes of their mothers. Their play could get rough, but seldom was anyone injured.

The calf was becoming a fairly accomplished swimmer. She often performed barrel rolls. Sometimes she swam upside down with the tips of her flippers cutting the surface. But she still stayed close to her mother most of the time, close enough to be carried along by the adult's pressure field. Whenever her mother picked up speed, the calf felt like she was flying underwater.

The weather was typically erratic for this time of year. Conditions could quickly go from glassy calm to ten-foot seas, especially when the wind swept in from the north. Then, just as quickly, the wind could swing around to the east, in the clockwise pattern typical of this region. On two days out of three the sky was darkly overcast, the wind strong enough to make the scarred female seek shelter for her baby in the lee of a coral reef. The surface noise was hard on the baby's sensitive ears. She was glad each time they could dive and reduce the cacophony of wind and waves to a muted sound like distant rolling thunder. She liked swimming submerged on sunny days most of all, when rays of sunlight were fanning down through the water, highlighting a profusion of suspended particles that created an underwater haze.

Sometimes, when conditions were calm, they swam close to the wrecked freighter. The baby liked to see the colors of the sunlit reef, with its seemingly limitless number of coral polyps, sea fans and anemones. The ship's hull extended about twenty feet underwater, its sheer vertical wall contrasting sharply with the tangled mounds of damaged coral around it. The baby humpback saw many creatures around the wreck. Damselfish swam in and out of the portholes. Trumpetfish concealed their slender bodies behind ladders, anchor chains and various other parts of the ship as they stalked small wrasses. Also abundant around the wreck were garfish, needlefish and halfbeaks, related to trumpetfish. She often saw barracuda near the ship, as well. The younger barracuda, even young adults three to four feet long, hunted in large schools, driving fish into shallow water and chopping them into bloody pieces as they fed. Mature barracuda, up to five and six feet long, usually hunted alone.

In deeper water, the young whale saw flying fish taking to the air to elude barracuda and other predators. In calm weather the fish became airborne by sculling rapidly along the surface with the lower lobes of their caudal fins, then spreading their winglike pectoral fins when they reached gliding speed—some forty miles per hour. In rough weather the fish could exit the peaks of high waves and become airborne without having to scull. The average flight of the two-winged flying fish lasted about ten seconds and covered four hundred to five hundred feet, but the four-winged species could glide for thirty or forty seconds and cover distances of a thousand feet or more.

In early March the scarred female and her calf were joined by a male escort who swam behind and a bit below them. If another male tried to join the group, the lead escort swam close to the scarred female and kept the challenger behind him. If the intruder persisted, the escort tried to warn him off with a series of escalating threats. First he blocked the challenger's approach and made loud rumbling sounds. If this failed to deter, he broke through the surface, engorging his throat pouch with water and air to make himself larger. His next step was usually to release an explosion of noisy bubbles, using air gulped into his mouth, as well as exhaling through his blowhole. This threatened the challenger and blocked his view of the scarred female. His next level of escalation was to scream, while slapping his tail hard against the surface or swishing it from side to side. When all else failed, the lead escort might ram the intruder, causing a great cloud of bubbles as he butted him with his head and knocked the wind out of him. Or he might strike the intruder with his tail. One day he hit another male so hard with his tail that the whale was propelled sideways for a distance of six feet.

These normally slow whales can move very quickly, at speeds up to fifteen knots, over short distances. And when males weighing thirty tons or more crash into each other at such speeds, severe internal injuries may result.

Sometimes the challengers came six at a time, each in turn harassing the lead escort and trying to assume his role, but this feisty male managed to drive off all competitors.

The scarred female was quick to distance her calf from the fighting. She was also quick to thump any male that came too close to her calf. And given her greater size—female mysticetes are larger than males—she could deliver quite a thump.

As winter passed into spring, the northward migration began.

Alison Deming

Woods Work

from *Temporary Homelands*

A photograph of an empty house. Weathered clapboards, two and a half stories, a simple peaked rectangular box, windows and doors gone, the interior open to the wind. On the roof, a foot of snow; in the dooryard, a three-foot drift. A few weedy blackberry canes poke through the white crust. Worn and leaning cedar fence posts run along the south wall. The neighbor's cows have been grazing where once a clothesline hung, where a garden of purple iris and oriental poppies made an annual spectacle. In the background, ice-blue sky. Two leafless apple trees, which, untended, have lost their shapeliness. The deadwood is tangled with a snarl of overgrown suckers, the bark scarred with woodpecker holes and burly scabs left from limb falls. In the foreground, a narrow dirt road packed hard with snow, overlapping lines of wheel-track where a few cars and the milk truck have passed. I stood across the road and snapped the picture from my yard.

That ruin was so beautiful to me it might have been the statue of a fallen god. I contemplated the varied patina of aging wood, the damaged fancywork under eaves and over the front door. I never walked inside because the floors, rotted through, had caved into the cellarhole. In the rubble one could see the remains of a lost domestic order—broken skeleton of a cast-iron cookstove, crockery shards, barrel staves, zinc-lidded canning jars, rags of clothing and feedsacks, battered sap buckets, and bullet-punctured tincans. Whoever the ghost neighbors were who had left this junk behind, they called up the America I wanted, a country where everyone was a farmer, no matter what else they did; a country where everyone lived next to nowhere and had to figure out from scratch how to make the land provide; a country where one could shape the future with the ache of one's own labor.

I moved to that borderland just south of the Canadian line in the winter of 1969, when my daughter was three years old and I was twenty-two. Vermont, until then, had meant playland to me. I skied there, often with free passes my father had gotten from advertisers on his radio or television shows. At one mountain I'd walk into the manager's office, tell him whose daughter I was, and walk out with a weekend pass for myself and my boyfriend of the moment. Our family had driven north to a Vermont resort one summer. I don't remember much about the trip. We must have gone swimming and played tennis and taken walks in the woods. What I do remember is that the owners had a dog who had just come home from the animal hospital. They'd made an entertaining joke out of the dog's experience; they'd ask him about his operation, coaxing a little, until he began to bay and whine. Then everyone would laugh at how smart the dog was, understanding so many words; how cute that he remembered his pain. Again and again, as new guests arrived, the loving owners put the little canine through his performance. Again and again, everyone laughed lovingly, exchanging knowing looks. That was the summer when the adult world began to look a bit perverse to me. And once, several years later, during the Summer of Love I had come to Vermont for a weekend with members of my tribe for a planned acid trip in the fern meadows of an isolated section of woods near Killington. That was the summer that planted some seed in my mind that grew into my moving north.

By then I had scandalized my family by dropping out of college, five months pregnant. I had endured and escaped a short and dismal forced marriage, committing myself to an extent I did not yet understand to an experimental life. Much of the experiment had to do with sex. I was unconvinced by fifties propriety in sexual matters—that Doris Day dream of feminine resistance against the Rock Hudson hounding of male seduction. I'd read enough great literature, seen enough Gilbert and Sullivan, Shakespeare and O'Neill—books and theater bestowed on me by parents who hoped to protect me from the evils of popular culture—to know that human passion was a mystery too complicated to be understood by ignoring it. In fumbling teenage attempts at intimacy, I learned fast that the body's responses are not contingent upon the heart or the head. That seemed good—a capacity to celebrate, not curtail. Erich Fromm's book *The Art of Loving* was passing among students like the flu. From it I got the idea that the shame of Adam and Eve was caused not by sex, but by their separateness, by the man and the woman remaining strangers to each other. One thing the sexes had in common was desire. It seemed a place to meet. In high school I admired an older couple (they must have been nineteen) who were openly sexual. Driving around with them one day, I was stunned to see her nestle her hand into his crotch and keep it there even though she knew I had noticed. That openness seemed a thing to strive for. I vowed to myself that the first time I went all the way would be intentional, loving, and unashamed—not a backseat fumble in which the lamb succumbed to the wolf.

But sex, like death, is hard to plan for, no matter what one wants or knows. I stumbled into what I hadn't planned on, got lost in the headlong sensations that a certain good-time boy could bring me to. We were seventeen and the only thing serious about the time we spent together was our passion. We may not have been particularly intelligent, or even in love, but at least we taught each other a thing or two about the pleasure our bodies were capable of. For that, I'm grateful. Our daughter was born on March 21, 1965, the spring after I had graduated from high school.

We spent a few years in Cambridge before the teenage marriage came apart; my husband and brother were students at Boston University. I had everything to prove about being a parent and I knew it. The guys got into psychedelics. Leary and Alpert had just been fired from Harvard. Before that no one had heard of hallucinogens. The drug talk was everywhere—"a structural regression of the ego . . . more in line with Zen thinking . . . mystic states as the function of a flexible ego." People tried blotter, buttons, and speed, as if each were a new album by the Stones. The streets were boiling. There was a cadre of us by then—a circle of tight friends, the circumference as permeable as a cell membrane. Many circles like that. Tribal parties of long-hairs, we met and trusted each other by signs. Weed, hair, clothes weren't fashion, but code to identify cultural revolutionaries working to make life our religion and our art. I read *Summerhill: A Radical Approach to Child Rearing* and began to take motherhood seriously. To love well, for fallible creatures, was a radical act. I felt frightened and exhilarated by the challenge.

My daughter and I ended up settling near the Cold Hollow Mountains, the largest unbroken range in Vermont, situated twenty miles south of the Canadian border. Dairy farm and maple syrup country. Some logging. Much poverty. I worked as a dishwasher at a ski resort—no longer the manager's darling. But there I began to meet other urban refugees who had settled in the hills. Our arrival predated the back-to-the-land movement: more farms were abandoned than working. Land could be bought for two hundred dollars an acre. I owned one savings bond worth a thousand dollars, which my grandmother had given me. With it I made the down payment on a house, barn, and three and a half acres of cleared land on a dirt road. In one direction, I looked out at the forested bowl of mountains where snow could last until July; in the other, at the large empty clapboard house gone to ruin. Our house, not a ruin, was just a dump. In the cellar snored a dinosaur of an old wood furnace used for central heat. There was no bathroom to speak of, a toilet in a closet when we started out; no insulation, no television, no phone. But families had lived this way for decades and I figured so could we.

The first frost came by Labor Day, the last at the end of May. In winter, weeks passed when the mercury didn't climb over zero—the snow and wind grew fierce. Nights fell to twenty, thirty below. In the deepest cold, nothing moved but smoke from the chimneys. Snow packed on the dirt road creaked under foot or wheels. In the gone-by orchard the trees were frozen stiff, icy twig tips clicking in the wind, chimes made of bones. The air itself seemed frozen. In the neighbor's barn, steam heat rose off the backs of stanchioned cows, their breath making warm clouds as they nuzzled in their grain—animals large enough, and enough of them, to keep their own space warm. I worked hard at it—splitting and hauling wood, wearing heavy woolen socks to bed. When pipes froze, I learned to use a blowtorch. Outside the bedroom window, the moon ran its light through giant icicles hanging from the roof. I thought they looked like glass teeth, as if I were trying to sleep inside the mouth of a beast.

In the miserably short summer, I grew gorgeous gardens—never perfectly tended, but productive nonetheless. I froze and canned vegetables, made cider and sauerkraut, dried herbs, raised hens and pigs. Like a cover photo for *Organic Gardening* magazine, I stood beaming knee-deep in comfrey, showing off a cabbage two feet wide, my cheeks as smooth as a butternut squash. I was home. Nothing makes one feel at home, and stay at home, like keeping animals and growing gardens. I was happy in my hardship. I built a desk out of barnboards in the living room, stripped the walls to find, under the plaster and lath, planking three feet wide. I brushed the rough-cut surface with linseed oil to heighten the grain. My daughter Lucinda's room was sprawled with Legos, Tonkas, Play-Doh, broken Crayolas, stuffed and plastic animals, a dripping easel and scattered sheets torn from jumbo newsprint pads. The gone-wild territory of her playing became a sovereign nation with a culture so ingrained it could not be suppressed with my cheerful colonizing dictum, "Time to clean up your room." There was much I could not give her. Yet I felt certain that she'd be all right if I gave her love as bedrock and the skill to deal with change. Nights I'd lie awake in bed, listening to the deep clarity and silence of the north. I'd listen to my heart and wonder if it was all right. When a lady from the church brought us a gift basket of fruit and nuts for Thanksgiving, I realized that we were poor.

I had come for the woods, not merely to live with a view of green felted hills, but to be nestled into that leafy profusion. The northeast woods, not grand, not intimidating like in the West, are comforting—the mountains old and worn, thickly green with second-growth forest. A century ago the Vermont hills had been a solid patchwork quilt of farms, houses dotting the tended pastures and meadows, hedgerows and a few marker trees growing along the fencelines. When I lived there, the forest had claimed back the majority of the farmland; stonewalls marked former boundary lines even in the densest woods; weedy roadbeds once used for logging and sugaring made the backcountry accessible. A mile in, one might find an overgrown cellar hole, the yard marked by huge maples and a single black walnut tree, a rose garden taken over by ragweed, daylilies tangled with timothy. In my own neighborhood there had been a sawmill, tannery, schoolhouse, and a Poor Farm with a barracks-like dormitory—all now vacant and ramshackle. The town had started in 1800, population thirty-six, and by 1859 had peaked at fifteen hundred. Much of the land was clear-cut during those sixty years, white pine six feet across logged off. The tallest and straightest trees went to ship builders; much of the rest were cut in segments and smoldered underground to make charcoal for industrial England. "The Iron Age was necessarily a Wood Age too," wrote Eric Sloane, "for our forests were stripped to make charcoal, then the only smelting fuel." What lumber remained was used for local building, or burned for potash, which was leached out and rendered into soap. French Canadians and Irish refugees had come to settle, raised turkeys and cows, banded together to drive them two hundred miles to market in Boston. And almost just as quickly the population had drained away. Many left to join the Gold Rush in the West; many died in the Civil War. In 1970, the population just over six hundred, someone painted on the broad side of a barn, BAKERSFIELD CLOSED DUE TO LACK OF INTEREST. Those who remained were either families who had accumulated land wealth by working a farm for several generations or those too poor and discouraged to try again somewhere else.

The maple trees generally fared better than the evergreens, since they produced a lucrative cash crop while alive. For two months of backbreaking woods work in the spring, a family could earn a large portion of its annual income from selling maple syrup. Without that crop, most of the farms would have long since gone the way of the sawmill and tannery. A tended sugarbush makes elegant woods; competing trees thinned out, the crowns of maple spread wide into the open space, making a canopy that shelters the ground. Underneath, islands of shoulder-high ferns proliferate and the leaf mold sends forth a scattering of trout lilies, trillium, and spring beauties—ephemeral blooms always a gift in rough terrain.

What I hadn't planned on during the quiet first years of that decade was community. Musicians, artists, writers, and scientists who'd left college or careers to strip down to essentials were setting up homesteads back in the hills. They bought up ramshackle places, cleared backlots, threw work parties and pig roasts when they needed help raising beams and walls. They turned barns into houses and houses into barns. They jammed, playing blues and bluegrass with the locals, got hired on farms, or a few with the means did the hiring. One musician, a high-school band director, had been fired because he taught the students to play "Sergeant Pepper's Lonely Hearts Club Band." A zoologist kept seagulls in his haybarn, thinking he might get around to completing his dissertation—something about how the red spot on a herring gull's beak is a code telling their babies where to peck for food. There were other children being raised in free-spirited households and communes. One group called themselves the Dreamers. They used to visit the local family planning clinic to get free condoms, which they used for air locks on jugs of home-brew. There were the ones we called "the bad hippies" who stole the firewood out of our yard; a Catholic priest who'd left the church to marry a Cherokee social worker; a woman who'd lived in an urban feminist collective and left to marry a leftist pediatrician who had worked the medical tents at the Democratic Convention in Chicago. Dreamers all, and we kept dreaming. We started a parent cooperative school, a natural foods co-op, a madrigal group, a sitting meditation circle, jug bands, jazz bands, and farming collectives. And there was visiting, lots of laid-back unannounced visiting over coffee and joints, while the children and the music played on. There were games of hide-and-seek in the woods, adults and children playing together; there were love affairs and domestic rearrangements. Everyone seemed to have time for this sociability, though most of us had no money. No one had moved there for a job. That was the point. To take time into our own hands, to rethink our lives right down to their family and economic basis.

In the early seventies, War on Poverty money began to flow into the county and a number of us found work on the public dollar. After having done time as a dishwasher, waitress, farm worker, linotype operator, and free-school teacher, I got hired to be a family planning worker for the clinic opening in the county seat. We set up shop once a month in the hallway and emergency room of a small hospital. The doctors and staff were volunteers. Not until 1972 were unmarried women legally eligible for contraception. Abortion was available only in New York. The clinic was controversial, but Christian fundamentalists had not yet started picketing, harassing patients, or bombing medical facilities. Much of the clinic's public rhetoric spoke of poverty and "family planning." We were morally defensive, citing the neediest case histories—a Catholic woman who'd had fourteen pregnancies by the age of twenty-nine, who had nine living children, an unemployed farm worker for a husband, and a physician ethically opposed to contraception. But the majority of the patients were single women and many were teenagers. Though we couldn't say so publicly, most of the clinic workers believed these women were entitled to a good sex life.

This job didn't help my reputation with the more traditional locals. Rumors came back to me, as they do in small towns—the matriarch of the most respected farm family in town saying, "She has a different man every night at her house," another calling our remote neighborhood "the red-light district." At the time, three single women lived in isolated houses several miles apart and the snowplow driver, who was a family man, a fiddle player and our friend, used to stop by to visit. Any one of us would brew up coffee and chat away a good half hour on his timecard. I had my share of sexual friendships in those years and most of them, in memory, I treasure. But no lover ever became a coparent; I think I resisted that because so much was at stake for me in being a mother. I didn't trust anyone as much as I trusted myself. And I believed (though this is difficult now to own up to) that monogamy was about as noble an ideal as totalitarianism. I wanted to earn the respect of country people, and I thought I could do it by working hard for what I wanted and by being a good mother. But certain cultural borders seemed unbridgeable, and clearly the idea of sexual autonomy as a morally responsible choice created one such boundary.

A few times during the decade I lived in the north, I worked in the woods. These jobs came as a great relief, usually after a funding cut meant I'd been laid off from what had seemed a more permanent job. The relief was not only economic, but a period of healing from the public tensions that women's health work increasingly entailed. I spent one spring near the end of that period working the sugaring season at the zoologists's farm. Actually three couples had bought the place, but (typical of the fluidity of the times) only three of those six individuals remained. Two of them were former zoologists (one—the gull guy), now raising families and sheep, odd-jobbing, and taking a good portion of their annual income out of the trees.

We started on the first of March. At sunrise the temperature was still below zero—cold for March, even there. But layering up to work outdoors was a sign of spring, even if the robins were a long way off. The workhorses had grown woolly and cantankerous from a hard winter. Thornette and Joker were not a well-matched team.

They had never worked together before, and Joker, a seventeen-year-old stocky black with a white blaze, had a bad reputation. He was wild, prone to prancing or bolting when what was needed was a steady pace. Thornette, a younger Belgian mare, preferred to nap on the job. We'd load the sleigh with firewood, then whip and whoop; she'd just stand there thigh-deep in crusty snow until we unloaded half of the burden. In harness together, Joker grew agitated, dancing and straining in the traces, while Thornette drooped in passive resistance. After several days of this, with the sun warming and the snow softening, the horses began to accept the inevitable: that they would have to work and that they would have to do so together—and they found a rhythm to match each other. Some early American farm machinery, reapers and combines, hitched sixteen or more horses together in harness. It's difficult to imagine how a contract was negotiated among so many equine personalities. But horses are herd animals, and so they are genetically prepared to work out their differences.

The sap didn't run until March 22, but we filled the weeks with hard days of labor—shimming the storage tank in the East Woods, gathering sled loads of firewood from the North Woods, adjusting and repairing the harnesses, drilling the tapholes (from one to eight taps per tree, depending on its girth), setting the spouts, and distributing thirty-five hundred lidded buckets throughout the woods. The ride was rough—stones, holes, and hummocks in the woods road or the natural tilt of the land pitching us off the sled and into the snow, stacks of buckets rolling down the hill. A bellyband or buckle, one of the traces or reins would break and someone would run back to the barn for the stuff to fix it, others heading indoors for coffee to wait out another delay. Conversation drifted from the weather, to gossip, to the owners' low-voiced hashing over of decisions—about a second mortgage, weighing the idea of setting up a land trust instead of private ownership, talk of a betrayal, arguments, the couple who'd left. For all the difficulties of their situation, they spoke with satisfaction of feeling closer to life than when they had studied it as scientists.

We waited and waited for the trees to loosen their juice. For sap to run sugar maples need warm sunny days and freezing nights. We had cold, cold, cold. Everything hip-deep in snow. We teamed out together into the sugarbush, the horses breaking roads through the snow. Then we fanned out separately to hang the buckets on the trees, sliding on lids to protect the sap from dirt, twigs, and rain, each one of us alone with thoughts and quiet. Then some slender music would drift up the hillside—birdcall, jangle of tugs, creak of sled-runners, rapping of stick against metal to separate the stacked buckets, birdsong of children arriving home from school. We found a porcupine den in a hollow tree in the Home Woods. Piss and shit by the entrance, twigs stripped bare and dropped out onto the snow, not a single pawprint farther than two feet from the tree, the creature's disgruntled assessment of the weather matching our own. Bird nests hung in the leafless trees like tangles in gray hair. Then we saw two robins, new orange against the black-and-white winter landscape (dark tree trunks against unmarred snow), and the mountains went pink in a bright sunset signaling a cold, clear night ahead and, we hoped, the necessary sunny day.

On the first day of gathering, the best tree in the bush had eight buckets all full, others had only an inch or two. We gathered the Home Woods, Heartbreak Hill, the Old Orchard, the names inherited from the family who had worked the sugarbush before us. Only a dozen people in the world know the names given to these clusters of trees, and they don't show up on any map, the names born from working, useful as tools. Trees are fifty years old before they are tapped; the best ones are two or three times that old. Someone who works the sugarbush for years gets to know how each tree runs, its relative productivity consistent over decades. The sap looks like clean water, tastes slightly sweet, and does not feel sticky. To make a gallon of maple syrup takes forty gallons of sap. We slogged through the snow each carrying two five-gallon pails, unhooked each bucket from the tree, poured the sap from bucket to pail, lugged pails from tree to tree until full, then to the steel tub on the sled, then teaming up to the next cluster of trees, and when the tub was full making a run to the gathering tank from which the sap would be piped downhill to the sugarhouse. We gathered nine tubs of sap and the first syrup came off Fancy, the highest grade, as light in color as clover honey.

Good sap runs come on only a handful of days each spring. By the time the trees bud, the sap is no good. If the day is too warm, the sap sours in the bucket. In the sugarhouse sap is boiled down on a wood-fired evaporator—the arch—which eats four-foot lengths of wood and sends billows of sweet steam out through the vented roof. On the good days we worked twelve backbreaking hours, gathering all morning, grading and canning the syrup into the night, and pasting on hand-lettered labels: HOME FARM: VERMONT MAPLE SYRUP. The rest of the time we waited, gathered firewood, and collected drizzle. In a season, an average sugar maple gives ten gallons of sap, some give as much as eighty gallons. Having set thirty-five hundred taps, we did our share of slogging and lugging. Some days other neighbors and friends would come by to help for an hour or two, taking home a quart of syrup in trade. We had more visitors as the snow gave way to mud, the sled to a wagon, and we could finally start the day without long johns, the seasonal milepost that didn't come until April 18.

Spring takes its time in the north. Old-timers still talk about the year it never came, 1816, the year with no summer, when it snowed in July and one farmer reportedly saved his cornfield by cutting and burning pine trees around it day and night. This year spring came, though it was in no hurry. One week we saw the Canadian geese return from their winter migration, and the next a few green shoots began to pierce the leaf rot on the forest floor. The horses shed their winter coats in scrappy patches. A woodchuck ventured out of its hole, then baby rabbits, then the green began to leak up the hillsides as if slow capillary action were transforming meadow, then pasture, then foothill, then slope—the mountains holding their gray expressions until June. The last sap of the spring is called the frog run because it coincides with the first nightsongs of peepers. Its flavor is poor, bearing the woody bitterness of new buds. During cleanup at the end of April, restacking the buckets, pulling out the taps to let the drill holes heal, we found the first trout lilies in bloom, little yellow trumpets hanging amidst their fish-speckled leaves.

Now, reflecting back on that period, I find myself looking for possible meanings and for the reasons I left. I used to have a recurring dream there in which I lived in a dilapidated house, depressing in its demands for constant repair that I could not afford and did not have the skill to tackle alone. It was always winter in the dream; the furniture was spare and tattered; cold seeped through the seams around windows and doors; ice worked its way under the roofing, then melted and seeped around the chimney; the ceiling was marked with a spreading creosote stain. I dragged myself through room after room, exhausted, fearful that this house of entropy would collapse. I opened a door expecting to find more of the same and instead entered a luxurious library—the walls lined with bookshelves, hardbacks with gold-lettered spines stacked to the ceiling, a mahogany ladder on runners, deep oxblood-red leather chairs, Persian rugs, an oak desk on which a brass lamp sat glowing. Each time I dreamed this room, I experienced the same shock in finding it. How could it have been here in my house all along without my knowing it? Why did I live in ruin when I owned such riches?

Our time in the north was not an idyll. I found myself longing, on my own behalf and on Lucinda's, for the cultural dimension we'd left behind. We had to drive an hour and a half (often enough through snow and ice) to get to a movie, a concert, a decent library, or a fancy dessert. The alternative school went only to grade six and the parents who'd run it were too overworked to start another for the upper grades. The open classroom experience had given our kids exceptional social skills and creativity. In math and science, they were shaky. My daughter spent two years at the public middle school, where she was the only kid with brown bread in her lunch box. She took her share of grief for that and other evidence of her family's difference, but she still managed to be a gifted student. With all the talent sequestered in the hills, we found private teachers for piano, ballet, and riding lessons. But as high school approached, I grew leery of the patchwork nature of her education. Most local kids were raised to work on farms or join the army. Only two or three each year went to college; no one at the high school expected more. Luckily we were poor enough for her to receive scholarship offers from several private schools. I hoped that she'd choose an experimental one, but she said, "No more hippie schools, Mom," and we packed her off to a traditional bastion of the New England elite.

For myself, though I never stopped imagining that I could be a full-time farmer, working the land was either a hobby or a stopgap job. My public health career burned out the year that federal money for sexually transmitted diseases (a hush-hush budget item even fifteen years ago) was diverted into the high-profile campaign to fight a nonexistent swine flu epidemic. I ended the seventies in an unhappy relationship, made the mistake of thinking a material solution would solve emotional problems, and sold my farm to buy one with my live-in love. We struggled for a few years to make that arrangement work. In my imaginative life, intimate relationship is central: I am constantly falling in love and living out the years in dynamic connection with a loved one. Yet by midlife a theme emerges from one's experience, which may be at odds with what one has imagined. I'm surprised to see how peripheral intimate relationships have been for me, coming and going like jobs, addresses, and seasons. What sense of continuity and connectedness I've known has come from being a mother, a writer, a gardener, and from friendship. I suppose my old neighbors would continue to find my experience either shocking or sad. I moved away from farm country to a small city that offered a good bakery, several bookstores, an ocean view, a university, walkable streets, and neighbors I did not know. It was a dark time. I was weighed down with grief for what I'd left. In a journal I wrote this entry: "*Skototropism,* meaning to grow toward darkness; a behavioral trait of vines in the tropical forest that enables them to find trees to climb. They head across the forest floor to the darkest spot, sun-shielded and wet, all their energy focused, an arrow pointed toward survival."

John Daniel

Cuttings

First publication

Sometimes the fallers would be working on a distant slope where we could see them, and when I wasn't wrestling a choker around a log I'd watch them drop the Douglas firs. As a tree toppled and then fell faster, its boughs would sweep back, the whole trunk would flex a little just before it hit the hillside, a flash of wood showing if it broke somewhere. Across the distance the sound came late, and small. The saws sounded like hornets.

The fallers worked in pairs, and they worked slowly. It's a dangerous job—the trees are big, the hills are steep. On any one day they never seemed to advance very far against the front of forest, but they worked slow and steady, and day by day they got the job done. They drove the back roads every morning, they laid the big trees down, they bucked them into standard lengths. All across Weyerhaeuser's Northwest empire, they turned the forest into pickup sticks.

There are forests on the rainy side of the Cascade Range where the best way you can walk is on the trunks of fallen trees. Some of the trunks are thicker through than you are tall. They make a random pathway through devil's club and thimbleberry, one to another and another, leading you nowhere except to more trunks with upthrust roots, more standing moss-coated stubs and skeletal snags, more bigleaf maples and western hemlocks and tall Douglas firs. The bark of the big trees is pocked and charred, and most of them lean, already beginning their eventual fall. The filtered light is clear and deep. The only sound you hear is the stepping of your feet among ferns and seedling trees that grow out of softening sapwood. And when you climb down from the pathway of trunks, your feet sink in to a yielding matrix of moss and needles and rotting wood—trees becoming earth, earth becoming trees, the forest falling and gathering itself, rising from the abundance of its dying.

Up on the landing the steel tower stands a hundred feet tall, a diesel yarder at its base with a reel of heavy cable. When we've set the chokers and scrammed out of the way, the rigging slinger sounds his whistle. The yarder roars, the chokers cinch, and two or three logs start stubbornly up the hill like things alive, plunging and rolling, snagging on stumps and lurching free, dragging and gouging the ground, then dangling in air as they approach the landing, where they're deftly dropped in a neat deck for the waiting trucks. Everything goes to the landing—butt-cuts ten feet through, mature saw logs, buckskin snags, measly pecker-poles, even half-rotted slabs and splintered chunks. Nothing is wasted. The operation scours the hillside, as far as the cables can reach, and by the time we lower the tower and trundle along to a fresh show, only stumps and sticks and boughs are left, patches of sun-struck fern and sorrel, long raw furrows in the barren ground.

Like the sea, like the streams full of salmon, the ancient forest gave plenty—totem poles, tool shafts, bows, fishing floats, baskets, dishes, robes, roots, tubers, medicine. A good red cedar might be felled by a storm, or the people would bring a tree down themselves by burning into its base. They hollowed the trunk with adzes, heated water in the cavity with hot stones, stretched out the softened sides with posts, lashed stern and bowsprit to the hull with cedar rope.

For their houses they split cedar logs into wide boards, tapping horn or hardwood wedges with a hammerstone. And sometimes they split large planks from standing trees and let the trees live on. They still live on. Here and there in the silence of the rainy forest you can find them, you can stand inside those spaces that yielded good wood, where human hands selected a careful portion of what the trees could give.

We started out from Bagby Hot Springs in Mount Hood National Forest. As I remember the trail, it climbed along a stream bed and topped out on a sunny ridge, then turned north along the far ridge flank, easy ups and downs through fir and hemlock, gray cliffs on the right. We walked a day like that, then camped in thicker woods where patches of old snow remained and small sounds stirred around our sleeping bags. In the morning after breakfast we walked on, following the trail toward no certain destination. We climbed for a while, still in trees, and then saw light ahead—a meadow, we thought, or a small lake. We walked into a glare of stumps and piled boughs, sap-smell heavy in the air. We worked around the far edge of the cut, trying to pick up the trail. We found the logging road, of course—dry and dusty white, unearthed boulders by its side—but we never found the trail. We sat on stumps awhile and walked back the way we had come.

I was new to the Northwest then. I'd been hearing about multiple-use on the public lands, and now I knew what multiple-use was. I decided that even a college drop-out could find better things to do than set chokers for a living.

The rain shadow east of the Cascades is the native home of the yellowbellies, ponderosa pines that can measure up to eight feet through and a hundred sixty feet tall. Where they've been left alone they tilt from the earth like great orange arrows, fletched with green, parceled out in a spacious array contrived by shallow soils and periodic sweeps of fire through the centuries. Logging here is usually called selective, like the fires, and sometimes that's exactly what it is. But clearcuts aren't too hard to find. The Forest Service has called them "group selections," and little blowdown patches sold for salvage have a way of expanding into sheared squares. The pine forest stands on gentle terrain. It's easy to get at. By the thirties many of the old yellowbelly groves were gone—*clean-cut,* in the usage of the day, the fat logs hauled out under ten-foot wheels. Now they're skidded out on chokers behind big Cats, and in most of ponderosa country, selective logging means that every thirty years or so the Cats drag out the biggest trees. It's called creaming, or high-grading, and it doesn't take everything. But the forest any kid sees is lesser than the one her father saw, diminishing toward little trees and big stumps, the ancient woods gradually brought down to human scale.

Junipers are stubby trees full of branches, and they often have several trunks. In most of them the grain is twisted, a naturally tendency accentuated by the big Great Basin winds. A man had to walk many dry hills and search many canyons to find a straight-grained tree, or a tree with one straight-grained trunk inside a thicket of outer trunks. He carefully stripped a length of bark to inspect the wood. With chiselstone and hammerstone he notched the top and bottom of the stave he wanted, about four feet long, two-and-a-half inches wide. He went away then, for a few years maybe, while the stave seasoned on the tree. When he came back, if it had seasoned well, without weather-checking, he split it from the tree with a tool of stone or antler. He carved and steamed and worked the stave until it curved in a deep belly and recurved at the ends. He boiled horn for glue, and glued on sinew fibers for strength and spring. He glued on rattlesnake skin to protect the backing, fashioned a grip of wrapped buckskin. He strung the bow with a length of sinew.

One juniper, a huge tree with several great trunks and limbs, shows scars of twelve staves removed. A scar heals as the tree lays in new wood, straight-grained wood laid down where straight-grained wood was taken. One scar shows clear evidence of having yielded four staves in sequence. The harvest interval was probably longer than a human life. In a crotch of one of the tree's big limbs, a hammerstone remains where it was placed.

Mount Adams, Mount Jefferson, Three Sisters, Diamond Peak—it doesn't matter which Cascade mountain you climb. From any of them you see a few singular volcanoes ranging away to north and south, studding an expanse of rolling green going blue in the distance. From most of the peaks you can see a lake, or several lakes. And always, more each year, on both flanks of the range and sometimes high up toward the crest, you can see the white squiggles of advancing roads and the bare geometric patches of sheared ground. From the highways you see mostly trees. From the summits you can see where all those trucks are coming from. And almost every acre in your view is public land, retained in the ownership of the American people, part of a national forest system established a hundred years ago to hold good woodlands in reserve against the aggressions of the timber barons.

Some of the cuts are greening up with a growth of genetically selected Douglas firs, which will yield a forest of identical clones, which will be cropped in sixty or eighty years and the clearcuts planted again, to raise another forest if they can. But many of the cuts are bare and brown, flecked with silver whiskers of culled wood. From this elevation they look neat and trim. Whenever I look down at them I search for a new metaphor. They aren't a quilt, not yet at least, but their clustered patchwork does suggest a farmer's fields. "Cascade crew cut" is a term you sometimes hear. *Mange* is the best that I've been able to do, a mange spreading through the mountains. But mange is scraggly and uneven. These clearcut barrens are too regular, too geometrical and clean-sided. Whatever is making them is working surgically, with fine precision. Mange doesn't know what it's doing to the animal. What's working at these mountains knows exactly what it's doing. As my friend grows older he feels himself turning from a farmer to a forester. He walks his wooded hillside, which about the time that he was born was cleared and planted in crops. Much of the topsoil ran away, the fields were left to scrub, and now he walks among the young trees that are reclaiming the hill. He names their kinds, delighting in their company. "Look at that oak there, isn't it pretty? That'll be an oak for a long time." He tells about a neighbor long ago who swung his dog on one of the wild grape vines, a story that ends badly for the dog but brings laughter to the hillside decades later. Stories grow here like the trees. My friend comes to walk and talk sometimes, and other times he comes to work. Low stumps are visible where he's thinned, the poles and logs hauled out behind his horses, seasoning now in neat piles below. In his mind he sees the cut wood forward to its good uses—fence posts, rafters, fuel for the winter—and the standing forest grows on in his mind too. "If I cut that sassafras," he says, "the little oak might grow." He opens such small spaces for the sun, opens and raises his hillside forest toward the beauty of the big hardwoods that once stood here, sunlight playing in their broad leaves, their roots grown deep in the rich soil of their making.

"No, it ain't pretty," a man said to me once, "but it's the only way to harvest these trees. It don't pay to go in there just for a few." We were standing in the rainy morning outside the Weyerhaeuser time shack. His tin hat battered by years in the woods, a lunch pail and steel thermos of coffee in his hands, he spoke those words with a certainty I remember clearly—just as I remember what a good man he was, how he cussed beautifully and told fine stories and was friendly to a green choker-setter, how he worked with an impossible appetite that left me panting and cussing unbeautifully behind him. I don't remember what I or someone said that drew his response, or whether he was answering some doubt he himself had raised. I only recall the authority of his voice, the rain dripping from his tin hat, and the idling crummies waiting to carry us out the muddy roads from camp, out through the stripped hills to another day of work.

The voice that spoke those words is my voice too. It's in all of us—the voice of practicality and common sense, the voice that understands that ugly things are necessary. It's a voice that values getting a hard job done and making an honest living. It has behind it certain assumptions, certain ideas about progress, economy, and standard of living, and it has behind it the evidence of certain numbers, of payrolls and balance sheets, of rotation cycles and board footage. It is not a heartless voice. It has love for wife and children in it, a concern for their future. It has love for the work itself and the way of life that surrounds the work. And it has at least a tinge of regret for the forest, a sense of beauty and a sorrow at the violation of beauty.

I must have nodded, those years ago, when a good man spoke those words. I didn't argue—against his experience and certainty, I had only a vague uneasiness. Now, I suppose, I would argue, but I know that arguing wouldn't change his mind. As he defined the issue, he saw it truly. Many of us define the issue differently now, and we think we see it truly, and all of us on every side have studies and numbers and ideas to support what we believe. All of us have evidence.

The best evidence, though, is not a number or idea. The land itself is not a number or idea, and the land has an argument to make. Turn off the highway, some rainy day in the Northwest, and drive deep into a national forest on the broad gravel roads and the narrow muddy roads. Drive in the rain through one of the great forests of Earth. Drive past the stands that are left, drive past the gentle fields of little trees and big stumps. Pass the yellow machines at rest, the gravel heaps and sections of culvert pipe, the steel drums here and there, a rusting piece of choker in the ditch. Drive until the country steepens around you, until you come to a sheer mountainside stripped of its trees—you will come to it—where puke-outs have spewed stone rubble across the road, where perhaps the road itself, its work accomplished, has begun to sag and slide.

Stand in the rainfall, look at the stumps, and try to imagine the forest. Imagine the great trees spiring skyward, imagine the creatures weaving their countless strands of energy into a living, shifting tapestry, from deep in the rooted soil through all the reaches of shaded light to the crowning twig-tips with their green cones. The trees are gone. The creatures are gone. And the very genius of these hills, that gathered the rain and changing light of untold seasons, that grew and deepened as it brought forth a green and towering stillness—it too is leaving. It's washing down in gullies to a muddy stream.

Nancy Lord

Two Lakes

First publication

My seventy-seven-year-old father and I sit on tree roots at the edge of the lake, surrounded by bird song and modest numbers of slow-moving mosquitoes. I've offered to take him out, away from the mosquitoes, in the rowboat that sits overturned beside us, but he says he's happy where he is. Ken has flown my mother off the lake in our small float plane; in a few minutes, after delivering her to an airport water lane across the inlet, he'll be back to ferry my father. For the last three late-June days, my parents have visited us at our fish camp, chewing hard-smoked salmon and walking miles of rocky beaches. Now they're on their way, beginning to return to the other side of the continent.

"God's country," my mother called it, a week ago, when I was townside with my parents and she was telling one of my Alaskan friends—a poet who has lived much of his life in the deep quiet and long distance of Alaska's bush—where they were from. She was speaking of New Hampshire, and she meant no irony. She has lived there all her life, and to her that country is endowed with a vast and sublime nature. I was born and lived my first twenty years there, all the time pinched by the smallness of the place, by its sense of having been used up long ago. What I saw around me were dying mill towns, the rivers into which they poured their poisons already dead, the air stinking of sulphur, blank faces of people who had never imagined another life. I wanted out. As soon as I was able, I headed west and then north, to find the space and untrammeled beauty I needed to live within. I don't think of it in terms of God's presence or preference, but it's clear to me that Alaska is pocketed with wild places where one can wonder at the generosity of life and be refreshed.

My father is a man of few words, emotionally reserved. I have, nevertheless, always felt secure in his love, and I sense that he is indeed comfortable in the morning quiet, the wait, the sun just cresting the hill behind us and beaming between trees. His white hair is longish and—at the moment—unruly, sticking up like the ruffled feathers of a bald eagle, and his cheeks, three days unshaved, look like he might have been swiped at by a porcupine. If he seems a little more stooped and frail than when I last saw him, he also looks relaxed, at ease in his life, and on this occasion. He wears his binoculars around his neck; these are part of his outdoors attire, part of what he puts on for his daily walks along the edge of a New Hampshire lake. Yesterday he pointed out the remains of adhesive tape on the side of the glasses—my name, my mother's handwriting. I so clearly remember my pleasure in being allowed to possess them the summer I'd attended a nature camp.

This is the third time my parents have traveled to Alaska, the second time they've come to the fish camp, the first time we've flown them in and off this lake. My father must believe this trip will be his last, if not to Alaska, then at least to share this particular place with us. This is not an easy spot to get to, and the trail from lake to beach cabin is a mile long, wet, and brushy, and, at its end, plunges down a slick, boulder-strewn stream bed. This summer is particularly dry, making travel easy, but when I mention this—what good shape the trail is in—my father looks astonished and shakes his head. The trails he knows back east are built, managed, and maintained, or old roads covered in pine needles. I grew up on such hiking trails in the White Mountains, undeniable thoroughfares, well marked with mileage signs, bridged and protected from erosion, and with other hikers just up ahead and just behind. On those long mindless hikes I used to imagine I was elsewhere, in a wild, uninhabited place where I'd need to find my own way, where I might be surprised at what lay ahead.

How is it that we find our homes, that sometimes these are the places we're born to, and that other times we need to search them out? How many times have I heard Alaskans say that when they first came to this state (or that mountain-rimmed town, or that tucked-away rocky cove) they had the overwhelming sense that they had at last found their home? I suppose people say this elsewhere too, perhaps everywhere, though I have a hard time imagining a person entering an eastern city and making this claim with the same heartfelt enthusiasm. To me, this sense of home-coming has to do with making very elemental connections, with responding through our senses to something we recognize on a visceral level—perhaps only from deep within the DNA. We come from somewhere else, but we recognize, from some remote human memory, the smell of budding cottonwood, the purple brilliance of fireweed fields, the snorting of bears, even the deep silences, the dark of moonless nights. We recognize it, and we want it—we need it. We need it more than we need what we are born to, the familiar, family. We may love our people, but we can't stay with them, not in a place that doesn't touch us on a deep enough level.

"Who cut down the tree?"

My father is studying the stump before us, at the edge of the lake. Who cut it? Ken and I are the only people who come here, certainly the only ones who needed to make room to park an airplane. I tell him we did it, it had to be done. In a forest where dozens of trees blow down every winter and others are felled by beaver, our removal of this one twisted spruce seems to me a small thing.

He acts surprised, nevertheless, that we would alter the landscape.

One tree, a necessity. I'm perhaps defensive. I'm well aware of the legacy of human settlement, the old story. People come to paradise, and then they cut trees, they kill things, they change the land and what grows on it and what can be sustained by it. Then it isn't paradise anymore; it isn't a place they want to stay. But this isn't our story. We don't pretend to leave *no* marks on this land, but we don't leave many.

The flattened stump, it's true, doesn't mimic anything in nature. It betrays our presence, as does the overturned rowboat we hauled up in pieces from the beach, the pack frame hung in another tree, the airplane itself, parked at the end of the lake most of the summer. I think of other stumps in the woods across the lake, rotted and grown over with moss, how it is to walk through those woods and come upon those stumps like ghosts. It's been twenty-five years since people lived back there, in a log cabin on the shore of a smaller lake. They cut house logs and firewood; the height of the stumps—some as high as my head—tells us how deep the snow was those winters. Rather than be offended by the old stumps, we readily accept them as a part of the history of the place, the human history as a part of the natural history. People lived here and are gone. They had a generator, a television, a TV antenna high on a pole. The television is there yet; in its plastic casing it's perhaps the most enduring of what remains. One side of the cabin's rotted roof is caved in, cans are rusted, bedding has been carried away in pieces and threads for the nests of birds.

The woods hold other, even older ghosts. Nearby we've come across the collapsed walls of a trapper's tiny shelter. Among thickets of alders and tangles of devil's club, we've measured out the hollows where an earlier people—the Dena'ina Athabascans—made their semi-subterranean homes in a time before any Europeans even set foot in this part of the country.

I admit I'd feel differently about this place if any of those other people were here now, if the drone of someone's generator carried across the water. Part of the beauty of this place, for me, is the privacy of it, the selfish possession of space. I stare down the length of the lake to mountains that rise as white and towering as cumulus clouds in the distance. There's not a person, as far as I know, between here and there.

I recall an occasion in New Hampshire long ago, one of many hikes in the White Mountains with my family. The trail passed through an area, I was told, of "virgin forest." I remember being very impressed by this, the very concept of a place that had not been disturbed, where the trees had never once been cut. The woods were not remarkable in any way obvious to a child, and yet I walked through in a sort of awe, sure that I was in a sacred, untouched place, a place allowed to find its own perfection.

In Alaska, one takes for granted that most lands are in a natural state, that this is the rule rather than the exception. This is not to say that the forests here are old, or that they aren't dynamic. Glaciers and volcanoes are still formative here, and the forests—a mix of alder, birch, and spruce—are only just developing on thin soil. Likely the land here was quite recently more open than today. From the air it's a patchwork of lakes, bogs, meadows, and woods, the outlines of eutrophied lakes now filled in to bogs, deciduous trees losing sunlight to taller spruce. We know that moose are new to the country, only migrating in when the right mix of food and shelter was available; the time when people on this side used to cross the inlet to hunt moose is still within the living memory of some Dena'ina elders.

Behind us, I show my father a beaver-girdled spruce, the chips at its base as big as crackers. It's hard to imagine how tools as simple as teeth can do that kind of work, and I don't know why a beaver would even take on a pitchy spruce, except perhaps to whittle down and sharpen its incisors. All around the lake the sharp-cut ends of alders glow like white labels, and leafy branches float in the shallows. Long-dead spruce, gray and smooth as flagpoles, stand in shallow water, victims of the beavers' industrious lake raising. A belted kingfisher sits in stately profile at the top of one, then loops into flight, raspy-voiced. Small trout flip among the yellow pond lilies, and I wonder if I shouldn't have urged my father to make a few casts from the rowboat.

"There's a beaver," my father says. Sure enough, one is streaming across the lake, small brown head, V-shaped wake. It crosses in front of us, a hundred feet off. We watch it navigate among lily pads and approach a bank overhung with alders.

My father asks, "Are there beaver houses on the lake, or are they bank beavers?"

I point down the lake. It's just possible to make out an old lodge, one dug out, presumably by bears, a couple of years ago. Across the lake, out of sight in a cove, there's an active one, and around the turn, also out of sight, is another. At the far end, there's one more, alongside the dam that separates lake from creek. There are many beavers here, in this lake and the next one over, and in the new ponds they've built farther down the creek, along the trail. Likely there are more beavers here now than at any time since the first people came through the mountains to the west and began to club them on the head for food and fur. No one has bothered these beavers in a long time.

Every spring we see young beavers in the inlet, as incongruous in the salt water as fish might be in trees. They are there only because there's not room for them in the lakes or ponds they were born to, and they've set off in search of new territory. One day we watched one head up our creek, climbing rocks and slithering through pools; the next day we saw it come back down and plunge again into the sea. It had not found space for another of its kind.

"We have beavers at home, but they're mostly bank beavers," my father says. "You don't see too many houses."

I wonder to myself if this has something to do with a sense of safety, if tucking one's beaver-self inconspicuously under a bank was safer in New Hampshire than building an obvious house. I remember, growing up, learning that beavers were nocturnal animals that came out only at night to feed and work on their dams. At the nature camp I attended we waited patiently in the dark beside a beaver lodge, hoping to catch a glimpse of its residents. When at last a beaver came out, it slapped its tail hard on the water, a warning, and then was gone again. When I arrived in Alaska I'd been surprised to see beavers at all hours, to know them as neither nocturnal nor wary. They commonly swim out to our rowboat to take a look at us; when we had a dog, the beavers and the dog swam together, playing a sort of tag for hours on end. It was many years before I learned that beavers became nocturnal in most of America only after they were nearly hunted and trapped out. They adapted, either learning safe behavior or making a very rapid evolution—survival of those who slept late.

I'm glad that this beaver has shown itself to my father. I had hoped he and my mother would see more wildlife on this visit. Before they came we'd had a couple of sea lions, rolling and diving in the inlet, far from their usual grounds, barking with a sound like foghorns. In another week or so we would sit on the end of the reef as hundreds of beluga whales passed, and we would look into their bulbous white faces as they rolled through the surface and snorted misty phoofing breaths. On the morning of the day my parents arrived Ken and I watched a young brown bear stroll up the beach at low water as we stood in front of our camp. It came to our running line and was puzzled by it, stepping around the two lines and then biting at one. It continued toward us, involved with the line, unaware it was being watched. I noted its pigeon-toed walk, knife-point claws clearly visible with each raised foot, and then Ken said, "How close are we going to let it come?" and we both, together, raised our arms and said, "Here we are. Hello." The bear brought up its head and stepped to the side. Only when it got windward of us, when it must have inhaled a whiff of our unlikely and disconcerting odor, did it suddenly look startled and break into a near-run. Its fur was golden brown, and it moved like something liquid, a smooth pouring of light and texture.

The beaver's recrossing the lake now. Perhaps it fed on underwater weeds, perhaps it was only reconnoitering. In any case, it knows we're here. It looks at us with an indifferent curiosity, like a cat. It dives once, without slapping its tail.

In New Hampshire, my parents are pleased to live now beside a lake that serves as a city water supply. Government owns most of the surrounding land, and trespassing is discouraged. My father skates over the ice in winter and keeps track all year of the bird life that comes and goes. When I visit there we walk the closed roads and an old railroad bed, and he stops to scan the waters for loons and the occasional blue heron. There's broken glass in the water and cairns of beer cans stacked after every sunny weekend, and the last time I was there someone left a used plastic diaper in the middle of the road. My parents now and then foray with garbage bags to pick up litter. They love that lake, but I only think of what it must once have been, when there were deer in the woods instead of people and dogs, bird song and the kerplunkings of turtles off logs instead of the sound of trucks downshifting on the highway.

Always, in the East, ever since I was a child, I felt I was too late; what I valued was already gone. The only bears I saw were chained to platforms, and people stuck peanuts and bubble gum into canisters the bears raised on pulleys. The polished granite basins were fenced off, accessible only for a fee, and bridged, and ramped, and painted with graffiti. There was only that one stand of untouched forest that moved me, and another time, a family visit to a heron rookery on an island. I remember thick forest and tall trees, nests that blocked the sun, screeches and a heavy thudding of wings. The ground was crusted with guano, eggshells, matted feathers, and dead, unfledged birds. I dreamed of this place—primeval territory, a stepping back to the beginning, dark and smelly and wild—for a long time with a sort of awed horror, a longing for deep mystery. I dream of it still.

My parents, during their visit, both remarked about the work Ken and I do, what they refer to as "hard physical labor," as though they can't believe we wouldn't prefer to avoid it. My father's people, I remind myself, came from Welsh coal mining, and I know he feels himself lucky to have advanced from both that and his own father's store clerking to become a physician. On his previous visit, after we had a particularly good day of fishing, he shook his head and said that, for the money, he'd much rather do a couple of hysterectomies.

But fishing's the work we do, what allows us to live here. It's hard at times, and I beat up my body pulling anchors and nets, diving in and out of the boat like a seal, just trying to keep my feet when we work the skiff in breakers that dump green water over the bow. Other days, the inlet's a sunny mill pond, the nets explode with fish, I taste salt on my lips and celebrate a perfect set, a job well done. No fishing day is like any other: always, the tide, the weather, the fish are different; always there is something we can do smarter, something more to look at. We see an eagle snatch a gull in midflight, find a thick piece of Asian bamboo, examine a salmon with deformed, gargantuan, kissy lips.

We live in beach time, a different passage than that measured in cities or towns, by clocks. Always I know the stage of tide and whether the tides are building or falling one day to the next. At night, even at the bottom of sleep, I know the water; I know whether it's coming in or going out, how rough or flat, whether it brings us fine new sand or berms of gravel, or whether it gnaws deeper around the beach rocks. It takes an entire day to walk to the neighbors and borrow a tool, to complete some small job of moving a log or jacking one corner of the cabin. I spend hours mending nets, with only the gulls cruising past, dried rockweed picked and eaten from the web, the snap of hot knots in my callused hands. My thoughts wander the world.

My parents, I suspect, wonder at more than why we choose such a tough line of work. The attractions of our modest cabin are, I expect, largely hidden to them. The walls are plywood, the floor stained with oil from the storage of our outboards, and dead flies tend to accumulate along the back edge of the table. The pots and pans are bent (a bear walked on them, I don't mention), and the only refrigeration comes from cool earth under the cabin. Our clothes are threadbare, rusty with old salmon blood, and our jackets are missing snaps. It's a small, grubby place, and if we lived like this anywhere else in the country we'd be thought poverty-stricken. But this is fish camp, and we're rich with the simple pleasures of collecting agates from the beach, licking the juice of smoked king salmon strips from our fingers, reading in bed while the surf pounds at our doorstep. It takes two hours to heat our hot tub—a horse-watering trough—with a wood fire, and when it rains into the tub we lie with our eyes just at water level and watch the raindrops bounce off the surface. Would I live anywhere else? I can't think where.

The beaver's back again, streaming directly toward us this time. It coasts to a halt, twenty feet off. Only its head extends from the water, its rodent stare and twitchy ears. My father and I sit silently, motionless except for brushing away mosquitoes.

Bored with us, the beaver at last swims away. Though we're still in shadow, the sun has cleared the trees behind us and shines down on the lake with a blue, fresh-water glow. Dragonflies with cellophane wings dip over the surface. In the distance, a woodpecker taps against a tree. I feel the calm, the sense of all being right, and I know it is this same sense my father seeks and finds on his own lake, each time he stops to watch the surface of the water ripple or brighten, or smells a freshness in the breeze. This we have in common, my father and I, our two lakes. Most likely I would never have come to this place, felt the need for what is here, if he hadn't shown me, in his own quiet way, what to look for, not just in lakes but in forests and fields and on the tops of mountains, in myself.

Partway down the lake, something catches my eye, and I point. A moose is swimming across, as smoothly as the beaver but with a higher profile, an ungainly head crossing the water like something being floated over on a platter. Its long narrow ears flick wildly front and back, trying to shake off mosquitoes. The beginnings of antlers show themselves as nobby spikes high on the animal's forehead.

The moose has only just reached the far side, where it stands in the shallows to shake itself like a large dog, when the sound of the plane, and then the plane itself, comes from behind the hill, and then the plane floats in over the lily-strewn neck of the lake and lands.

We hug good-bye and I see my father off, buckled safely in. When all is quiet again, I turn and make my way back down the trail. My mother, I know, will be worrying that I'll be eaten by a bear. Back in New Hampshire, she'll continue to clip any newspaper article that mentions local wildlife—the occasional moose that fixates on someone's cow, an eagle spotted somewhere, a single salmon reintroduced to an urban river—as she has for twenty years, as though this will seduce me back. Homeward, I whistle my bear protection, "The Teddy Bears' Picnic," again and again.

When next I see my parents, it will be on their ground. My father and I will circle their lake and look for birds, and I'll enjoy the looking, perhaps spotting a loon or a heron, listening to the chatter of red-winged blackbirds, poking under dead leaves for the first pink mayflower blossoms. I'll think again of beaver, and how the young ones go out to find new, roomier territory, and I'll be glad to have learned, growing up, what it was I needed in a place, and then have been allowed to have found it. I know that both my parents have only ever wanted me to be happy, and I trust that they understand, if not always why, at least that I am.

Jim Miller

The Valley of the Crane

First publication

I

. . . and so grey-eyed Athene swept through the host of the Achaians, urging them forward into battle . . . and they were like the multitudinous nations of birds winging, of geese, and of cranes, and of swans long-throated in the Asian meadows beside the Kaystrian waters, as this way and that they make their flights in the pride of their wings, then settle in clashing swarms and the whole meadow echoes with them, so did the Greeks from their ships and shelters pour forth unto the plain of Skamandros, thousands of them . . . Homer, *The Iliad,* Book II

As I stepped from the cottonwoods under the last March stars I expected to see cranes, large numbers of cranes. Instead, I saw only the river—black water in the gray pre-dawn. A chilly breeze was blowing and I raised the collar of my jacket as I approached the ruined wooden bridge. The single narrow lane had not seen any traffic in a long time, but the bridge afforded a good view of the country in all directions. Here the river was maybe half a mile wide and divided by several sandbars, the largest of which separated the channel into two parts, and these islands were mostly overgrown with willows and sedges. On either bank the cottonwoods and alders grew thickly in the deep soil of the flood plain. Once these sandy bottomlands knew the moccasins of dancing Pawnee villagers and visiting French *coureur du bois,* the splayed paws of prairie wolves and the autumnal thunder of bison hooves. Now, the valley of the Platte was dedicated largely to agriculture, and otherwise supported only a few reclusive deer and curious opossums, the occasional raccoon or coyote.

For some reason the area around the bridge must have been unattractive to the cranes; perhaps it had served as a vantage point for hunters in the days when cranes were still a game species in Nebraska. Or perhaps some fool had harassed the birds in more recent times—I'd heard about people driving their cars in darkness to the water's edge and then hitting the headlights in order to give their children a close-up view of the roosting cranes. Whatever the reason, I couldn't see a single bird, although the swelling cacophony downstream left little doubt as to their whereabouts—just out of sight, but certainly not trying to hide.

Despite being forewarned, I was unprepared for the sheer volume of their calls, and it was getting louder by the minute. My overall impression was of a riotous free-for-all, out of control, about to explode. It was a din unlike any that I had ever heard, a haunting, otherworldly sound. And it was a sound that had already been heard for ages when this river, the Platte River, was born.

For 60 million years, the call of the sandhill crane has echoed across the world's wetlands and waterways, and it's been heard in North America for at least 9 million years. Sandhill cranes, the oldest living bird species, have seen the violent birthing of entire mountain ranges, and then watched these same massifs experience slow death at the hands of wind and rain. These enduring birds have witnessed the ebb and flow of vast seas of water and ice. Long before man first took feeble steps on two legs, or raised a rock in anger, sandhills were already ancient. Many species that were once contemporaries of sandhill cranes now survive only as fossils in museum collections or as hatch marks on geologic timelines. Today, cranes occur on every continent except South America, but of the fourteen extant species, most are rare, including the only other North American species, the highly endangered whooping crane. Still, sandhills survive in great numbers. And each spring 80 percent of the world's population, half a million strong, descend on an eighty-mile stretch of the Platte River in south-central Nebraska.

The sun had not yet broken the horizon when the first cranes began to rise from their riverine night roost. A few isolated groups ascended at first and then gradually they increased in frequency, taking off to the southeast and into the wind. While an entire roosting flock numbers in the thousands, I estimated most of these groups to be about fifty or sixty birds. Once airborne, the flocks scattered to all points of the compass. One after another, in an endless procession they rose. Some flocks wheeling and turning in such a tight circle that the lead birds were flying in the opposite direction from the cranes bringing up the rear, their wings nearly touching. Occasionally there would be a lull in take-off activity accompanied by a decrease in the volume of calls, and I thought that perhaps I had seen the last. But soon the general clamor would again rise in volume and yet another bunch would take to the wing.

The formations appeared quite fluid with individuals shifting and trading positions—heads thrust forward, necks straight, and legs trailing. Some angled overhead, flying low but never directly upriver, and I could see individual birds in dusky gray plumage and hear distinct voices clearly as they passed. The typical call was a ratchety three-note trill. My friend Howard, who's read everything on cranes from the popular literature to the ornithological journals, but insists that he's learned the most by just watching, told me that the birds mate for life and that through their incessant calling are able to keep track of one another in all the commotion, at least that's the idea.

Indeed, crane music plays an important role in mediating many social interactions. Calls are used to advertise territories and to coordinate take-offs and landings, in pair bonding and pair maintenance, to signal the presence of a potential threat, and to synchronously bring pair members into sexual readiness. The sandhill crane is uniquely equipped to produce calls with subtle harmonic nuances. The trachea, or windpipe, of a typical adult is about forty-eight inches long, more than twice the length of its neck, and this remarkable piece of sandhill anatomy allows the bird to produce a rich variety of vocalizations at a fairly high volume.

Now and then I'd see a lone crane flying back and forth, apparently seeking a familiar answer to its forlorn cries. According to Howard, when mates become separated or if a juvenile loses its parents, the birds will search in earnest until the family is reunited. My heart went out to these loners—I felt as though I'd been through this sort of thing myself a time or two.

The sun was up now and activity began to wane. I made my way back through the cottonwoods, periodically looking up to catch a glimpse of a few passing stragglers.

II

The Platte, called by the Otoes Ne-braska, (Flat river, or water) is, as its name imports, almost uniformly broad and shoal. It is fordable at almost any place, except when swollen by freshets, which occur in the Spring season, from melting of snow . . . its bed is composed almost exclusively of sand, forming innumerable bars . . . Large herds of bison were in every direction . . . blackening the whole surface of the country through which we passed.

Edwin James, botanist and geologist for the 1820 expedition of Major Stephen H. Long

"Check it out!"

It was mid-afternoon and I had connected with Howard. He was pointing to a long, undulating flock, circling just above the tall grass about half a mile out. Not cranes this time. Howard stopped the pickup and poked his 10 × 50 Redfields out of the driver's side. He was a big, red-bearded man, maybe six-foot-five, and any repositioning in the cramped cab was an effort attended by a certain amount of grunting and groaning.

"White-fronted geese."

We'd been driving for several hours through an area called the

Rainwater Basin, which covers 4,200 square miles in central Nebraska just south of the Platte River. It's a mosaic of private agricultural land, used intensively for dryland farming and deep well irrigation, as well as grasslands, wetlands, a wildlife refuge, and forty-five WPAs (waterfowl production areas). Administrated by the U.S. Fish and Wildlife Service, these scattered parcels consist of wet meadows and uncultivated fields, some flooded to form expansive, shallow lakes that serve as critical staging areas for between 7 million and 9 million geese, ducks, and shorebirds on their way north during spring migration. Howard was giving me the grand tour.

It was a little past three when we turned north into one of these WPAs and began zigzagging our way slowly across a grid of gravel roads. Just as we passed a cottonwood that was showing the first green buds of the year, I glimpsed a Swainson's hawk quick-diving into an irrigation ditch adjacent to the road, out of sight. We'd been seeing quite a few raptors all day—mainly Swainson's and harriers, but more than a few redtails and several eagles, both golden and bald.

"Good Lord."

Howard stopped the truck on a one-lane causeway, flooded meadows on either side. On the left, coots bobbed close to the road. But about halfway out, the lake on the right turned white from shore to shore.

"Snow geese. There must be 20,000 of them."

I stepped out of the cab and into ankle-deep mud. Another couple of feet and it would have been knee-deep water. Howard was right, this avian carpet was about 80 percent snow geese, but through the binoculars I could see that at least half a dozen other waterfowl species were also represented. We stood and stared for about fifteen minutes, when I noticed a Chevy sedan sitting behind us. The couple inside were waiting patiently. Waiting was their only option unless they wanted to drive about a quarter-mile in reverse. We moved on.

Howard and I first met in Boulder, Colorado, in the early 1980s and became fast friends. I was a house painter at the time, and Howard was a finish carpenter and custom furniture maker. One of the best. He moved back to his native Nebraska in 1985 and married a local girl, Drew. Two wise and well-considered choices. He wasn't bringing down the same kind of money that he'd been accustomed to in upscale Boulder, but that was okay. He'd inherited a little cottage and a piece of bottomland on the Platte. An intelligent and down-to-earth wife (and damned pretty), low overhead, working at a craft he enjoys, plenty of free time—all in all, success. With the river pretty much in his backyard, he'd taken quite an interest in the Platte ("the great lost river" as he calls it), and especially in the cranes, the same cranes that he largely took for granted as a kid.

As we bounced along, I thought of the bridge and turned to Howard.

"Why the Platte?"

Howard smiled.

"Why the great lost river? Picture an hourglass. These birds come in from Texas, New Mexico, Mexico, the Gulf coast, ultimately bound for their breeding grounds on the northern plains or on the arctic coast from Canada to Siberia, depending on which subspecies we're talking about. Three subspecies of sandhills share the Platte River Valley. Mostly the lesser, but also the Canadian and the greater sandhill. They come together to rest and build up fat reserves, maybe 10 percent of their body weight in a month, for the trip north and for breeding. It's a long trip, maybe 6,000 miles. They need two things—a reliable source of food and a safe place to roost between meals."

I could tell that Howard, like a practiced university hall lecturer, had given this spiel a time or two, and that, unlike most of the lecturers that I'd been exposed to, he enjoyed giving it.

"They used to rely on the marshes and wet meadows along the river, but those are mostly gone now—no money in wetlands. But the fact that cranes are opportunists has allowed them to continue making a living around here. It's kind of ironic that one of the land use practices that's largely to blame for bleeding that river dry, namely agriculture, has also provided an alternate food source. Today the cranes feed on waste grain for the bulk of their diet, and the farmers don't mind because the birds mainly take what the cattle leave behind. But they still need the protein and minerals that are essential for successful reproduction, and can only get that from the few marshes that are left. Protein in the form of invertebrates such as worms, snails, and grubs, and minerals, especially calcium, in the form of precipitates."

We were beginning to see cranes in the cornfields again. A flock passed high overhead, navigating unseen currents. Howard leaned over the steering wheel and looked up through the windshield, straining to get a better view.

"They say that the crane formations were the inspiration for Mercury when he made up the Greek alphabet."

According to Howard, the birds left the river at sunrise to feed in the fields until about ten in the morning, then retired to more secluded areas and lazed away the day until mid-afternoon, when they again foraged until returning to their river roost around sunset.

"We can't afford to lose any more of those wetlands—not if we have any sense of responsibility to these birds."

And a host of other species, plant and animal. The tone of his voice was more serious.

"We're on the edge now, maybe past the edge." Howard gave the impression that his own fate was tied to that of the cranes, which in a way maybe it is.

"Of course, if they keep bleeding the river, it won't matter anyway. Good Lord."

It was the Platte that pointed the way west for hundreds of thousands of migrants in the middle of the last century, searching for their individual and collective Manifest Destiny. Since then, "the great lost river" has undergone a number of profound transformations. More than forty dams were built in the Platte River Basin, mainly on the North Platte and the mainstem, and this resulted in an 80 percent reduction in flows from presettlement days.

I was acquainted with the type of changes that more than a half-century of building dams and water diversions can cause. A few years back, I worked with some folks at the University of Wyoming on a cooperative research project that focused on the changes along the North Platte, changes caused primarily by the construction of five major reservoirs starting with Pathfinder, completed in 1909, and ending with Glendo in 1957.

Throughout the Platte River Basin, the sequence of events was essentially the same. With large reductions in both peak and annual flows, the river narrowed and cottonwoods invaded the former channel. Historically, snow-melt in the Rockies resulted in large floods that prevented seedlings from becoming established. Early explorers and settlers described the Platte River as a mile wide, an inch deep, and virtually treeless. Spring meltwater carried large amounts of sediment downstream, leading one traveler to remark that the Platte was "too thick to drink and too thin to plow." These large sediment loads gave the Platte a braided character, with multiple channels that were continually shifting and redefining themselves.

But the floods were controlled now, the river much narrower and deeper, and the grassy banks had become a cottonwood-lined corridor across the Great Plains. This corridor permitted the eastern and western faunas, formerly isolated by the barrier of the "Great American Desert," to mix and in some cases to hybridize.

Of course, without floods, many of the gallery forests are gradually dying out because cottonwood seedlings need open patches with water near the surface in order to reproduce. Sediment deposited by the high flows used to serve this purpose. Today, some scientists speculate that the Russian olive, an exotic tree that escaped cultivation and is now colonizing riparian areas throughout the West, will eventually replace the cottonwood as the climax vegetation on the Platte.

Howard explained that the narrowing of the Platte and the encroachment of vegetation caused the cranes to abandon large reaches of the river.

"They roost on sandbars in shallow water, but only where the channel's wide and only where the vista is unobstructed, giving them a sense of security. Careless species don't generally hang around for 60 million years."

Fewer sandbars are created now because of the reduced flows, the incising of the channel, and because the dams trap most of the sediment. Many of the remaining sandbars are being colonized by cottonwood and willows.

The eighty-mile stretch of the Big Bend between Overton and Grand Island remains viable for the birds because of the intensive efforts of groups such as the Audubon Society and the Platte River Whooping Crane Trust. These organizations have purchased approximately 10,000 acres of critical riparian habitat. They mechanically clear the sandbars and attempt to minimize disturbance by limiting human access.

Still, as the cranes are forced to crowd into progressively smaller portions of the river, the chances of the population being drastically reduced by a natural disaster, such as a tornado, or by disease, such as avian cholera, increase greatly. All the while, new plans are being devised for even more impoundments and more diversions, for ways to turn a profit with river water.

"A perforated artery in need of a tourniquet. What kind of a society wants rivers with no water? Good Lord."

III

Our ability to perceive quality in nature begins, as in art, with the pretty. It expands through successive stages of the beautiful to values as yet uncaptured by language. The quality of cranes lies, I think, in this higher gamut, as yet beyond the reach of words.

Aldo Leopold, *A Sand County Almanac* ("Marshland Elegy")

I crawled out of the blind and joined Drew sitting in the tall grass and milkweed. I figured that "Drew" was short for something, but for the life of me I couldn't figure out what. She taught at the local middle school and seemed to approach life with a certain wide-eyed curiosity and enthusiasm that, while certainly not limited to teachers, is usually found in the good ones. She was in her early forties and a handsome woman, possessing the type of beauty and self-confidence that neither youth nor plastic surgery can provide. I hoped that Howard realized how damn lucky he was.

We could hear the cranes gathering in the nearby fields but none were coming to the river just yet. We sat quietly. The sun was very low now, giving the Johnson grass a beautiful crimson glow. The Platte was calm and suddenly I was feeling quite fortunate. Fortunate to be in this place, at this time, and with these good people. A dozen cranes passed over the cottonwoods and glided down to the river, just downstream from the blind. Howard poked his head out and motioned for us to join him. The show was about to begin.

The blind was small but well built, as I would expect from my capable friend. It was partially excavated so that, while an adult could stand comfortably inside, only the upper half of the structure was above ground. A plywood pentagon on a concrete slab, maybe sixty square feet in all, with three sides affording a view of the river. One for each of us.

The sun was gone now and light was quickly fading. Here and there, small groups of cranes landed on sandbars, nearby. We could see them, silhouettes in the twilight, tall and graceful, long necks turning this way and that, wary and watchful. More and more flocks began to speckle the sky. One after another, they passed. Some landed in this stretch of the river, while others moved downstream. No one spoke, except for an occasional "Good Lord" from Howard. How many times had he witnessed this spectacle? Dozens? Hundreds? Still, he reacted as though it were the first.

The river was beginning to get crowded. Howard said that there might be 15,000 to 20,000 birds in this stretch before it was all said and done—a typical roosting flock. The sky was now filled with sandhill cranes. Line after line, in all directions, as far as the eye could see. An infinite variety of formations, all with a common destination after a day of foraging—the Platte River. The din from the river was rising in intensity and the trumpeting was deafening. The birds were packed in, separated from one another by only a few feet. Not much space—in addition to being the oldest avian species, the sandhill crane is also one of North America's largest, up to four feet tall with a six-foot wingspan. While standing on submerged sandbars with those long spindly legs, the cranes gave the appearance of walking on water as the congregation stretched across the entire channel.

It was nearly dark. Surely this nightly invasion must be nearing completion. I scanned the sky, straining and squinting to see in the fading light. Nothing had changed. The numbers of incoming flocks had not diminished and, according to Howard, probably wouldn't for a while yet. I felt that I was sharing an experience with others who had gone before. The Pawnee and Sioux with their wild ponies and sun-bleached teepees. The early trappers from Cincinnati and St. Louis, who told of bison herds from horizon to horizon. The pioneering naturalist Audubon, who wrote of endless processions of passenger pigeons, a single flock darkening the skies for three days; he painted these doomed birds as he painted the doomed grizzlies and wolves of the grasslands. The Conestoga trekkers of the Oregon Trail, whose wagons took up to two weeks to pass a single prairie dog town. Exaggeration and hyperbole? Who can say? As for the cranes, well, I've seen them for myself.

But numbers alone don't guarantee a future. In North America, we've demonstrated this time and time again, reducing the world's largest animal assemblages, rivaling any in history, to mere curiosities—or worse. Our powers, fantastic; our foresight, limited.

As we left the blind, silent in the cool darkness, I thought of the future. Of the Platte, of crane watchers yet unborn. I thought of sandhill cranes, a miraculously long thread in the fabric of time. Their comings and goings, as Aldo Leopold wrote with characteristic eloquence, are "the ticking of the geologic clock."

We live in a society that's increasingly rootless; fewer and fewer walk in the footsteps of their father or their father's father. In such a world, the spectacle of uncountable numbers of cranes has the capacity to bind generations together, to remind us of what we have in common, rather than what we can count as yours or mine. If we could ever reach beyond trickle-down and trickle-out economics, see beyond our own pathetically short lives, maybe we could rediscover a piece of the lost river, and in the process find something that we've lost in ourselves.

It was nearly midnight. As I climbed into the truck cab, the sound of thousands of cranes voicing that now-familiar ratchety trill echoed loudly in the night air and drowned out the serious little voice in my head. Good Lord.

Peggy Shumaker

Poems

from *American Poetry Review*

The Run of Silvers

If, inside me,
his one cell swam among millions
as if it knew the way,
met the ripe star falling
through my thick clouded sky

then plunged in headlong
renouncing even the tail that allowed it
to make the swim,

then I will tell our new
daughter or son, the one
taking shape, taking over
inside and out
that one afternoon

a run of silvers surged
through Resurrection Bay,
such hurry toward death!

Their potent ballet—muscular
dazzling leaps into the blinding
sparkle of an air they can't breathe—

how they hovered
in blue air—angels, perhaps,
messengers surely

sent to nourish and teach
those of us who might listen . . .

They did not know where
they were going,
they simply found their way.

We did not catch our supper that day.
Glacial spray from crashing falls
chilled our faces, cleared our eyes.

In never-ending daylight
sea otters rocked
belly up on the incoming
tide, swallowing whole
blue mussels
stone pounded
against their chests.

We never had touched each other
in quite such tender danger.

from *Wings Moist from the Other World*

Glacier, Calving

Kachemak Bay, Alaska

We picked through shoulder high
wide blade grasses, listening to the fading
snicker and he-yup of the trainer
posting a skittish foal. The massive
hooves of unshod Morgans turned the soil,
carved hollows to catch timothy seed,
grave half-moons to cradle rain.

A sweet-water stream emptied across rock beach
into Kachemak Bay. Across the way, glaciers
thrust splintered shale into black-shined
moraine, quick rivers charging inside them.
The bay caught the light, threw it back.

Something inside you let go.
You spoke of your father, who never learned to read,
grinding his teeth as you helped his hand
scrawl the letters of his painful name.
You told of the grandmother who wished you
never born, for fear you'd be like him. I held you.
That bitter river coursed.

At sunset we hiked to the rough lumber cabin.
Mud daubers under the eaves

dove for our faces, then banked
and soared over the unfenced field.
All night mosquitoes drilled through sleep—

each slap of little death
awake, and wet, and echoing.

Edward O. Wilson

Biodiversity Threatened

from *The Diversity of Life*

Hidden among the western Andean foothills of Ecuador, a few kilometers from Rio Palenque, there is a small ridge called Centinela. Its name deserves to be synonymous with the silent hemorrhaging of biological diversity. When the forest on the ridge was cut a decade ago, a large number of rare species were extinguished. They went just like that, from full healthy populations to nothing, in a few months. Around the world such anonymous extinctions—call them "centinelan extinctions"—are occurring, not open wounds for all to see and rush to stanch but unfelt internal events, leakages from vital tissue out of sight. Only an accident of timing led to an eyewitness account of the events on Centinela.

The eyewitnesses were Alwyn Gentry and Calaway Dodson, working out of the Missouri Botanical Garden, St. Louis. Gentry and Dodson made their discovery because they are born naturalists. By that I mean they are members of a special cadre of field biologists, those who do not practice science in order to be a success but try to succeed in order to practice science—at least this kind of science. Even if they have to pay for the trip themselves, they will go into the field to do biology, to blend sun and rain with the findings of evolution and to give memory thereby to places like Centinela.

When Gentry and Dodson visited the ridge in 1978, they were the first to explore it botanically. Centinela is only one of a vast number of little-known spurs and saddles arrayed on either side of the Andes for 7,200 kilometers from Panama to Tierra del Fuego. At middle to high elevations in the tropical latitudes these mountain buttresses are covered by cloud forests. A traverse reveals that they are ecological islands, closed off above by the treeless paramos, surrounded below by the lowland rain forests, and segregated from one another by deep mountain valleys. Like conventional islands in the ocean, they tend to evolve their own species of plants and animals, which are then the endemics of that place, found nowhere else or at most in a few nearby localities. On Centinela Gentry and Dodson discovered about 90 such plant species, mostly herbaceous forms growing under the forest canopy, along with orchids and other epiphytes on the trunks and branches of trees. Several of the species had black leaves, a highly unusual trait and still a mystery of plant physiology.

In 1978 farmers from the valley below were moving in along a newly built private road and were cutting back the ridge forest. This is standard operating procedure in Ecuador. Fully 96 percent of the forests on the Pacific side have been cleared for agriculture, with little notice taken by conservationists outside Ecuador and no constraining policy imposed by local governments. By 1986 Centinela was completely cleared and planted in cacao and other crops. A few of the endemic plants have persisted in the shade of the cacao trees. Several others hold on in the forest of neighboring ridges, which themselves are in danger of clear-cutting. I don't know if any black-leaved plant species survived.

The revelation of Centinela and a growing list of other such places is that the extinction of species has been much worse than even field biologists, myself included, previously understood. Any number of rare local species are disappearing just beyond the edge of our attention. They enter oblivion like the dead of Gray's *Elegy,* leaving at most a name, a fading echo in a far corner of the world, their genius unused.

Extinction has been much greater even among larger, more conspicuous organisms than generally recognized. During the past ten years, scientists working on fossil birds, especially Storrs Olson, Helen James, and David Steadman, have uncovered evidence of massive destruction of Pacific Island landbirds by the first human colonists centuries before the coming of Europeans. The scientists obtain their data by excavating fossil and subfossil bones wherever the dead birds dropped or were thrown, in dunes, limestone sinkholes, lava tubes, crater lake beds, and archaeological middens. On each of the islands the deposits were mostly laid down from 8,000 years ago up to nearly the present, bracketing the arrival of the Polynesians. They leave little room for doubt that in the outer Pacific in particular, from Tonga in the west to Hawaii in the east, the Polynesians extinguished at least half of the endemic species found upon their arrival.

This vast stretch of Pacific islands was colonized by the Lapita people, ancestors of the modern Polynesian race. They emigrated from their homeland somewhere in the fringing islands of Melanesia or Southeast Asia and spread steadily eastward from archipelago to archipelago. With great daring and probably heavy mortality, they traveled in single outrigger or double canoes across hundreds of kilometers of water. Around 3,000 years ago they settled Fiji, Tonga, and Samoa. Stepping from island to island they finally reached Hawaii, with Easter the most remote of the habitable Pacific islands, as recently as 300 A.D.

The colonists subsisted on crops and domestic animals carried in their boats but also, especially in the early days of settlement, whatever edible animals they encountered. They ate fish, turtles, and a profusion of bird species that had never seen a large predator and were easily caught, including doves, pigeons, crakes, rails, starlings, and others whose remains are only now coming to light. Many of the species were endemics, found only on the islands discovered by the Lapita. The voyagers ate their way through the Polynesian fauna. On Eua, in present-day Tonga, twenty-five species lived in the forests when the colonists arrived around 1000 B.C., but only eight survive today. Nearly every island across the Pacific was home to several endemic species of flightless rails before the Polynesian occupation. Today populations survive only on New Zealand and on Henderson, an uninhabited coral island 190 kilometers northeast of Pitcairn. It used to be thought that Henderson was one of the few virgin habitable islands of any size left in the world, never occupied by human beings. But recently discovered artifacts reveal that Polynesians colonized Henderson, then abandoned it, probably because they consumed the birds to less than sustainable levels. On this and other small islands lacking arable soil, birds were the most readily available source of protein. The colonists drove the populations down, erasing some species in the process, then either starved or sailed on.

Hawaii, last of the Edens of Polynesia, sustained the greatest damage measured by lost evolutionary products. When European settlers arrived after Captain Cook's visit in 1778, there were approximately fifty native species of landbirds. In the following two centuries, one third disappeared. Now we know from bone deposits that another thirty-five species identified with certainty, and very likely twenty other species less well documented, had already been extinguished by the native Hawaiians. Among those identified to date are an eagle similar to the American bald eagle, a flightless ibis, and a strange parliament of owls with short wings and extremely long legs. Most remarkable of all were bizarre flightless forms evolved from ducks but possessing tiny wings, massive legs, and bills resembling the beaks of tortoises. Helen James and Storrs Olson record that

> although they were terrestrial and herbivorous, like geese, we now know from the presence of a duck-like syringeal bulla that these strange birds were derived either from shelducks (Tadornini), or more likely from dabbling ducks (Anatini), quite possibly from the genus *Anas.* They may have had an ecological role similar to that of the large tortoises of the Galápagos and islands of the western Indian Ocean. Because we now recognize three genera and four species of

> these birds, and because they are neither phyletically geese nor functionally ducks, we have coined a new word, *moa-nalo*, as a more convenient general term for all such flightless, goose-like ducks of the Hawaiian Islands.

The surviving native Hawaiian birds are for the most part inconspicuous relicts, small, elusive species restricted to the remnant mountain forests. They are a faint shadow of the eagles, ibises, and moa-nalos that greeted the Polynesian colonists as the Byzantine empire was born and Mayan civilization reached its zenith.

Centinelan extinctions also occurred on other continents and islands as human populations spread outward from Africa and Eurasia. Mankind soon disposed of the large, the slow, and the tasty. In North America 12,000 years ago, just before Paleo-Indian hunter-gatherers came from Siberia across the Bering Strait, the land teemed with large mammals far more diverse than those in any part of the modern world, including Africa. Twelve millennia back may seem like the Age of Dinosaurs, but it was just yesterday by geological standards. Humanity was stirring then, some eight million people alive and many seeking new land. The manufacture of hooks and harpoons for fishing was widespread, along with the cultivation of wild grains and the domestication of dogs. The construction of the first towns, in the Fertile Crescent, lay only a thousand years in the future.

In western North America, just behind the retreating glacial front, the grasslands and copses were an American Serengeti. The vegetation and insects were similar to those alive in the west today—you could have picked the same wildflowers and netted the same butterflies—but the big mammals and birds were spectacularly different. From one spot, say on the edge of riverine forest looking across open terrain, you could have seen herds of horses (the extinct, pre-Spanish kind), long-horned bison, camels, antelopes of several species, and mammoths. There would be glimpses of sabertooth cats, possibly working together in lionish prides, giant dire wolves, and tapirs. Around a dead horse might be gathered the representatives of a full adaptive radiation of scavenging birds: condors, huge condor-like teratorns, carrion storks, eagles, hawks, and vultures, dodging and threatening one another (we know from the species that survived), the smaller birds snatching pieces of meat and waiting for the body to be whittled down enough to be abandoned by their giant competitors.

Some 73 percent of the large mammal genera that lived in the late Pleistocene are extinct. (In South America the number is 80 percent.) A comparable number of genera of the largest birds are also extinct. The collapse of diversity occurred about the same time that the first Paleo-Indian hunters entered the New World, 12,000 to 11,000 years ago, and then spread southward at an average rate of 16 kilometers a year. It was not a casual, up-and-down event. Mammoths had flourished for two million years to that time and were represented at the end by three species—the Columbian, imperial, and woolly. Within a thousand years all were gone. The ground sloths, another ancient race, vanished almost simultaneously. The last known surviving population, foraging out of caves at the western end of the Grand Canyon, disappeared about 10,000 years ago.

If this were a trial, the Paleo-Indians could be convicted on circumstantial evidence alone, since the coincidence in time is so exact. There is also a strong motive: food. The remains of mammoths, bison, and other large mammals exist in association with human bones, charcoal from fires, and stone weapons of the Clovis culture. These earliest Americans were skilled big-game hunters, and they encountered animals totally unprepared by evolutionary experience for predators of this kind. The birds that became extinct were also those most vulnerable to human hunters. They included eagles and a flightless duck. Still other victims were innocent bystanders: condors, teratorns, and vultures dependent on the newly devastated populations of heavy-bodied mammals.

In defense of the Paleo-Indians, their counsel might argue the existence of another culprit. The end of the Pleistocene was a time not only of human invasion of the New World, but also of climatic warming. As the continental glacier retreated across Canada, forests and grasslands shifted rapidly northward. Changes of this magnitude must have exerted a profound effect on the life and death of local populations. Between 1870 and 1970, by way of comparison, Iceland warmed an average 2°C in the winter and somewhat less in the spring and summer. Two Arctic bird species, the long-tailed duck and the lesser auk, declined to near extinction. At the same time, lapwings, tufted ducks, and several other southern species established themselves on the island and began to breed. There are hints of similar responses during the great Pleistocene decline. Mastodons, for example, were apparently specialized for life in coniferous forests. As this belt of vegetation migrated northward, the proboscideans moved with it. In time they became concentrated along the spruce forest zone in the northeast, then disappeared. Their extinction might have stemmed not only from overkill by hunters but also from fragmentation and reduction of the populations forced by a shrinking habitat.

Let the defense now speak even more forcefully: for tens of millions of years before the coming of man, mammal genera were born and died in large numbers, with the extinction of some accompanied by the origin of others to create a rough long-term balance. The changes were accompanied by climatic shifts much like those in evidence 11,000 years ago, and perhaps they were driven by them. During the last 10 million years, David Webb has pointed out, six major extinction episodes leveled the land mammals of North America. Among them the terminating event of the Pleistocene (the Rancholabrean, named after Rancho La Brea, in California) was not the most catastrophic. The greatest, according to available records,

> was the late Hemphillian (nearly five million years ago) when more than sixty genera of land mammals (of which thirty-five were large, weighing more than 5 kg) disappeared from this continent. The late Rancholabrean extinction pulse (about 10,000 years ago) was the next greatest; over forty genera became extinct, of which nearly all

> were large mammals . . . Some evidence shows that these extinction episodes were correlated with terminations of glacial cycles, when climatic extremes and instability are thought to have reached their maxima.

In at least two of the great extinction spasms, the large browsing mammals were destroyed as the climate deteriorated and the broad continental savannas gave way to steppes. At the end of the Hemphillian, even grazing mammals such as horses, rhinos, and pronghorns precipitously declined.

It may seem that the debate between experts who favor overkill by humans and those who favor climatic change resembles a replay, in a different theater, of the debate over the end of the Age of Dinosaurs. The Paleo-Indians have replaced the giant meteorite in this new drama. Circumstantial evidence is countered by other circumstantial evidence, while both sides search for a smoking gun. The dispute is the product of neither ideology nor clashing personalities. It is the way science at its best is done.

That said, I will lay aside impartiality. I think the overkill theorists have the more convincing argument for what happened in America 10,000 years ago. It seems likely that the Clovis people spread through the New World and demolished most of the large mammals during a hunters' blitzkrieg spanning several centuries. Some of the doomed species hung on here and there for as long as 2,000 years, but the effect was the same: swift destruction, on the scale of evolution that measures normal lifespans of genera and species in millions of years.

There is an additional reason for accepting this verdict provisionally. Paul Martin, who revived the idea in the mid-1960s (a similar proposal had been made a century earlier for the Pleistocene mammals of Europe), called attention to this important circumstance: when human colonists arrived, not only in America but also in New Zealand, Madagascar, and Australia, and whether climate was changing or not, a large part of the megafauna—large mammals, birds, and reptiles—disappeared soon afterward. This collateral evidence has been pieced together by researchers of various persuasions over many years, and it points away from climate and toward people.

Before the coming of man around 1000 A.D., New Zealand was home to moas, large flightless birds unique to the islands. These creatures had ellipsoidal bodies, massive legs, and long necks topped by tiny heads. The first Maoris, arriving from their Polynesian homeland to the north, found about thirteen species ranging in size from that of large turkeys to giants weighing 230 kilograms or more, the latter among the largest birds ever evolved. There had in fact been a moa radiation, filling many niches. It was of the kind normally occupied by medium-sized and large mammals, of which there were none on New Zealand. The Maoris proceeded to butcher the birds in large numbers, leaving conspicuous moa-hunting sites all over New Zealand. On South Island, where most of the remains occur, the deposits are piled with moa bones dating from 1100 to 1300. During this brief interlude the colonists must have obtained a substantial portion of their diet from cooked moa. The peak kills began on the northern part of the island, the Maori point of entry, and spread slowly to the southern districts. Several Europeans claimed to have seen moas in the early 1800s, but the records cannot be verified. Archaeological and public opinion alike hold the Maori hunters responsible, as declared in the popular New Zealand song:

> No moa, no moa,
> In old Ao-tea-roa.
> Can't get 'em.
> They've et 'em;
> They've gone and there aint no moa!

The moa extinction was only part of the New Zealand carnage. A total of twenty other landbirds, including nine additional flightless species, were also wiped out in short order. The tuatara, only living member of the reptilian order Rhynchocephalia, along with unique frogs and flightless insects, were driven to the edge of extinction. Their demise was partly due to the deforestation and firing of large stretches of land. It was hastened by rats that came ashore with the Maoris and bred in huge numbers, against which the autochthons had few natural defenses. In the 1800s the British settlers came upon a beautiful but already much-damaged archipelago. As elsewhere, they proceeded to reduce its biodiversity still further, with a pernicious ingenuity of their own.

Madagascar, fourth largest island in the world, is a small continent virtually on its own. Fully isolated during a northward drift through the Indian Ocean for 70 million years, it was the theater for a biological tragedy like New Zealand's. Despite the proximity of Africa, the first human colonists came to Madagascar not from that continent but from far-off Indonesia. They arrived around 500 A.D. In the centuries immediately following, the megafauna of the great island vanished. No important climatic change accompanied this event; it appears to have been solely the work of the Malagache pioneers. Six to a dozen elephant birds, large and flightless like the moas, disappeared. They included the heaviest birds of recent geological history, *Aepyornis maximus,* a feathered giant almost 3 meters tall with massive legs. Its eggs, the size of soccer balls, can still be pieced together from fragments piled around Malagache archaeological sites. Also erased were seven of the seventeen genera of lemurs, primates most closely related among living mammals to monkeys, apes and men. The lemuroids had undergone a spectacular adaptive radiation on Madagascar. The forms that disappeared were the largest and most interesting of all. One species ran on all fours like a dog, and another had long arms and probably swung through the trees like a gibbon. A third, as big as a gorilla, climbed trees and resembled an oversized koala. Also erased were an aardvark, a pygmy hippopotamus, and two huge land tortoises.

Essentially the same story of destruction was repeated when aboriginal human populations came to Australia about 30,000 years ago, also by way of Indonesia. A number of large mammals soon vanished, including marsupial lions, gigantic kangaroos 2.5 meters (8 feet) tall, and others separately resembling ground sloths, rhinos, tapirs, woodchucks, or, perhaps more accurately expressed, blends of these more familiar types of World Continent fauna. The case for overkill by the aboriginal Australians, however, is complicated by the remote time of their arrival, the longer period during which the extinctions took place, and the scarcity of fossils and kill sites to document the role of hunting. It is also true that Australia experienced a severe arid period from 15,000 to 26,000 years ago, during which the greatest number of animal extinctions occurred. We know that the Australian aboriginals hunted skillfully and burned large stretches of arid land in their search for prey. They still do. Men must have played a role in extinction, but the evidence does not yet allow us to weigh their influence against the drying out of the continent's interior.

In 1989 Jared Diamond summed up for the prosecution in the case of the extinguished megafaunas. Climate, he said, cannot be the principal culprit. He asked: how could changes in climate and vegetation during the retreat of the last glacier lead to mass extinction in North America but not in Europe and Asia? The differences between the land masses were not climatic but the first-time colonization of America, confronting a megafauna with no previous experience of human hunters. And in North America, why did this hecatomb occur at the end of the last glacial cycle, which closed the Quaternary period, but not at the end of the twenty-two glacial cycles preceding it? Again, the difference was the coming of the Paleo-Indian hunters. How, Diamond pressed, did Australia's reptiles manage to survive the prehistoric human invasions better, as did the smaller mammals and birds? And, finally, why did such large forms as the marsupial wolf and giant kangaroos disappear about the same time from both Australia's arid interior and rain forests, as well as from nearby New Guinea's wet mountain forests?

> Quaternary extinctions were selective in space and time because they appear to have occurred at those places and times where naive animals first encountered humans. It is further argued that they were selective in taxa and in victim size because human hunters concentrate on some species (e.g. large mammals and flightless birds) while ignoring other species (e.g., small rodents). It is argued that Qua-

> ternary extinctions befell species in all habitats because humans hunt in all habitats, and human hunters help no species except as an incidental consequence of habitat changes and of removing other species.

"Human hunters help no species." That is a general truth and the key to the whole melancholy situation. As the human wave rolled over the last of the virgin lands like a smothering blanket, Paleo-Indians throughout America, Polynesians across the Pacific, Indonesians into Madagascar, Dutch sailors ashore on Mauritius (to meet and extirpate the dodo), they were constrained by neither knowledge of endemicity nor any ethic of conservation. For them the world must have seemed to stretch forever beyond the horizon. If fruit pigeons and giant tortoises disappear from this island, they will surely be found on the next one. What counts is food today, a healthy family, and tribute for the chief, victory celebrations, rites of passage, feasts. As the Mexican truck driver said who shot one of the last two imperial woodpeckers, largest of all the world's woodpeckers, "It was a great piece of meat."

From prehistory to the present time, the mindless horsemen of the environmental apocalypse have been overkill, habitat destruction, introduction of animals such as rats and goats, and diseases carried by these exotic animals. In prehistory the paramount agents were overkill and exotic animals. In recent centuries, and to an accelerating degree during our generation, habitat destruction is foremost among the lethal forces, followed by the invasion of exotic animals. Each agent strengthens the others in a tightening net of destruction. In the United States, Canada, and Mexico, 1,033 species of fishes are known to have lived entirely in fresh water within recent historical times. Of these, 27 or 3 percent have become extinct within the past hundred years, and another 265 or 26 percent are liable to extinction. They fall into one or the other of the categories utilized by the International Union for Conservation of Nature and Natural Resources (IUCN), which publishes the *Red Data Books:* Extinct, Endangered, Vulnerable, and Rare. The changes that forced them into decline are:

Destruction of physical habitat	73% of species
Displacement by introduced species	68% of species
Alteration of habitat by chemical pollutants	38% of species
Hybridization with other species and subspecies	38% of species
Overharvesting	15% of species

(These figures add up to more than 100 percent because more than one agent impinges on many of the fish populations.) When habitat destruction is defined as both the physical reduction in suitable places to live and the closing of habitats by chemical pollution, then it is found to be an important factor in over 90 percent of the cases. Through a combination of all these factors, the rate of extinction has risen steadily during the past forty years.

In fishes and in all other groups of which we have sufficient knowledge, the depredations were started in prehistory and early historical times and are being pressed with a vengeance by modern generations. Early peoples exterminated most of the big animals on the spot. They also decimated less conspicuous plants and animals on islands and in isolated valleys, lakes, and river systems, where species live in small populations with their backs to the wall. Now it is our turn. Armed with chainsaws and dynamite, we are assaulting the final strongholds of biodiversity—the continents and, to a lesser but growing extent, the seas.

Will it ever be possible to assess the ongoing loss of biological diversity? I cannot imagine a scientific problem of greater immediate importance for humanity. Biologists find it difficult to come up with even an approximate estimate of the hemorrhaging because we know so little about diversity in the first place. Extinction is the most obscure and local of all biological processes. We don't see the last butterfly of its species snatched from the air by a bird or the last orchid of a certain kind killed by the collapse of its supporting tree in some distant mountain forest. We hear that a certain animal or plant is on the edge, perhaps already gone. We return to the last known locality to search, and when no individuals are encountered there year after year we pronounce the species extinct. But hope lingers on. Someone flying a light plane over Louisiana swamps thinks he sees a few ivory-billed woodpeckers start up and glide back down into the foliage. "I'm pretty sure they were ivorybills, not pileated woodpeckers. Saw the white double stripes on the back and the wing bands plain as day." A Bachman's warbler is heard singing somewhere, maybe. A hunter swears he has seen Tasmanian wolves in the scrub forest of Western Australia, but it is probably all fantasy.

In order to know that a given species is truly extinct, you have to know it well, including its exact distribution and favored habitats. You have to look long and hard without result. But we do not know the vast majority of species of organisms well; we have yet to anoint so many as 90 percent of them with scientific names. So biologists agree that it is not possible to give the exact number of species going extinct; we usually turn palms up and say the number is very large. But we can do better than that. Let me start with a generalization: *in the small minority of groups of plants and animals that are well known, extinction is proceeding at a rapid rate, far above prehuman levels. In many cases the level is calamitous: the entire group is threatened.*

To illustrate this principle, I will present a few anecdotes, out of many available: whenever we can focus clearly, we usually see extinction in progress. Then I will take a more theoretical approach, using models of island biogeography, to arrive at an estimate of extinction rates in tropical rain forests, which contain half or more of the world's species of plants and animals. Here are the examples:

- One fifth of the species of birds worldwide have been eliminated in the past two millennia, principally following human occupation of islands. Thus instead of 9,040 species alive today, there probably would have been about 11,000 species if left alone. According to a recent study by the International Council for Bird

Preservation, 11 percent or 1,029 of the surviving species are endangered.

- A total of 164 bird species have been recorded from the Solomon Islands in the southwest Pacific. The *Red Data Book* lists only one as recently extinct. But in fact there have been no records for twelve others since 1953. Most of these are ground nesters vulnerable to predators. Solomon Islanders who know the birds best have stated that at least some of the species were exterminated by imported cats.
- From the 1940s to the 1980s, population densities of migratory songbirds in the mid-Atlantic United States dropped 50 percent, and many species became locally extinct. One cause appears to be the accelerating destruction of the forests of the West Indies, Mexico, and Central and South America, the principal wintering grounds of many of the migrants. The fate of Bachman's warbler will probably befall other North American summer residents if the deforestation continues.
- About 20 percent of the world's freshwater fish species are either extinct or in a state of dangerous decline. The situation is approaching the critical stage in some tropical countries. A recent search for the 266 species of exclusively freshwater fishes of lowland peninsular Malaysia turned up only 122. Lake Lanao on the Philippine Island of Mindanao is famous among evolutionary biologists for the adaptive radiation of cyprinid fishes that occurred exclusively within the confines of the lake. As many as 18 endemic species in three genera were previously known; a recent search found only three species, representing one of the genera. The loss has been attributed to overfishing and competition from newly introduced fish species.
- The most catastrophic extinction episode of recent history may be the destruction of the cichlid fishes of Lake Victoria, which I described earlier as a paradigm of adaptive radiation. From a single ancestral species 300 or more species emanated, filling almost all the major ecological niches of freshwater fishes. In 1959 British

colonists introduced the Nile perch as a sport fish. This huge predator, which grows to nearly 2 meters in length, has drastically reduced the native fish population and extinguished some of the species. It is projected eventually to eliminate more than half of the endemics. The perch affects not only the fishes but the lake ecosystem as a whole. As the alga-feeding cichlids disappear, plant life blooms and decomposes, depleting oxygen in the deeper water and accelerating the decline of cichlids, crustaceans, and other forms of life. A task force of fish biologists observed in 1985, "Never before has man in a single ill advised step placed so many vertebrate species simultaneously at risk of extinction and also, in doing so, threatened a food resource and traditional way of life of riparian dwellers."

- The United States has the largest freshwater mollusk fauna in the world, especially rich in mussels and gill-breathing snails. These species have long been in a steep decline from the damming of rivers, pollution, and the introduction of alien mollusk and other aquatic animals. At least 12 mussel species are now extinct throughout their ranges, and 20 percent of the remainder are endangered. Even where extinction has not yet occurred, the extirpation of local populations is rampant. Lake Erie and the Ohio River system originally held dense populations of 78 different forms; now 19 are extinct and 29 are rare. Muscle [sic] Shoals, a stretch of the Tennessee River in Alabama, once held a fauna of 68 mussel species. Their shells were specialized for life in riffles or shoals, shallow streams with sandy gravel bottoms and rapid currents. When Wilson Dam was constructed in the early 1920s, impounding and deepening the water, 44 of the species were extinguished. In a parallel development, impoundment and pollution have combined to extinguish two genera and 30 species of gill-breathing snails in the Tennessee and nearby Coosa rivers.
- Freshwater and land mollusks are generally vulnerable to extinction because so many are specialized for life in narrow habitats

and unable to move quickly from one place to another. The fate of the tree snails of Tahiti and Moorea illustrates the principle in chilling fashion. Comprising 11 species in the genera *Partula* and *Samoana,* a miniature adaptive radiation in one small place, the snails were recently exterminated by a single species of exotic carnivorous snail. It was folly in the grand manner, a pair of desperate mistakes by people in authority, which unfolded as follows. First, the giant African snail *Achatina fulica* was introduced to the islands as a food animal. Then, when it multiplied enough to become a pest, the carnivorous snail *Euglandina rosea* was introduced to control the *Achatina. Euglandina* itself multiplied prodigiously, advancing along a front at 1.2 kilometers a year. It consumed not only the giant African snail but every native tree snail along the way. The last of the wild tree snails became extinct on Moorea in 1987. On nearby Tahiti the same sequence is now unfolding. And in Hawaii the entire endemic tree-snail genus *Achatinella* is endangered by *Euglandina* and habitat destruction. Twenty-two species are extinct and the remaining 19 are endangered.

- A recent survey by the Center for Plant Conservation revealed that between 213 and 228 plant species, out of a total of about 20,000, are known to have become extinct in the United States. Another 680 species and subspecies are in danger of extinction by the year 2000. About three fourths of these forms occur in only five places: California, Florida, Hawaii, Puerto Rico, and Texas. The predicament of the most endangered species is epitomized by *Banara vanderbiltii.* By 1986 this small tree of the moist limestone forests of Puerto Rico was down to two plants growing on a farm near Bayamon. At the eleventh hour, cuttings were obtained and are now successfully growing in the Fairchild Tropical Garden in Miami.
- In western Germany, the former Federal Republic, 34 percent of 10,290 insect and other invertebrate species were classified as threatened or endangered in 1987. In Austria the figure was 22

percent of 9,694 invertebrate species, and in England 17 percent of 13,741 insect species.

- The fungi of western Europe appear to be in the midst of a mass extinction on at least a local scale. Intensive collecting in selected sites in Germany, Austria, and the Netherlands has revealed a 40 to 50 percent loss in species during the past sixty years. The main cause of the decline appears to be air pollution. Many of the vanished species are mycorrhizal fungi, symbiotic forms that enhance the absorption of nutrients by the root systems of plants. Ecologists have long wondered what would happen to land ecosystems if these fungi were removed, and we will soon find out.

For species on the brink, from birds to fungi, the end can come in two ways. Many, like the Moorean tree snails, are taken out by the metaphorical equivalent of a rifle shot—they are erased but the ecosystem from which they are removed is left intact. Others are destroyed by a holocaust, in which the entire ecosystem perishes.

The distinction between rifle shots and holocausts has special merit in considering the case of the spotted owl (*Strix occidentalis*) of the United States, an endangered form that has been the object of intense national controversy since 1988. Each pair of owls requires about 3 to 8 square kilometers of coniferous forest more than 250 years old. Only this habitat can provide the birds with both enough large hollow trees for nesting and an expanse of open understory for the effective hunting of mice and other small mammals. Within the range of the spotted owl in western Oregon and Washington, the suitable habitat is largely confined to twelve national forests. The controversy was engaged first within the U.S. Forest Service and then the public at large. It was ultimately between loggers, who wanted to continue cutting the primeval forest, and environmentalists determined to protect an endangered species. The major local industry around the owl's range was affected, the financial stakes were high, and the confrontation was emotional. Said the loggers: "Are we really expected to sacrifice thousands of jobs for a handful of birds?" Said the environmentalists: "Must we deprive future generations of a race of birds for a few more years of timber yield?"

Overlooked in the clamor was the fate of an entire habitat, the old-growth coniferous forest, with thousands of other species of plants, animals, and microorganisms, the great majority unstudied and unclassified. Among them are three rare amphibian species, the tailed frog and the Del Norte and Olympic salamanders. Also present is the western yew, *Taxus brevifolia,* source of taxol, one of the most potent anticancer substances ever found. The debate should be framed another way: what else awaits discovery in the old-growth forests of the Pacific Northwest?

The cutting of primeval forest and other disasters, fueled by the demands of growing human populations, are the overriding threat to biological diversity everywhere. But even the data that led to this conclusion, coming as they do mainly from vertebrates and plants, understate the case. The large, conspicuous organisms are the ones most susceptible to rifle shots, to overkill and the introduction of competing organisms. They are of the greatest immediate importance to man and receive the greater part of his malign attention. People hunt deer and pigeons rather than sowbugs and spiders. They cut roads into a forest to harvest Douglas fir, not mosses and fungi.

Not many habitats in the world covering a kilometer contain fewer than a thousand species of plants and animals. Patches of rain forest and coral reef harbor tens of thousands of species, even after they have declined to a remnant of the original wilderness. But when the *entire* habitat is destroyed, almost all of the species are destroyed. Not just eagles and pandas disappear but also the smallest, still uncensused invertebrates, algae, and fungi, the invisible players that make up the foundation of the ecosystem. Conservationists now generally recognize the difference between rifle shots and holocausts. They place emphasis on the preservation of entire habitats and not only the charismatic species within them. They are uncomfortably aware that the last surviving herd of Javan rhinoceros cannot be saved if the remnant woodland in which they live is cleared, that harpy eagles require every scrap of rain forest around them that can be spared from the chainsaw. The relationship is reciprocal: when star species like rhinoceros and eagles are protected, they serve as umbrellas for all the life around them.

And so to threatened and endangered species must be added a growing list of entire ecosystems, comprising masses of species. Here are several deserving immediate attention:

Usambara Mountain forests, Tanzania. Varying widely in elevation and rainfall, the Usambaras contain one of the richest biological communities in East Africa. They protect large numbers of plant and animal species found nowhere else, but their forest cover is declining drastically, having already been cut to half, some 450 square kilometers, between 1954 and 1978. Rapid growth of human populations, more extensive logging, and the takeover of land for agriculture are pressing the last remaining reserves and thousands of species toward extinction.

San Bruno Mountain, California. In this small refuge surrounded by the San Francisco metropolis live a number of federally protected vertebrates, plants, and insects. Some of the species are endemics of the San Francisco peninsula, including the San Bruno elfin butterfly and the San Francisco garter snake. The native fauna and flora are threatened by offroad vehicular traffic, expansion of a quarry, and invasion by eucalyptus, gorse, and other alien plant species.

Oases of the Dead Sea Depression, Israel and Jordan. These humid refuges in a quintessentially desert area, called *ghors,* are isolated tropical ecosystems sustained by freshwater springs. They contain true pockets of an ancient African fauna and flora cut off by the dry terrain of the Jordan Rift Valley. Species that flourish thousands of kilometers to the south are joined here by others restricted to the vicinity of ghors or even to single springs. In 1980 I walked most of the length of Ein Gedi, one of these sites, through the lush bankside vegetation, marveling at the crystalline water of the spring-fed brook, with its endemic cichlid fish and emerald algae. I studied large weaver ants that nest in the banks—a little slice of Africa an hour's drive from Jerusalem. Climbing away from the bank trail for a hundred meters, I was back in the desert terrain of the Middle East. The ghors are of exceptional scientific interest because they bring an African fauna and flora into direct contact with a different set of species that together range from Europe across the Middle East to temperate Asia. The oases are threatened by overgrazing, mining, and commercial development. In an exquisitely symbolic reflection of the region's politics, several are used as minefields.

If species vanish en masse when their isolated habitats collapse, they die even more catastrophically when entire systems are obliterated. The logging of a mountain ridge in the Andes may extinguish scores of species, but logging all such ridges will erase hundreds of thousands. Such broad areas were labeled "hot spots" by Norman Myers in 1988. The emergency-care cases of global conservation, they are defined as areas that both contain large numbers of endemic species and are under extreme threat; their major habitats have been reduced to less than 10 percent of the original cover or are destined to fall that low within one to several decades. Myers has listed eighteen hot spots. Although they collectively occupy a tiny amount of space, only half a percent of the earth's land surface, they are the exclusive home of one fifth of the world's plant species. The hot spots comprise a far-flung array of forests and Mediterranean-type scrubland and are represented on every continent except Antarctica. Each deserves special and immediate mention.

California floristic province. This familiar Mediterranean-climate domain, stretching from southern Oregon to Baja California and recognized by botanists as a separate evolutionary center, contains one fourth of all the plant species found in the United States and Canada combined. Half, or 2,140 species, are found nowhere else in the world. Their environment is being rapidly constricted by urban and agricultural development, especially along the central and southern coasts of California.

Central Chile. South America's preeminent Mediterranean vegetation contains 3,000 plant species, slightly over half of the entire Chilean flora, crowded into only 6 percent of the national territory. The surviving cover is only one third that of the original and unfortunately is located in the most densely populated part of the country. It is being pressed especially hard by rural families, who rely on natural vegetation for fuel and livestock fodder.

The Colombian Chocó. The forest of Colombia's coastal plain and low mountains extends the entire length of the country. The Chocó, as the region is called after the state it includes, is drenched with extreme rainfall and blessed with one of the richest but least explored floras in the world. At present, 3,500 plant species are known but as many as 10,000 may grow there, of which one fourth are estimated to be endemic and a smaller but still substantial fraction are new to science. Since the early 1970s, the Chocó has been relentlessly invaded by timber companies and, to a lesser extent, by poor Colombians hungry for land. The forests are already down to about three quarters of their original cover and are being destroyed at an accelerating rate.

Western Ecuador. The wet forests of the lowlands and foothills of Ecuador west of the Andes, including the small portion that formerly clothed the Centinela ridge, once contained about 10,000 plant species. Of these one quarter, as in the closely similar Chocó region to the north, were endemic. The forests, so notable for the richness of their orchids and other epiphytes, have been almost completely wiped out. They are, in Myers' expression, among the hottest of the hot spots.

> An idea of the former biotic diversity may be gained from the Rio Palenque Science Center at the southern tip of the area, where less than one square kilometer of primary forest survives. In this fragment there are 1200 plant species, 25 percent of them endemic to western Ecuador. As many as 100 of these Rio Palenque species have proved to be new to science; 43 are known only from the site, and a good number exist in the form of just a few individuals, some as a single individual.

Daniel Janzen has referred to these and other species reduced to a population too small to reproduce as the "living dead."

Uplands of western Amazonia. The western reaches of the Amazon Basin stretching in an arc from Colombia south to Bolivia contain what some biologists believe to be the largest fauna and flora of any place on earth. And the richest of the rich in endemic species are the uplands of the region, which form a belt 50 kilometers wide between 500 and 1,500 meters' elevation along the Andean slopes. On each mountain ridge there are still largely unstudied concentrations of unique local plants and animals. The Amazonian uplands, like the western side of the Andes in Colombia and Ecuador, are being rapidly settled. In Ecuador's sector alone the population has grown from 45,000 to about 300,000 during the past forty years. About 65 percent of the upland forests have already been cleared or converted into palm-oil plantations. The loss is projected to approach 90 percent by the year 2000.

Atlantic coast of Brazil. A unique rain forest once reached from Recife southward through Rio de Janeiro to Florianópolis, of which the young Charles Darwin once wrote, "twiners entwining twiners—tresses like hair—beautiful lepidoptera—silence—hosanna—silence well exemplified—lofty tree . . . Wonder, astonishment, & sublime devotion, fill & elevate the mind." That was 1832 when, as naturalist on the *Beagle,* Darwin first put ashore in South America and jotted his impressions in a notebook. The Atlantic forests originally covered about a million square kilometers. Geographically isolated from the Amazonian forests to the north and west, they contain one of the most diverse and distinctive biotas in the world. But Brazil's south Atlantic coast is also the agriculturally most productive and densely populated part of the country. The forests have been reduced to less than 5 percent of the original cover, and that part survives mostly in steep mountainous regions. A good part of this remnant is protected as parks and reserves, a last glimpse of Eden for future generations teeming around it.

Southwestern Ivory Coast. The towering rain forest of the Ivory Coast and adjacent areas of Liberia, a distinct botanical province of West Africa, once covered 160,000 square kilometers. Unrestricted logging and slash-and-burn farming have reduced it to 16,000 square kilometers. What remains is being cleared at the rate of up to 2,000 square kilometers a year. Only the Taï National Park, with 3,300 square kilometers, is officially protected, and even this solitary reserve is under pressure from illegal logging and gold prospecting.

Eastern arc forests of Tanzania. The Usambara forest, described earlier, is one of nine sections of montane forests strung across eastern Tanzania. Isolated to some extent since prehuman times, these habitats are the sites of profuse local evolution. They are the native home, for example, of 18 of the known 20 species of African violets and 16 of the species of wild coffee. The forests are down to half their original cover and shrinking fast from the incursions of Tanzania's exploding population.

Cape floristic province of South Africa. At the southern tip of Africa is a specialized heathland called *fynbos,* which is graced with one of the world's most unusual and diverse floras. In the 89,000 square kilometers of the environment still surviving, 8,600 plant species can be found. Of these, 73 percent exist nowhere else in the world. A third of the fynbos has been lost to agriculture, development, and the incursion of exotic plant species. The remainder is being rapidly fragmented and degraded. Most of the native species occur in local areas of a square kilometer or less in extent. At least 26 are known to be extinct and another 1,500 are rare and threatened, a total exceeding the entire flora of the British Isles. Unless swift action is taken, South Africa will lose a large part of its greatest natural heritage.

Madagascar. Madagascar, the most isolated of the great islands of the world, has a fauna and flora independently evolved to a corresponding degree: 30 primates, all lemurs; reptiles and amphibians that are 90 percent endemic, including two thirds of all the chameleons of the world; and 10,000 plant species of which 80 percent are endemic, including a thousand kinds of orchids. The impoverished Malagasy people have relied heavily on slash-and-burn agriculture on poor rain forest soils to sustain their growing populations, causing them to grind their way through and destroy most of the world-class biological environment they inherited. In 1985 the forest remaining intact was down to a third of the cover encountered by the first colonists fifteen centuries ago. The destruction is accelerating along with population growth, with most of the loss having occurred since 1950.

Lower slopes of the Himalayas. A girdle of lush mountain forest encircles the southern and eastern edges of the Himalayas, from Sikkim in northern India across Nepal and Bhutan to the western provinces of China. It comprises a complex mixture of tropical species of southern origin and temperate species from the north. A seemingly endless succession of deep valleys and knife-edge ridges breaks the fauna and flora into large numbers of local assemblages, containing for example about 9,000 plant species of which 39 percent are limited to the region as a whole. The original extent of the forests was roughly 340,000 square kilometers. Occurring in or near some of the most densely populated regions of the world, the forests are down by two thirds and disappearing quickly through unregulated logging and conversion to farmland.

Western Ghats of India. Along the seaward slopes of the Western Ghat mountains, extending the length of peninsular India, is a zone of tropical forest covering about 17,000 square kilometers. It is home to 4,000 known plant species, of which 40 percent are endemic. The pressure from the expanding local populations is intense, and clearing for timber and agriculture has been rapid. About a third of the cover is gone already, and the remainder is disappearing at a rate of 2–3 percent a year.

Sri Lanka. The wet forests of this island off the southern tip of India are relicts of an ancient, largely vanished floristic province that once covered all of the Indian peninsula. The Sri Lankan remnant itself contains over a thousand plant species, of which half are endemic. With a population density of 260 persons per square kilometer and timber and agricultural land in heavy demand, the forest cover has been reduced to slightly less than 10 percent of its original area. Much of the primary forest growth is limited to a 56-square-kilometer tract within the Sinharaja forest near the southwestern corner of the island. This sector is also the most densely settled part of the island. To make matters worse, most of the local people depend on shifting cultivation and forest products for their livelihood.

Peninsular Malaysia. Most of the Malay peninsula was once covered by tropical forest. It contained at least 8,500 plant species, of which as many as a third were endemic. By the mid-1980s half the forest was gone. Almost all of the remaining lowland sector, the richest repository of diversity, had been degraded to some degree. About a half of the endemic tree species are now classified as endangered or extinct.

Northwestern Borneo. In earlier times Borneo was equated in lore with the perfect image of vast pristine jungle. That image has mostly faded. The forest is being stripped back swiftly, and many of the resident 11,000 plant and uncounted animal species are under siege. The northern third of the island, where biodiversity is deep and plant endemicity approaches 40 percent, has been extensively cleared by logging. In the state of Sarawak, part of Malaysia, the forest cover has been reduced by nearly a half, and most of the remainder has been consigned to timber companies.

The Philippines. This island nation is at the edge of a full-scale biodiversity collapse. Isolated from the Asian mainland but close enough to Indonesia to receive many plant and animal colonists, fragmented into 7,100 islands in a pattern that promotes species formation, the Philippines had evolved a very large fauna and flora with high levels of endemicity. In the past fifty years, two thirds of the forest has been cleared, including all but 8,000 square kilometers of the original lowland cover. From island to island intensive logging was pursued until it became uneconomical, to be followed in lockstep by full agriculture settlement. The demand for new land by a growing population endangers the remaining upland forest. Preserves are planned for 6,450 square kilometers, 2 percent of the nation's land surface. At best the ultimate losses will be heavy. As I write, the Philippine or monkey-eating eagle, majestic symbol of the nation's fauna, is down to 200 or fewer individuals.

New Caledonia. My favorite island: far enough off the east coast of Australia to spawn a unique fauna and flora; large enough to accommodate large numbers of animals and plants; and close enough to Melanesian archipelagoes to the north to have received elements from that different biogeographical realm. For the naturalist, New Caledonia is a melting pot and a place of mystery. One of the finest days of my life was spent climbing Mt. Mou and then hiking along the summit ridge in mist-shrouded araucaria forest, where I found a pure native biota, not a single species of which I had ever seen in the wild before. The forests of New Caledonia hold 1,575 species of plants, of which an astonishing 89 percent are endemic. The New Caledonians, including the colonial French, have exploited the environment with abandon, logging, mining, and setting brushfires that push back the edges of the drier woodlands. Less than 1,500 square kilometers of undisturbed forests survive, covering 9 percent of the island. To see New Caledonia as it was, you must climb to mountain slopes too remote or steep for the loggers to clear.

Southwestern Australia. The extensive heathland west of the Nullarbor Plain evolved in a Mediterranean climate and state of isolation similar to those of the South African fynbos. It also resembles the fynbos in physical appearance and rivals it in diversity, harboring 3,630 plant species of which 78 percent are found nowhere else in the world. When I visited it in 1955, the environment was in nearly pristine condition. You could stand in the midst of the waist-high scrub in many places and see an unbroken horizon in all directions. In spring the flowers bloomed in splendid profusion. The cover has been reduced by half since then, mostly through agricultural conversion. It is being degraded further by mining operations, invasion of exotic weeds, and frequent wildfires. One quarter of its species are now classified as rare or threatened.

These are the eighteen hot spots, but the list is not closed. There are other candidates among forested regions, including the remnant rain forests of Mexico, Central America, West Indies, Liberia, Queensland, and Hawaii. To them can be added a large assemblage of entirely different habitats: the Great Lakes of East Africa and their counterpart in Siberia, Lake Baikal; virtually every river drainage system in the world near heavily populated regions, from the Tennessee to the Ganges and even some of the tributaries of the Amazon; the Baltic and Aral seas, the latter dying not just as an ecosystem but as a body of water; and a myriad of isolated tracts of species-rich tropical deciduous forests, grasslands, and deserts.

Then there are the coral reefs. These fortresses of biological diversity in the shallow tropical seas are giving way to a combination of natural and human assaults. The reefs have a permanent look but are highly dynamic in composition. Subject to the vagaries of weather and climate, they have always experienced local advances and retreats. Hurricanes periodically turn portions of the Caribbean reefs into rubble, but they grow back. El Niño events, the warming of water currents in the equatorial eastern Pacific, cause widespread mortality. The 1982–83 phenomenon, strongest recorded during the past two centuries, killed huge quantities of coral along the coasts of Costa Rica, Panama, Colombia, and Ecuador.

In normal circumstances, the reefs recover from natural destruction within a few decades. But now these natural stresses are being augmented by human activity, and the coral banks are being steadily degraded with less chance for regeneration. Reefs of twenty countries are affected around the world, from the Florida Keys and the West Indies to the Gulf of Panama and the Galápagos Islands, from Kenya and the Maldives east across a large swath of tropical Asia and south to Australia's Great Barrier Reef. In some places the reduction of reef area approaches 10 percent. Off Florida's Key Largo it is 30 percent, with most of the damage having occurred since 1970. In no particular order the principal causes are pollution (the oil spill during the Persian Gulf war being a disastrous example), accidental grounding of freighters, dredging, mining for coral rock, and harvesting of the more attractive species for decoration and amateur collections.

The decline of the reefs has been accompanied by coral bleaching. The loss of pigment is due to the failure of the zooxanthellae, the single-celled algae that live in the tissues of the coral animals and share a large fraction of the energy fixed by photosynthesis. The algae either die or lose much of the photosynthetic pigment they hold in their own cells. Like etiolated and dwarfed green plants germinated in the dark, the corals are as sickly as they look, and unless the process is reversed they die. Bleaching is a generalized stress reaction. It results variously from excessive heat or cold, chemical pollution, or dilution by fresh water, all of which are promoted by human activity.

During the 1980s, coral-reef bleaching occurred over a large part of the tropics. Rapid change most often proceeded in places where water temperatures rose conspicuously. It has been estimated that if the shallow tropical seas warm by as little as one or two degrees Celsius over the next century, many coral species would become extinct (three were lost from the eastern Pacific during the El Niño event of 1982–83 alone) and some reefs might disappear altogether. It is therefore possible that the bleaching of the last decade was the first step toward a catastrophe foretold by the rising levels of carbon dioxide in the atmosphere—possible, but still unproved. Coral bleaching in the 1980s occurred in some localities around the world but not in others. It was probably due to a variety of causes of which warming was only one. As they await further developments, marine biologists are inclined to agree that the greatest immediate peril for coral reefs comes from physical damage and pollution, not a worldwide warming trend.

But the long-term danger from climatic change looms in the decades ahead, for most ecosystems. If even the more modest projections of global warming prove correct, the world's fauna and flora will be trapped in a vise. On one side they are being swiftly reduced by deforestation and other forms of direct habitat destruction. On the other side they are threatened by the greenhouse effect. Whereas habitat loss on the land is most destructive to tropical biotas, climatic warming is expected to have a greater impact on the biotas of the cold-temperature and polar regions. A poleward shift of climate at the rate of 100 kilometers or more each century, equal to one meter or more a day, is considered at least a possibility. That rate of progression would soon leave wildlife preserves behind in a warmer regime, and many animal and plant species simply could not depart from the preserves and survive. The fossil record supports this forecast of limited dispersal. As the last continental ice sheet retreated from North America 9,000 years ago, spruce managed to spread at a rate of 200 kilometers a century, but the ranges of most other tree species spread at rates of only 10 to 40 kilometers. This history suggests that unless transplantings of entire ecosystems are undertaken, many thousands of native species are likely to be dislocated. How many will adapt to the changing climate, not having emigrated northward, and how many will become extinct? No one knows the answer.

It seems to follow that the organisms of the tundra and polar seas have no place to go even with a modest amount of global warming; the north and south poles are the end of the line. All the species of the high latitudes, reindeer moss to polar bears, risk extinction.

In another arena, large numbers of species around the world, at all latitudes, are restricted to low-lying coastal areas that will be flooded as the sea rises from the melting of polar ice. Various estimates have bracketed the rise somewhere between half a meter and two meters. In the United States, Florida will be the hardest hit region biologically. More than half of the rare animals and plants specialized for existence on the extreme coastal fringe live there. In the western Pacific many atolls, and even two small island nations, Kiribati and Tuvalu, would be largely covered by the sea.

Human demographic success has brought the world to this crisis of biodiversity. Human beings—mammals of the 50-kilogram weight class and members of a group, the primates, otherwise noted for scarcity—have become a hundred times more numerous than any other land animal of comparable size in the history of life. By every conceivable measure, humanity is ecologically abnormal. Our species appropriates between 20 and 40 percent of the solar energy captured in organic material by land plants. There is no way that we can draw upon the resources of the planet to such a degree without drastically reducing the state of most other species.

An awful symmetry of another kind binds the rise of humanity to the fall of biodiversity: the richest nations preside over the smallest and least interesting biotas, while the poorest nations, burdened by exploding populations and little scientific knowledge, are stewards of the largest. In 1950 the industrialized nations held a third of the world's population. The proportion fell to a quarter by 1985 and is expected to decline further to a sixth by 2025, when the total world population will have risen by 60 percent to 8 billion. One cannot help being struck with an irony, that if nineteenth-century technology had been born midst tropical rain forests instead of temperate-zone oaks and pines, there would be very little biodiversity left for us to save.

But what precisely is the magnitude of the crisis—how many species are disappearing? Biologists cannot tell in absolute terms because we do not know to the nearest order of magnitude how many species exist on earth in the first place. Probably fewer than 10 percent have even been given a scientific name. We cannot estimate the percentage of species going extinct each year around the world in most habitats, including coral reefs, deserts, and alpine meadows, because the requisite studies have not been made.

It is possible, though, to get a handle on the richest environment of all, the tropical rain forests, and to make a rough estimate of the extinction rates of species there. That much is possible because, thanks to the efforts of the Food and Agriculture Organization of the United Nations and a few pioneer researchers, such as Norman Myers, the rate of destruction of the rain forests has been ascertained. From the loss in forest area we can infer the rates at which species are being extinguished or doomed. And since the tropical forests contain more than half the species of plants and animals on earth, estimates pertaining to them allow us to make a rough qualitative assessment of the general severity of the biodiversity crisis.

Before attempting this projection, I am obliged to say something about the regenerative powers of rain forests. Despite their extraordinary richness, despite their reputation for exuberant growth ("the jungle quickly reclaimed the settlement as though nothing had existed there before"), these forests are among the most fragile of all habitats. Many of them grow on "wet deserts"—an unpromising soil base washed by heavy rains. Two thirds of the area of the forest surface worldwide consists of tropical red and yellow earths, which are typically acidic and poor in nutrients. High concentrations of iron and aluminum form insoluble compounds with phosphorus, decreasing the availability of that element to plants. Calcium and potassium are leached from the soil soon after their compounds are dissolved in the rain water. Only a tiny fraction of the nutrients filters deeper than 5 centimeters (2 inches) beneath the soil surface.

During the 150 million years of their existence, rain-forest trees have nevertheless evolved to grow thick and tall. At any given time, most of the carbon and a substantial fraction of the nutrients of the ecosystem are locked up in the tissue and dead wood of the vegetation. So the litter and humus on the ground are, in most cases, as thin as in any forests in the world. Here and there, patches of bare earth show through. At every turn there are signs of rapid decomposition by termites and fungi. When the forest is cut and burned, the ash and decomposing vegetation flush enough nutrients into the soil to support vigorous new herbaceous and shrubby growth for two or three years. Then the nutrients decline to levels too low to support healthy crops and forage. Farmers must add artificial fertilizer or move on to the next patch of rain forest, perpetuating the cycle of slash-and-burn.

The regeneration of rain forests is also limited by the fragility of the seeds of its trees. Those of most species germinate within a few days or weeks. They have little time to be carried by animals or water currents across the stripped land into sites favorable for growth. Most sprout and die in the hot, sterile soil of the clearings. The monitoring of logged sites indicates that regeneration of a mature forest may take centuries. Even though the forest at Angkor, for example, dates back to the abandonment of the Khmer capital in 1431, it is still structurally different from even older forests in the same region. The process of rain-forest regeneration is generally so slow, particularly after agricultural development, that few projections of its progress have been possible. In some areas, where the greatest damage is combined with low soil fertility and no native forest exists nearby to provide seeds, restoration might never occur without human intervention.

The ecology of rain forests stands in sharp contrast to that of northern temperate forests and grasslands. In North America and Eurasia, organic matter is not locked up so completely in the living vegetation. A large portion lies relatively fallow in the deep litter and humus of the soil. Seeds are more resistant to stress and able to lie dormant for long periods of time until the right conditions of temperature and humidity return. That is why it is possible to cut and burn large portions of the forest and grassland, graze cattle or grow crops for years on the land, and then see the vegetation grow back to nearly the original state a century after abandonment. Ohio, in a word, is not the Amazon. On a global scale, the north has been luckier than the south.

In 1979 tropical rain forests were down to about 56 percent of the prehistoric cover. Surveys made by satellite, by low-altitude overflights, and on the ground disclosed that the remainder, along with the much less extensive monsoon forests, was being removed at the rate of approximately 75,000 square kilometers, or 1 percent of the cover a year. Removal means that the forest is completely destroyed, with hardly a tree standing, or else degraded so severely that most of the trees die a short time later. The main causes of deforestation continue to be small-scale farming, especially slash-and-burn cultivation that leads to permanent agricultural settlement; only somewhat less important are commercial logging and cattle ranching.

During the 1980s the rate of deforestation was accelerated everywhere. It soared to tragic proportions in the Brazilian Amazon. There the people recognize three seasons, the dry, the wet, and the *queimadas,* or burnings. During the last brief period, armies of small farmers and peons employed by land barons set fires to clear the land of fallen trees and brush. About 50,000 square kilometers in four states of the Amazon (Acre, Mato Groso, Pará, Rondonia) were cleared and burned during four months, July through October, in

1987. A similar amount was destroyed the following year. Deforestation was driven by government-sponsored road building and settlement, sanctioned as government policy. It approached holocaust proportions, with effects spreading outward across larger parts of Brazil. "At night, roaring and red," observed the journalist Marlise Simons, "the forest looks to be at war." According to a report of the Institute for Space Research, "The dense smoke produced by the Amazonian burnings, at the height of the season, spread over millions of square kilometers, bringing health problems to the population, shutting down airports, hampering air traffic, causing various accidents on riverways and on roads, and polluting the earth's atmosphere in general." Global pollution did indeed occur. The Brazilian fires manufactured carbon dioxide containing more than 500 million tons of carbon, 44 million tons of carbon monoxide, over 6 million tons of particles, and a million tons of nitrogen oxides and other pollutants. Much of this material reached the upper atmosphere and traveled in a plume eastward across the Atlantic.

By 1989 the tropical rain forests of the world had been reduced to about 8 million square kilometers, or slightly less than half of the prehistoric cover. They were being destroyed at the rate of 142,000 square kilometers a year, or 1.8 percent of the standing cover, nearly double the 1979 amount. The loss is equal to the area of a football field every second. Put another way, in 1989 the surviving rain forests occupied an area about that of the contiguous forty-eight states of the United States, and they were being reduced by an amount equivalent to the size of Florida every year.

What impact does this destruction have on biodiversity in the tropical forests? In order to set a lower limit above which the species extinction rate can be reasonably placed. I will employ what we know about the relation between the area of habitats and the numbers of species living within them. Models of this kind are used routinely with science when direct measurements cannot be made. They yield first approximations that can be improved stepwise as better models are devised and more data added.

The first model is based on the widely observed area-species curve earlier given, $S = CA^z$, where S is the number of species, A is the area of the place where the species live, and C and z are constants that vary from one group of organisms to another and from one place to another. For purposes of calculating the rate of species extinction, C can be ignored; z is what counts. In the great majority of cases the value of z falls between 0.15 and 0.35. The exact value depends on the kind of organism being considered and on the habitats in which the organisms are found. When species are able to disperse easily from one place to another, z is low. Birds have a low z value, land snails and orchids a high z value.

The higher the z value, the more the species numbers will eventually fall after the area is reduced. I say "eventually fall": whereas some doomed species may vanish quickly when a forest is trimmed back or a lake partly drained, other species decline slowly and linger a while before disappearing. In more precise language, when an area is reduced, the extinction rate rises and stays above the original background level until the species number has descended from a higher equilibrium to a lower equilibrium. The rule of thumb, to make the result immediately clear, is that when an area is reduced to one tenth of its original size, the number of species eventually drops to one half. This corresponds to a z value of 0.30 and is actually close to the number often encountered in nature.

In 1989 the area of the combined rain forests was declining by 1.8 percent each year, a rate that can be reasonably assumed to have continued into the early 1990s. At the typical z value, 0.30, each year's area reduction can be expected to reduce the number of species by 0.54 percent. Let us try to bracket the extinction rate for most kinds of organisms by estimating the minimal and maximal numbers possible. At the lowest likely z value, 0.15, this extinction rate would be 0.27 percent a year; at the highest likely z value, 0.35, the extinction rate would be 0.63 percent. *Very roughly, then, reduction in the area of tropical rain forest at the current rate can be expected to extinguish or doom to extinction about half a percent of the species in the forests each year.* More precisely, groups with a low *z* value will be affected the least, those with high *z* values the most. If most groups of organisms have low *z* values, the overall extinction rate will be closer to 0.27 percent; if most have high *z* values, the overall extinction rate will approach 0.63 percent. Not enough data exist to guess where the true overall value falls between these extremes.

If destruction of the rain forest continues at the present rate to the year 2022, half of the remaining rain forest will be gone. The total extinction of species this will cause will lie somewhere between 10 percent (based on a *z* value of 0.15) and 22 percent (based on a *z* value of 0.35). The "typical" intermediate *z* value of 0.30 would lead to a cumulative extinction of 19 percent over that span of time. Roughly, then, if deforestation continues for thirty more years at the present rate, one tenth to one quarter of the rain-forest species will disappear. If the rain forests are as rich in diversity as most biologists think, their reduction alone will eliminate 5 to 10 percent or more—probably considerably more—of all the species on earth in thirty years. When other species-rich but declining habitats are added, including heathland, dry tropical forests, lakes, rivers, and coral reefs, the toll mounts steeply.

The area-species relation accounts for a great deal of extinction, but not for all of it. We need a second model. As the last trees are cut, the last patch turned into a pasture or cornfield, the area-species curve plunges off the extrapolated line down to zero. So long as a small remnant of forest exists somewhere, say on a ridge in western Ecuador, a substantial number of species will hang on, most in tiny populations. Some may be doomed unless heroic efforts are made to culture and transplant them to new sites. But for the moment they hang on. When the last bit of forest or other natural habitat is removed and the area falls from 1 percent to zero, a great many species immediately perish. Such is the condition of legions of Centinelas around the world, the silent extinctions occurring as the last trees are felled. When Cebu in the Philippines was completely logged, nine of the ten bird species unique to the island were extinguished, and the tenth is in danger of joining them. We don't know how to assess global species loss from all these small-scale total extinctions. One thing is certain: because they do occur, the estimation of global rates based purely on the area-species curve must be on the low side. Consider the impact of removing the final few hundred square kilometers of natural reserves: in most cases, more than half of the original species would vanish immediately. If these were the refuges of species found nowhere else, the circumstance for so many rainforest animals and plants, the loss in diversity would be immense.

The concept of a world peppered by miniature holocausts can be extended. Take the extreme imaginary case in which all species dwelling in the rain forests are local in distribution, limited to a few square kilometers, in the manner of the endemic plant species of Centinela. As the forest is cut back, the percentage loss in species approaches but never quite equals the percentage loss in forest area. In the next thirty years, the world would lose not only half of its forest cover but nearly half of the forest species. Fortunately, this assumption is excessive. Some species of animals and plants dwelling in rain forests have wide geographical distributions. So the rate of species extinction is less than the reduction in area.

It follows that the amount of species loss from halving of the rainforest area will be greater than 10 percent and less than 50 percent. But note that this range of percentages is the loss expected from the area effect only, and it is still on the low side. A few species in the remnant patches will also be lost by rifle-shot extinction, the hunting out of rare animals and plants in the manner of Spix's macaw and the New Zealand mistletoe. Others will be erased by new diseases, alien weeds, and animals such as rats and feral pigs. That secondary loss will intensify as the patches grow smaller and more open to human intrusion.

No one has any idea of the combined magnitude of these additional destructive forces in all habitats. Only the minimal in the case of tropical rain forests—10 percent extinction with a halving of area—can be drawn with confidence. But because of the generally higher z values prevailing and the additional and still unmeasured extinction factors at work, the real figure might easily reach 20 percent by 2022 and rise as high as 50 percent or more thereafter. A 20 percent extinction in total global diversity, with all habitats incorporated, is a strong possibility if the present rate of environmental destruction continues.

How fast is diversity declining? The firmer numbers I have given are the estimates of species extinctions that will *eventually* occur as rain forests are cut back. How long is "eventually"? When a forest is reduced from, say, 100 square kilometers to 10, some immediate extinction is likely. Yet the new equilibrium described by the equation $S = CA^z$ will not be reached all at once. Some species will linger on in dangerously reduced populations. Elementary mathematical models predict that the number of species in the 10-kilometer-square plot will decline at a steadily decelerating rate, swiftly at first, then slowing as the new and lower equilibrium is approached. The reasoning is simple: at first there are many species destined for extinction, which therefore vanish at a high overall rate; later only a few are endangered and the rate slows. In ideal form, with species going extinct independently of one another, this course of events is called *exponential decay.*

Employing the exponential-decay model, Jared Diamond and John Terborgh approached the problem in the following way. They took advantage of the fact that rising sea levels at the end of the Ice Age 10,000 years ago cut off small land masses that had once been connected to South America, New Guinea, and the main islands of Indonesia. When the sea flowed around them, these land masses became "land-bridge islands." The islands of Tobago, Margarita, Coiba, and Trinidad were originally part of the South and Central American mainland and shared the rich bird fauna of that continent. In a similar manner, Yapen, Aru, and Misool were connected to New Guinea and shared its fauna before becoming islands fringing its coast. Diamond and Terborgh studied birds, which are good for measuring extinction because they are conspicuous and easily identified. Both investigators arrived at the same conclusion: after submergence of the land bridges, the smaller the land-bridge island, the more rapid the loss. The extinctions were regular enough to justify use of the exponential-decay model. Extending the analysis in the American tropics, Terborgh turned to Barro Colorado Island, which was created by the formation of Gatun Lake during the construction of the Panama Canal. In this case the clock started ticking not 10,000 years ago but fifty years before the study. Applying the land-bridge decay equation to an island of this size, 17 square kilometers, Terborgh predicted an extinction of 17 bird species during the first 50 years. The actual number known to have vanished during that time is 13, or 12 percent of 108 breeding species originally present.

For a process as complex as the decline of biodiversity, the conformity of the Barro Colorado bird data to the same equation based on much larger islands and longer times, even if just within a factor of two, seemed too good to be true. But several other studies of new islands have produced similar results, which are at least consistent with the decay models, and depressing. The islands are patches of forest isolated in cleared agricultural land. When the islands are in the range of 1 to 25 square kilometers, the extinction rate of bird species during the first hundred years is 10 to 50 percent. Also, as predicted by theory, the extinction rate is highest in the smaller patches and rises steeply when the area drops below a square kilometer. Three patches of subtropical forest in Brazil surrounded by agricultural land for about a hundred years varied in area from 0.2 to 14 square kilometers; the resident bird species suffered a 14 to 62 percent extinction, in reverse order. On the other side of the world, a 0.9-square-kilometer forest patch, the Bogor Botanical Garden, was also isolated by clearing. In the first fifty years it lost 20 of its 62 breeding bird species. Still another example in a different environment: comparable rates of local extinction of bird species occurred in the wheat belt of southwestern Australia when 90 percent of the original eucalyptus woodland was removed and the remainder was broken into fragments.

There is no way to measure the absolute amount of biological diversity vanishing year by year in rain forests around the world, as opposed to percentage losses, even in groups as well known as the birds. Nevertheless, to give an idea of the dimension of the hemorrhaging, let me provide the most conservative estimate that can be reasonably based on our current knowledge of the extinction process. I will consider only species being lost by reduction in forest area, taking the lowest z value permissible (0.15). I will not include overharvesting or invasion by alien organisms. I will assume a number of species living in the rain forests, 10 million (on the low side), and I will further suppose that many of the species enjoy wide geographical ranges. Even with these cautious parameters, selected in a biased manner to draw a maximally optimistic conclusion, the number of species doomed each year is 27,000. Each day it is 74, and each hour 3.

If past species have lived on the order of a million years in the absence of human interference, a common figure for some groups documented in the fossil record, it follows that the normal "background" extinction rate is about one species per one million species a year. Human activity has increased extinction between 1,000 and 10,000 times over this level in the rain forest by reduction in area alone. Clearly we are in the midst of one of the great extinction spasms of geological history.

Eva Saulitis

The Burden of the Beach

First publication

It's been nearly three years, but I can't get Molly's question out of my mind. "Eva, what do you think it means that we have to do this? What does it mean for us to find this dead whale?" The whale is long-gone now, washed off the sloping beach where we found it. The shoreline has recovered itself from the imprint of its body by the roiling of stones resettling themselves as the tide rises again and again. It's floating body has dissolved into the blue-green coldness of salt water. An everyday thing, a carcass is, in the life of a biologist. But this dead whale just won't leave me alone; this being of the deep, unconscious ocean, heaved up on land. One can ask it a question and it will lie there, or one may never see it at all, hidden in a crook of an island, visited only by gulls and eagles, ravens and bears.

The dead whale asks more of me. More than why it died, or how it arrived, or what had it been eating, more than was it poisoned by oil. Three years ago, Molly listened and heard the questions, and asked them of me. And then she left me to listen, to learn to ask. She left me to answer, in my own voice.

I dreamed that it was night, and I was at the ocean. I walked onto a long, wooden boardwalk that went straight out, miles out to sea. I walked along the wet planks, and there was no railing at the sides, just the blackened waves very close to me and the wind, and clouds torn open across the moonlit sky. Suddenly, I was surrounded by killer whales, their exhalations sounding on both sides of me. There were many whales and I could dimly see their blackness, blacker even than the waves, the sky. I sat down on the boardwalk, afraid I would lose control of myself, plunge recklessly into the dark water. I held my breath. My blood pounded in my ears. In that moment, someone could have put an ear to the shell of my ear and heard the sound of the sea.

Our gum-boots roll and slide off the algae-slicked stones of the beach as we approach the whale. Faltering steps mimic the tentative fear I feel inside. "Halloooo, bears, coming throoooough, bears . . ." We send our calls with the southwest day-breeze blowing across the body of the whale, carrying our warning with the smell of decay over the island of bears.

Egged on by our resolve, we lay our buckets down and walk in opposite directions, circling the carcass. Molly stands near the withered dorsal fin. "God, it reeks!" Her face is contorted in a grimace of disgust, and I have to laugh. But underneath it all, I think, *Can I do this?*

Our instruction: to find this body, measure it, photograph it, cut it open and place pieces of its blubber in buckets, remove its stomach and take what is inside. The dead orca offers up no instruction of its own.

The whale's body roasts in the heat of the sun: skin cracked and dripping grease, its normally starkly contrasted black and white colors melted away to a streaked bronze. Its heaviness weights the beach. Its blood penetrates the stones.

I look past the rye grass above the rocks, into the moving green screen of the forest. I imagine invisible bears, whose eyes watch from the trees. "Halloooo, bears," I cry, remembering, suddenly, our invasion. I feel a cold cylinder of fear in my chest when I confront myself with our predicament. Montague Island represents for me fierceness, wildness, like the wind over the island grasses, it is uncompromising and irrevocable. The dead orca has, by chance or design, come to rest on the watery edge of the homeland of bears.

Three islands in Prince William Sound are inhabited by brown bears: Montague, Hinchinbrook, and Hawkins. Hinchinbrook and Montague are separated from each other by a notorious strait of water called Hinchinbrook Entrance. Ten miles across at the point where the islands are the closest, it opens like a wide whale's mouth to the Gulf of Alaska. The Entrance is streaked by currents and rip tides; winds rise unexpectedly. Through the mouth, storms enter, whirling off the Gulf.

Several years ago, a strong-willed bear made the crossing of the Entrance. It had been transplanted to Montague Island by the Fish and Wildlife Service, after raiding garbage cans in Cordova. Weeks later, the bear showed up again in town.

The Chugach Eskimo people tell of bears swimming in the opposite direction. One story involves a woman living at the now-abandoned village of Nuchek. She was betrayed by her husband, so transformed herself into a brown bear and killed him. Four fur seals disguised as men bore her by baidarka to Hinchinbrook Entrance. From there she swam into the Gulf, creating Middleton Island out of seaweed so she could rest. She finally arrived at Montague, her fury intact. That is why, say the Chugach, the brown bears on Montague are so fierce. I imagine these descendants of the betrayed woman: beings that shift from human to animal, volatile changelings.

The alders wave wildly, forming a visually impenetrable, moving curtain of green. Surely the smell of the carcass is passing through the cool forest air, bending around trees and into passages between boulders. I hope that the whale is too rancid for bears. Behind the green, are there eyes, watching?

Molly and I regroup. "Let's get this over with as fast as we can," I say, opening the top of a bucket. "Let's make a plan." Molly's thoughts are elsewhere. "Eva, why do you think we have to do this? What does it mean that we have to cut open this whale?" Her question inserts itself into my mind, trying to find purchase. I'm in science mode, nervous about bears, unsure of the task before us, wanting to do it right. I know what she is asking. As always, what she asks of me is to look deeper, beyond the surface, beyond science and task. I don't always know if I'll be able to live up to the challenges she poses. I load the question like film into my consciousness, hoping the picture will be taken, the moment preserved for later consideration.

We bend to the buckets, one of us rearing our head up every few minutes to shout our incomprehensions toward the edge of trees. Before we left the boat, we had changed into expendable clothing. In Valdez, eighty miles distant and a day's journey away, we had foraged through the local second-hand shop for clothing we knew we would burn after our encounter. Ill-fitting jeans, a dollar a pair. Pink sweatshirt with too-short arms, fifty cents, discarded T-shirts only a tourist would buy.

We prepared ourselves as best we could in Valdez. But looking at the sheer weight of the whale's carcass, the unimagined flesh, I realize that we could never be prepared for such a death. We could never be prepared for the eyes of bears we cannot see, for the impossibility of detachment in the face of the manifold implications of ourselves on this beach. Wildness accepts no predictions.

We pull on raingear and reach in for the fillet knives we bought in town. I glance at the enormity of the whale. The knives are absurd, but they will have to do. We move toward the carcass. "Maybe one of us should watch for bears, while the other cuts," suggests Molly. I agree, looking back down the beach to our inflatable raft, and then to the *Whale One,* floating blankly at anchor fifty yards offshore. I imagine scrambling down to the raft and paddling like mad for the boat. At least with the receding tide, it is floating closer to the beach. I turn away and, knife in hand, press its tip into the crisp skin of the whale's throat.

From a cartographer's perspective, this beach is part of a sickle-shaped peninsula separating Port Chalmers from Stockdale Harbor.

These names hint at the commerce and the busy industry of the first half of this century in Prince William Sound. They do not apply to the current wildness of these two wide bays. They are shunned by most mariners. In 1964, the earthquake lifted the entire coastline of Montague Island; in some areas, the island rose thirty feet. Charts warn of hundreds of underwater dangers—reefs and ledges not marked on maps. At low tide, water curls whitely over shallow areas, and waves break themselves against the exposed rocks.

Montague Island is forty miles long, a jagged backbone of mountains. It bears along its length the force of the Gulf, protecting, and actually creating, the shelter of the Sound. Storms pile up along its south-facing coastline. We watch weather meet the mountains and spill down their sides like waterfalls of steam. Where clouds are held in the valleys, rain falls endlessly.

To me the tiny crook of island where we stand has always looked like a beckoning finger. I have placed my feet on Montague only a few times in eight years. The submerged rocks, unsuitable anchoring spots, and dangerous waters surrounding the island hold me away. The promises of the unknown—bears, huge trees, expansive green valleys, permanent snowfields—draw me closer.

Earlier in the summer, I ventured onto the island with three friends. In the late afternoon, I sat alone in a rye grass meadow, not facing the sea as I usually do, but facing the island, into an alder and salmonberry thicket. The meadow was a resting place for bleached and scattered logs, and I leaned my back against their sun-warmed solidity. Facing the thicket, I thought of the bears that inhabit the island, and wondered where the closest one was. I imagined its eyes among the alders, its tongue tasting the berries. I imagined the spirits of all the bears who had ever lived on the island watching me. Closing my eyes, fear left me. I thought of the ancient stories of women who coupled with bears, and with a strange, floating serenity, I asked to be filled with the spirit of the brown bear. For that brief drift of time, I wanted a bear to come to me. Before the thought could leave my mind and depart to wherever it was headed, I snapped to.

Are you crazy? I asked myself, quickly sitting up and looking around the meadow, with its graveyard of logs. I was suddenly terrified of the unknown power of my own thoughts. But that momentary letting go of the fear that I expected of myself asked me questions. What empty place inside myself could be filled by this fearful presence, what it represented: strength, a sense of territory, a fierce need for solitude, fidelity to place.

The heat of the sun sears my face and dampens my clothes with sweat as I push the knife blade through the leathery skin of the whale. I stand awkwardly, a few feet away, my arm extended, trying to keep my distance. As the knife penetrates the blubber layer, juice oozes out of the cut. I can feel its heat as it runs across my gloved hand. Inside this whale minute organisms are working, softening, consuming, dissolving the whale. They generate another kind of heat. I saw away a square of skin and hot, melting fat and drop it into the bucket that Molly holds toward me. A lab will whirl this flesh in test tubes and, by a process I can hardly imagine, gas chromatography, render it into data on hydrocarbon levels borne by the whale.

The open wound releases the thick, sweet rotten smell of decay. Molly's voice rings out as she paces the pale cobbles, calling to the bears. "How are you doing?" she asks. "It's so hot," I reply, wiping moisture from my forehead with the back of my gloved hand. "And this smell. . . . I'm trying not to judge it. If I describe it to myself, it's not so bad." I turn my face into the wind, gulping breaths of clean, salt-laden air.

She offers to start off cutting for the stomach. I hand her the gloves. We stand side by side, looking at the bulk of the whale. "Let's just cut it like we're gutting a fish," I suggest. I try to imagine where the stomach would be—above the chewed-open flesh near the belly button, and below the chest cavity. The giant, paddlelike pectoral flippers fold together like hands in prayer, blocking access to the upper belly. "Let's just lift the top one out of the way," says Molly, striding up and grasping the peeling slab with both hands. With both of us heaving, the flipper is unyielding, as improbable and unmoving as a grand piano. Molly bends down, crawls as far as she can under the flipper, and begins the cut.

Several moments have passed since we've shouted, so I send out calls to the trees as I walk around to the whale's head. The flesh is puckered where birds have picked out the skyward-facing eye. The mouth gapes, its rows of evenly spaced, conical teeth grinning. I bend down and stroke my fingers along their marble smoothness. They are cold to my touch.

I guess I should cut one out for aging, I think, and fetch our small hacksaw from the bucket. After several minutes of vigorous rasping I let my arm drop to check out my progress. The tooth is barely scratched. The hacksaw, like the knife, like ourselves, has been daunted by the reality of the whale. This tooth will resist my futile attempt at thieving. I leave it intact and move close to Molly.

She has emerged from under the flipper and is jerking the knife along, making a jagged cut through the blubber layer. She is on her knees, wallowing in the stiffness of the raingear, her face inches away from the whale. Her rubber-suited arms are smeared with juice and blobs of grease. The split-open rinds of flesh on the whale's belly pull away from the underlying layer of muscle.

We approach this task from a hundred different perspectives, Molly and I. I watch her working, her small form dwarfed by the whale. She is six years younger than I, but I often feel diminished by the power of her imagination and insights. Her small stature is belied by her physical strength and endurance. She grew up crewing on her father's fishing boat, the *Sweet Sage.* As a young child, she woke at 4:00 A.M. with her two sisters to set out for the fishing grounds in Cook Inlet.

Molly is my companion of three summers in the Sound. We share a wall-tent home looking out on the passage where we scan for whales. She is my companion of stretched-out days on the water in our small boat. She always asks the important questions, unwrapping me from anxiety over the quality of our work. She pulls me back from my worries and, my hand in hers, leads me toward the edges of things. She challenges me to peer over the side, to plumb the deeper waters. On this day, she calls me to the shadow side of what is before us: this body on the beach, on the island of bears, edged by waters of whales and fish and deepness and unknown. Sometimes, we speak the same language. Sometimes no words are necessary.

We take walks often, stretching our legs after long days on the boat. We explore stretches of beach, deer trails leading up to ridges, depressions in the forest that hint of hidden lakes where we might swim. On beaches, we search for Japanese glass fishing floats: round globes of colored glass that survive wave-driven landings. On the same fog-bound day last summer, we each found our first glass balls, on two separate beaches. In the afternoon, we lounged in the boat, holding them up to the light, peering through them. Molly's was small, fitting perfectly in the palm of her hand. The glass was a clear blue-green. My ball was larger, and the glass was opaque, with a scratched look. "See how these balls are different in the way we are, Mol," I pondered. "Yours is so clear-sighted and compact; mine is cloudy and uncertain, a little battered." We laughed. "I think yours is beautiful," Molly said.

This summer, I must face the certainty of Molly's decision that this will be her last season working with me in the Sound. She is a writer by vocation and avocation, and a scientist by neither. She moves on, toward her writing, and away from the eclipsing silences, the hourless days. She moves on from the precarious balancing act between science and pure experience.

Her absence asks of me why I stay. For I cannot imagine not staying. Our friendship has been the anchor point from which I have explored my place in the Sound. Within it, I have been able to move in this in-between place of conflict. In the world we have created together, questions of detachment and implication can live side by side.

The question of the whale, as she posed it, was to ask me how to be more authentic in this place. To let go of the easily resolvable. To climb into the body of the whale, to be not afraid of bears, of experience, of questions that have no answers. Of being alone. She left me with the challenge of seeing through my own eyes, and not relying on hers.

I take my turn at the whale. Molly lurches up, her face glistening with sweat. "I have to get away from this and breathe some fresh air," she says, stumbling down the beach to move the buckets closer to the edge of the water. "Heeeeyooo . . ." she yells over her shoulder.

I slice at the exposed muscle layer. The juice from the cut sizzles up. The meat is brown, softened, and fibrous. The huge body of a whale retains heat for days after death, cooking the flesh from the inside. The sun bakes it from without.

I think of the living whale that once moved this body through the secret realms of water. The streamlined form swam effortlessly, the once blood-red muscles conveying a life of constant, undulating motion; the ability to travel a hundred or more miles in a single day, to capture silver flashes of salmon, twirling porpoises. This is what happens to a body that has been supported by the sea when it is cast upon land, the realm of gravity. It falls, as the whale falls back to water mightily during a breach. It sags, collapses, breaks down. I am self-conscious for this whale's spirit. I am suddenly aware of our intrusion into the privacy of death. This slashed body reviles me.

So many times my own presence as a scientist in the Sound or amongst the animals feels repellent. It's an ever-present contradiction, the desire to learn about the whales, to "do science," and the conviction that the animals should be left alone. I hover above myself, watching this efficient persona, scanning with binoculars, wielding cameras and knives, scratching notes on wet paper with a mechanical pencil.

And sometimes I see myself from a different set of eyes. And I feel real. I watch the mountains of Montague in the distance, the streaked lenses of rock eddied by ice and snow. I want to imprint myself there on those slopes. And the image of the mountains pools inside of me, carves in me a certain solidity.

I pivot back and forth constantly, between my scientist self and the self that feels more true: the witness. There must be a balancing point there with the integrity of stone. I don't believe it's wholly the domain of a scientist to want to know why. It is a universal human quality, one that I can't separate myself from.

The mountain or the ocean itself cannot be asked with the hope of receiving an answer. And this is what holds me here. The sea is vast and yields its secrets randomly, slowly, if at all. It is willful, like a sleeping animal, wakening with heavy breathing, shaking itself. I peer down into the water, straining to see what is yielded up: the eye of a whale, or its shoulder, a flash of black and white in the greening world.

Two hours have passed. "We should go faster," I tell Molly. "Maybe we can both cut and yell at the same time." The sun has dipped to the west. "Sure," says Molly, grasping a knife. My blade glides along the taut, gray membrane that lines the cavity holding the organs. We carve away rinds of fat and muscle to expose a rectangle of lining. I push the tip of my knife through the shiny elastic surface. An instant whoosh of fetid air rushes out, and the membrane loses its tautness. We hold our breath and turn our heads away. "Jesus," says Molly, releasing air in a gasp. "That was awful." I slice away a patch of lining. Cuts through the inner skin of membrane reveal the coils of glistening, veined intestines. My knife penetrates a loop and it oozes orange slime, the color of sulphur fungus.

The stomach is deep inside the whale. I stand back and pull the intestines onto the beach to make a space. We take turns grasping and feeling for the stomach, our arms reaching in to the pits. I feel for the end of the intestines; it seems impossible that there is an end. Finally, I feel the widening flask that welds into the stomach. My arms extend as far as they can into the body of the whale, bending under the ribs, lost in the mass of intestines. "How are we going to get this out?" I ask Molly. "We need a bigger opening," she says, knifing off more slabs of blubber and muscle, widening our rectangle. I wield the hacksaw, trying to carve away ribs to reach the stomach. As with the teeth, the saw makes nearly imperceptible scratches on the two-inch-thick bone.

Our only choice is to climb on top of the whale and heft the stomach up from under the lowest rib. Molly uses the pectoral fin as a step; she skids along the whale's side. I reach the knife into the body cavity, cutting away the transparent membranes holding the stomach pouches to the wall. When I have loosened a mound of stomach, I lean back and pull the slippery mass out from under the rib, and heave it to Molly. Bending her knees, she strains upward until the sack rests on the whale's side.

I climb onto the whale to help Molly pull the rest of the stomach out and up. My foot slips on the greasy skin, and I slide down into the body cavity. I am drenched in sweat, but am thankful for the protection of raingear now. I look up and see for the first time that we have an audience. A cadre of eagles and ravens looks down on us from the trees.

I try to imagine the sight: two ungainly humans, slipping, sliding, shimmying, cutting, probing, hefting, slicing. Do they wonder, what is the purpose, what is our place? We of the buckets and bags, notebooks, cameras. I often feel out of place in the eyes of the animals we encounter. Once, I stared over the bow of the boat at my reflection in the water. This is what the whale sees, looking up. An odd, flickering, white-faced shape flapping its orange wings, jabbering noisily in the bright, blinding air.

It takes both of us pulling, but soon we have hauled many sections of stomach up through the ribs and onto the side of the whale's belly. We reach for our knives, and draw them back and forth across pouches. The knives have dulled. Through the thick, outer skin of the muscled sack is a crenulated surface, like the underside of a mushroom. This pouch is empty, surprisingly white and clean.

"I think I've found something," Molly says quietly. Her two palms rest on a bulging section of stomach. It is hard and knobby, like the crop of a bird. The knife slices, and the contents spill out: a brown slimy soup of whiskers, claws, and shriveled strips of skin. We pull out handfuls of long, quill-like sea lion whiskers, and the white, pearly ones of seals.

Something curious catches my eye. I reach into the jumble of remains and pull out three square tabs. "What the heck . . ." I begin. They look disconcertingly like buckles from Helly Hansen raingear. It takes me a moment to recognize that they are numbered flipper tags. Somewhere, biologists snapped them to the flesh of living seals or sea lions, to trace their movements and fate.

We are excited at our success. We work quickly, slicing open more pouches, scraping the contents out with our fingers, and filling Zip-loc bags. We don't want to miss tiny fish scales that may cling to the stomach walls. When we finish, we slide off the side of the whale, our boots crunching down on the cobbles.

Stepping back from the carcass, its full view is shocking. Streaks of intestine have begun to dry, sticking to the rocks. The pull of gravity on the internal organs has caused them to sag toward the ground. The pit of the body cavity is filling with brownish fluid. I want to leave, to relish our accomplishment of what had at first seemed an insurmountable task. But my feelings are mixed with shame at seeing the gash in the whale's side, its innards spilling out of our jagged cuts. It seems a reckless, violent piece of work.

Later that summer we would get a radio call about an orca carcass floating in Montague Strait. The caller described a huge opening in its belly, so I knew it was the whale from the beach. But he also told us the carcass was headless. The picture flashed in my mind of a chain-saw-wielding someone, after the ivory teeth or perhaps the skull. How was this person different from me? Both of us, wanting something, and taking it, from the whale.

The gashed body of the whale offers up no reckoning. I remember a story. The Chugach Eskimos believed that when killer whales came into a bay with a village, death would come. The people were sad.

The whales were after someone's spirit. There are spirits on this island, including those of the whale, the bears. My own spirit wants taking up. It is too full of contradictions.

Back on the boat, we prepare for our departure. Molly fills buckets with soap and salt water. Still in our raingear, we stand on the bow and pour water over each other, scrubbing away the offal of the whale with long-handled deck brushes. Several washes later, the smell remains, as it will for weeks to come. We peel down to our damp clothing, strip it off, and pile it in a plastic garbage bag for later burning. We take quick dives from the boat after soaping our bodies, but the scent of the whale has permeated our skin.

I pull up the anchor and Molly backs the boat away from the shore. The tide rises again, seeping up the beach. I look at the strange shape resting on the stones. "Remember that time we bowed to the forest, Molly?" I ask.

We had been on a hike in the high country. We stood on the beach afterward, looking back toward the stream-cut valley we had followed. "I feel the need to bow to that place, Eva," Molly had ventured. So we stood, side by side, our palms pressed together, like the hands of prayerful monks. We bent at our waists, with our faces turned up to the forest. We kneeled on the beach and touched our foreheads to the wet gravel. And then we turned and walked away.

As we depart, we see the whale from the vantage from which we first saw it. The marks of our probing are not visible from this distance. The impression we had when we stood beside it, that the whale was cast from its element, dissolves. It is an illusion, in which our defilement of the whale disappears as the conflicts fade to the ordinary, day-by-day of our water life.

On one of the wooden supports inside our wall-tent is pinned a fragment of a poem by Rilke. It instructs us emphatically to live the questions. And doing so, he writes, *perhaps you will then gradually, without knowing it, live along some distant day into the answer.*

For this moment, the coppery form of the whale rests on the wild fringe of the island, with eagles perched in the high trees above it. The image imprints on my mind as the weight of the whale imprints its memory onto the beach. We leave the burnished form to the solitude of its resting place, to the company of waving grasses, patient birds, the spirits of ponderous bears. I imagine them biding time, waiting to reclaim what is theirs, their eyes in the alders, watching.

Contributors

Rick Bass is the author of several noted works of nonfiction and fiction, including *The Deer Pasture, Wild to the Heart, Ninemile Wolves, The Watch,* and, most recently, *Platte River.* His long-awaited first novel, *Where the Sea Used to Be,* is due to be published by Houghton Mifflin in 1995. Rick Bass resides in the northwestern mountains of Montana with his wife, Elizabeth, and daughter, Mary Katherine.

Susan Brownmiller is one of the leading feminist writers of our time. Her books, such as *Against Our Will: Men, Women and Rape,* have influenced thinking on the complex intergender issues facing men, women, and society. In 1992 she visited Vietnam and wrote *Seeing Vietnam: Encounters of the Road and Heart,* a meditation on war, nature, and human culture.

Lyn Buckley graduated with a Master of Fine Arts degree in poetry from the University of Hawaii. She currently teaches creative writing and environmental literature at Feather River College in Davis, California. She has published her poetry in literary journals and is preparing her first book of poetry.

John Daniel studied creative writing under Wallace Stegner at Stanford University, where Daniel later taught for many years. He is the author of *The Trail Home,* an acclaimed book of nature essays, and several books of poetry. He is the poetry editor for *Wilderness* magazine. Daniel lives with his wife in Portland, Oregon, where they both are avid gardeners.

Alison Deming is director of the poetry center at the University of Arizona in Tucson. For many years she has been active in the arts community in the Southwest. Her poetry has been widely published and celebrated. Her awards include the Walt Whitman Award from the Academy of American Poets and a Pushcart Prize. In 1994 her first book of nature essays, *Temporary Homelands,* was published to acclaim by Mercury House in San Francisco.

Clarice Dickess is happiest when she is kayaking a whitewater canyon in Central America, bicycling on some epic cross-country trek, or ascending a sheer rock face that no one has climbed yet. Originally from Connecticut, she currently makes her home in a cabin outside Fairbanks, Alaska. She has published essays in periodicals and in an anthology, *Another Wilderness,* and is writing a book about her many exciting experiences in the North American outback.

John Gierarch lives in a house on the banks of the St. Vrain River in Lyons, Colorado. His books on angling—*Trout Bum, The View from Rat Lake,* and *Sex, Death, & Fishing*—have revolutionized the genre. Unlike many of the more traditional writers of early decades, Gierarch is refreshingly informal and personal in his essays. *Dances with Trout* is his latest book. Gierarch's thoughts on fishing can be found in regular columns in the *New York Times* and in *Flyfishing* magazine.

Gerard Gormley, a former submariner and science writer, began his career as a nature writer with *A Dolphin Summer,* a book rated by *Library Journal* as one of the best of 1986. Subsequently he wrote *Orcas of the Gulf* about the killer whales in the seas around Martha's Vineyard and Nantucket Island. He has received fellowships from Bread Loaf Writers Conference, Millay Colony for the Arts, and Yaddo. Mr. Gormley makes his residence in Manchester-by-the-Sea, Massachusetts.

John Haines—poet, naturalist, and essayist—lived for more than forty years on a homestead along the Tanana River in northern Alaska. His book of essays on that experience, *The Stars, The Snow, The Fire,* is one of the finest memoirs ever written about life in the far north. Haines has taught at a number of universities and holds an honorary doctorate from the University of Alaska. He was formerly Alaska's poet laureate. His volume of collected poems, *The Owl in the Mask of the Dreamer,* won the 1993 Western Writer's Award for best book of poetry.

Carolyn Kremers, a native of Colorado, graduated from Stanford University with a degree in music and subsequently played the flute semiprofessionally for many years. She has taught in the Yupik Eskimo communities of Tununak and Bethel and has received a Master of Fine Arts degree from the University of Alaska. Her creative nonfiction and poetry have earned her a citation from the PEN/Jerad Fund Award for emerging women writers of nonfiction and a fellowship from the Alaska State Council on the Arts.

Barry Lopez grew up in New York City and southern California and later graduated from the University of Notre Dame in Indiana. He is one of the most important nature writers of our century. He has authored such seminal works as *Of Wolves and Men, Arctic Dreams* (winner of the National Book Award), *Crossing Open Ground, Winter Notes, Desert Notes,* and *The Rediscovery of North America.* He lives with his wife, an artist, in the Cascade Mountains of Oregon.

Nancy Lord commercially fishes for salmon in Homer, Alaska. She is the author of the critically acclaimed short story collection *Survival,* which explores the lives of maritime people interacting with the land and the sea. Her fiction and essays have been published widely in literary periodicals.

Peter Matthiessen, one of the founding members of the *Paris Review,* has devoted his life to writing about humankind and nature. His many classic books include *The Snow Leopard, Sand Rivers, The Tree Where Man Was Born, The Cloud Forest,* and, most recently, *African Silences.* Matthiessen is also an accomplished novelist whose works include *The Far Tortuga, Killing Mister Watson,* and *At Play in the Fields of the Lord* (recently a motion picture).

Rick McIntyre has one of the best collections of wild wolf photographs in the world, taken during fifteen years as a ranger in Denali National Park. McIntyre currently works as a ranger at Big Bend in the winter and Yellowstone in the summer. His books include *Grizzly Cub* and *The Society of Wolves.* McIntyre is well known for his wolf program, an exciting lecture/slide show that has delighted crowds from the American Museum of Natural History in New York to the California Academy of Sciences in San Francisco.

Jim Miller is a doctoral student in biology at Colorado State University. His dissertation explores new ways of managing fragmented landscapes. Miller has published several scientific articles and has also delivered papers on conservation biology at technical meetings. For the past twenty years he has backpacked widely in the West.

Adele Ne Jame, originally from New York City and of Lebanese-American descent, has lived in Honolulu, Hawaii, for the past twenty years. She teaches English at the University of Hawaii and at Hawaii Pacific University. She has received an NEA award and in 1991 was a writer-in-residence at the University of Wisconsin. Her poetry is published often in quarterlies and periodicals.

Doug Peacock is one of today's most respected defenders of bears. Since returning from the Vietnam War in the late 1960s—a tour that included front-line duty as a Green Beret—Peacock has sought out and studied the grizzlies of Yellowstone and Glacier. His memoir *Grizzly Years* was published to immediate critical acclaim; the first edition sold out in a month. Edward Abbey based the character of Hayduke in *The Monkey Wrench Gang* on his good friend Doug Peacock.

David Petersen lives in a cabin with his wife, Carolyn, in the San Juan Mountains of Colorado. His books include *Among the Aspen, Racks, Among the Elk,* and *Big Sky, Fair Land: The Environmental Essays of A. B. Guthrie.* He is also editor of the journals of Edward Abbey, *Confessions of a Barbarian,* as well as the collected poems of Edward Abbey. Petersen is currently writing a book about the grizzly bears of Colorado's San Juan Mountains.

Brenda Peterson—novelist, naturalist, and essayist—makes her home in Seattle, Washington, where she writes about nature and human life in the Pacific Northwest. Her first nature book, *Living by Water,* was warmly received, and her articles are frequently featured in popular periodicals such as *Sierra* and *Outside.* Her latest book is *Nature and Other Mothers.*

Eva Saulitis has spent her summers for the past eight years on Prince William Sound, where she is engaged in long-term studies of killer whales. She bases her research boat, the *Whale II,* in Cordova. In 1993 she received her Master of Science degree in wildlife biology from the University of Alaska. Her thesis documented the natural history of the northern Pacific killer whale and explored the effects of the *Exxon Valdez* oil spill on the species.

Peggy Shumaker lives in a log cabin home in Ester, Alaska. Shumaker has taught creative writing at the University of Arizona, the University of Alaska, Fairbanks, and Arizona State University. Her books of poetry include *Esperanza's Hair, The Circle of Totems,* and *Wings Moist from the Other World.*

Jane Smiley teaches fiction in the writing program at Iowa State University in Ames, Iowa. Several years ago her novel *A Thousand Acres* was awarded the Pulitzer Prize for fiction. Smiley is also an environmental activist and accomplished nature essayist.

Cindy Van Dover was educated at Rutgers University, UCLA, and the Massachusetts Institute of Technology. For several years she was one of the pilots for the *Alvin,* the deep-sea submarine used by researchers for exploring the ocean floor. Her doctoral dissertation was devoted to the exotic life forms that are associated with geothermal vents. Her memoir of life as a submarine pilot, *Octopus's Garden,* is forthcoming from Addison-Wesley. She is currently based as a project scientist at Woods Hole Oceanographic Institute in Massachusetts.

David Rains Wallace is the author of nine works of natural history, including *The Dark Range, Idle Weeds, The Klamath Knot, Bulow Hammock,* and *The Quetzal and the Macaw. The Klamath Knot* was awarded the John Burroughs Medal for Nature Writing in 1983. Wallace has also authored two novels, *The Turquoise Dragon* and *The Vermilion Parrot.* He and his wife, Betsy, an artist, make their home in Berkeley, California.

Terry Tempest Williams has authored four acclaimed nature books: *Pieces of White Shell: A Journey to Navajoland, Coyote's Canyon, Refuge: An Unnatural History of Family and Place,* and *An Unspoken Hunger.* She works as a naturalist for the Utah Museum of Natural History. Her writings appear often in *Outside, Sierra,* and other periodicals. She and her husband live in the mountains outside Salt Lake City.

Edward O. Wilson is Baird Professor of Science at Harvard University. He has devoted his life to the study of nature in tropical regions. His books include *Sociobiology, On Human Nature, Biophilia, The Ants,* and *The Diversity of Life.* Professor Wilson has twice been awarded the Pulitzer Prize for general nonfiction and is mentioned increasingly as a Nobel candidate for his tireless work and leadership on the biodiversity issue.

Periodicals Consulted

Alaska Quarterly Review, Department of English, 3221 Providence Drive, Anchorage, Alaska 99508

American Poetry Review, 1721 Walnut Street, Philadelphia, PA 19103

Antaeus, Ecco Press, 26 West 17th Street, New York, New York 10011

The Antioch Review, P.O. Box 148, Yellow Springs, Ohio 45387

Arizona Quarterly, Department of English, University of Arizona, Tucson, Arizona 85721

The Atlantic Monthly, 745 Boylston Street, Boston, Massachusetts 02116

Audubon, 700 Broadway, New York, New York 10003

Backpacker, 33 East Minor Street, Emmaus, Pennsylvania 18098

Chicago Review, 5801 South Kenwood, Chicago, Illinois 60637

Cimarron Review, 205 Morril Hall, Oklahoma State University, Stillwater, Oklahoma 74078

Colorado Review, 360 Eddy Building, Colorado State University, Fort Collins, Colorado 80523

Denver Quarterly, Department of English, University of Denver, Denver, Colorado 80210

Esquire, 1790 Broadway, New York, New York 10019

Florida Review, Department of English, University of Central Florida, Orlando, Florida 32816

The Georgia Review, University of Georgia, Athens, Georgia 30602

The Gettysburg Review, Gettysburg College, Gettysburg, Pennsylvania 17325

Harper's Magazine, 2 Park Avenue, New York, New York 10016

Hawaii Pacific Review, 1060 Bishop St., Honolulu, HI 96813

Hawaii Review, Department of English, University of Hawaii, 1733 Donaghho Road, Honolulu, Hawaii 96822

Indiana Review, 316 North Jordan Avenue, Indiana University, Bloomington, IN 47405

Kansas Quarterly, Department of English, Denison Hall, Kansas State University, Manhattan, Kansas 66506

The Kenyon Review, Kenyon College, Gambier, Ohio 43022

Manoa, Department of English, University of Hawaii, 1733 Donaghho Road, Honolulu, Hawaii 96822

The Massachusetts Review, Memorial Hall, University of Massachusetts, Amherst, Massachusetts 01002

Michigan Quarterly Review, 3032 Rackham Building, University of Michigan, Ann Arbor, Michigan 48109

Minnesota Monthly, 15 South 9th Street, Suite 320, Minneapolis, Minnesota 55402

The Missouri Review, 1507 Hillcrest Hall, University of Missouri, Columbia, Missouri 65211

Nebraska Review, Department of English, University of Nebraska, Omaha, Nebraska 68182

New England Review, Middlebury College, Middlebury, Vermont 05753

New Mexico Humanities Review, Department of English, New Mexico Tech., Socorro, New Mexico 57801

The New Yorker, 20 West 43rd Street, New York, New York 10036

Nimrod, Arts and Humanities Council of Tulsa, 2210 South Main, Tulsa, Oklahoma 74114

The North American Review, University of Northern Iowa, 1227 West 27th Street, Cedar Falls, Iowa 50613

North Atlantic Review, 15 Arbutus Lane, Stony Brook, New York 11790

North Dakota Quarterly, University of North Dakota, Box 8237, Grand Forks, North Dakota 58202

The Ohio Review, Department of English, Ellis Hall, Ohio University, Athens, Ohio 45701

Orion, 136 East 64th Street, New York, New York 10021

Outside, 1165 North Clark Street, Chicago, Illinois 60610

Pacific Discovery, Golden Gate Park, San Francisco, CA 94118

The Paris Review, 541 East 72nd Street, New York, New York 10021

Prairie Schooner, Andrews Hall, University of Nebraska, Lincoln, Nebraska 68588

Puerto Del Sol, Department of English, New Mexico State University, Las Cruces, New Mexico 88003

Santa Monica Review, Center for the Humanities at Santa Monica College, 1900 Pico Boulevard, Santa Monica, California 90405

The Sewanee Review, University of the South, Sewanee, Tennessee 37375

Sierra, 730 Polk Street, San Francisco, California 94109

Sonora Review, Department of English, University of Arizona, Tucson, Arizona 85721

South Carolina Review, Department of English, Clemson University, Clemson, South Carolina 29634

South Dakota Review, Box 111, University Exchange, Vermillion, South Dakota 57069

Southern Humanities Review, Department of English, Auburn University, Auburn, Alabama 36830

The Southern Review, Drawer D, University Station, Baton Rouge, Louisiana 70803

Southwest Review, Southern Methodist University, Dallas, Texas 75275

Tampa Review, Box 19F, University of Tampa, 401 West Kennedy Boulevard, Tampa, Florida 33606

The Threepenny Review, P.O. Box 9131, Berkeley, California 94709

The Village Voice Literary Supplement, 842 Broadway, New York, New York 10003

The Virginia Quarterly Review, Department of English, University of Virginia, Charlottesville, Virginia 22903

Wilderness, 900 17th Street N.W., Washington, D.C. 20006

ZYZZYVA, 41 Sutter Street, Suite 1400, San Francisco, California 94104

Permissions

Rick Bass: "Creatures of the Dictator," first appeared in *Men's Journal.* Copyright © 1994 by Rick Bass. Reprinted with permission of the author.

Susan Brownmiller: "Flying to Vietnam," first appeared in *Audubon.* Copyright © 1994 by Susan Brownmiller. Reprinted with permission of the author.

Lyn Buckley: "Elegy for Vincent," first publication. Copyright © 1994 by Lyn Buckley. Used with permission of the author.

John Daniel: "Cuttings," first appeared in *Wilderness.* Copyright © 1994 by John Daniel. Reprinted with permission of the author.

Alison Deming: "Woods Work," first appeared in *Temporary Homelands.* Copyright © 1994 by Mercury House. Reprinted with permission of the publisher.

Clarice Dickess: "Learning to Breathe," first publication. Copyright © 1994 by Clarice Dickess. Used with permission of the author.

John Gierarch: "Scotland," first appeared in *Dances with Trout* Copyright © 1994 by Simon & Schuster. Reprinted with permission of the publisher.

Gerard Gormley: "The Winged Whales," first publication. Copyright © 1994 by Gerard Gormley. Used with permission of the author.

John Haines: "Shadows and Vistas," first publication. Copyright © 1994 by John Haines. Used with permission of the author.

Carolyn Kremers: "Native Store," first appeared in *Indiana Review.* Copyright © 1994 by Carolyn Kremers. Reprinted with permission of the author.

Barry Lopez: "Offshore: A Journey to the Weddell Sea" first appeared in *Orion.* Copyright © 1994 by Barry Lopez. Reprinted with permission of Sterling Lord Literistic, Inc.

Nancy Lord: "Two Lakes," first publication. Copyright © 1994 by Nancy Lord. Used with permission of the author.

Peter Matthiessen: "At the End of Tibet," first appeared in *Audubon*. Copyright © 1994 by Peter Matthiessen. Reprinted with permission of the author.

Rick McIntyre: "The Gift of a Wolf," first publication. Copyright © 1994 by Rick McIntyre. Used with permission of the author.

Jim Miller: "The Valley of the Crane," first publication. Copyright © 1994 by Jim Miller. Used with permission of the author.

Adele Ne Jame: "A Bedouin's Dream," first appeared in *Manoa* (Winter 1993). "Dance of the Areca" and "The Wedding Feast" first appeared in *Hawaii Pacific Review* (Spring 1993). Copyright © 1993 by Adele Ne Jame. "Phosphorescence, North Shore, O'ahu" and "Saba and the Songs We Hear," first publication. Copyright © 1994 by Adele Ne Jame. All poems appear with permission of the author.

Doug Peacock: "Walking Point in White Bear Country," first appeared in *Pacific Discovery*. Copyright © 1994 by Doug Peacock. Reprinted with permission of the author.

David Petersen: "Blood, Hair, and the Ground Tore Up," from the forthcoming *Ghost Grizzlies* (Boston: Houghton-Mifflin, 1995). Copyright © 1994 by David Petersen. Reprinted with permission of the author.

Brenda Peterson: "Animal Allies," first appeared in *Orion*. Copyright © 1993 by Brenda Peterson. Reprinted with permission of the author.

Eva Saulitis: "The Burden of the Beach," first publication. Copyright © 1994 by Eva Saulitis. Used with permission of the author.

Peggy Shumaker: "Glacier, Calving," appears in *Wings Moist from the Other World* (Pittsburgh, PA: University of Pittsburgh Press, 1993). "The Run of Silvers" first appeared in *American Poetry Review* (Sept./Oct. 1993). Poems copyright © 1993 by Peggy Shumaker. Both poems appear with permission of the author.

Jane Smiley: "So Shall We Reap," first appeared in *Sierra*. Copyright © 1994 by Jane Smiley. Reprinted with permission of the author.

Cindy Van Dover: "Octopus's Garden," first publication. Copyright © 1994 by Cindy Van Dover. Used with permission of the author.

David Rains Wallace: "The Crowded Desert Islands," first appeared in *Manoa.* Copyright © 1994 by David Rains Wallace. Reprinted with permission of the author.

Terry Tempest Williams: "The Erotic Landscape," first appeared in *Harper's.* Copyright © 1994 by Terry Tempest Williams. Reprinted with permission of the author.

Edward O. Wilson: "Biodiversity Threatened," first appeared in *The Diversity of Life.* Reprinted by permission of the publishers from *The Diversity of Life* by Edward O. Wilson, Cambridge, Mass.: The Belknap Press of Harvard University Press, Copyright 1992/1994 (paper) by the President and Fellows of Harvard College.